Sourcing Practices in the Apparel Industry

Implications for Garment Exporters in Commonwealth Developing Countries

Marlon Lezama
Brian Webber
Charles Dagher

D1413350

THE COMMONWEALTH SECRETARIAT

This report is published by the Special Advisory Services Division
of the Commonwealth Secretariat

Commonwealth Secretariat
Marlborough House
Pall Mall, London SW1Y 5HX, United Kingdom

Designed and published by the Commonwealth Secretariat
Printed in Britain by Formara Ltd.

Wherever possible, the Commonwealth Secretariat uses paper sourced from
sustainable forests or from sources that minimise a destructive impact on the environment.

ISBN 0-85092-809-5   Price: £16.99

Web site: http//www.thecommonwealth.org

The Authors

Marlon Lezama is Chief Programme Officer (Trade), Special Advisory Services Division (SASD) of the Commonwealth Secretariat and Team Leader of the apparel sourcing study. Marlon is responsible for developing, implementing and managing a range of trade-related technical assistance programmes for Commonwealth developing countries.

Brian Webber is Director of Saican Consultants Inc. (Montreal, Canada), a member of the Strategy Analysis International Group, an international consultancy specialising in market and enterprise development.

Charles Dagher is CEO of Dagher Consulting Group Inc. (Montreal, Canada), a consultancy firm that provides manufacturing management and industrial engineering services on an international scale to the garment industry.

Acknowledgements

This study was undertaken as part of the Commonwealth Secretariat's ongoing trade-related technical assistance to member countries. It focuses on the apparel industry in Commonwealth developing countries and the implications for garment manufacturers of the removal of the Multi-Fibre Arrangement post-2004.

Many people in the apparel industry, their industry associations and government agencies were consulted during the course of this study and provided important insights into the challenges faced in the evolving environment. The authors wish particularly to thank the sourcing executives in North America who gave so generously of their time to discuss the issues addressed in this study. This was a rare opportunity to gain valuable insights into the intricacies of strategic global sourcing in the apparel industry. We also draw attention to the support and encouragement provided by the apparel manufacturers and their industry representatives in the six Commonwealth developing countries that were the focus of the fieldwork.

We also wish to express our thanks to Md. Akmal Hossain, Claudia Wynter and Costa Theo for their critical inputs to the assessments in Bangladesh, Jamaica and South Africa, respectively.

Finally, we wish to acknowledge the assistance of the International Trade Centre (UNCTAD/WTO) in providing pertinent statistics for apparel exports from Commonwealth developing countries.

Contents

Charts

Abbreviations

AGOA	African Growth and Opportunities Act
AISA	American Import Shippers Association
BGMEA	Bangladesh Garment Manufacturers and Exporters Association
BKMEA	Bangladesh Knitwear Manufacturers and Exporters Association
BOI	Board of Investment (Sri Lanka)
CAD	Computer-aided design
CAM	Computer-aided manufacturing
CBI	Caribbean Basin Initiative
CBTA	Caribbean Basin Trade Development Act
CLOFED	Clothing Federation
C&M	Cut and make
CMT	Cut, make and trim
CTPAT	United States Customs Trade Partnership Against Terrorism
CTC	Clothing Textile Centre
EDB	Export Development Board
EDI	Electronic Data Interchange
EMPD	Export Market Development Programme
EPB	Export Promotion Bureau
EPZ	Export Processing Zone
EPZDA	Export Processing Zones Development Authority
ERP	Enterprise Resource Planning
EU	European Union
FOB	Free on Board
FTZ	Free trade zone
GSD	General Sewing Data
GSP	Generalised System of Preferences
ISO	International Standards Organisation
ITC	International Trade Centre
IVTB	Industrial Vocation Training Board
LDC	Less developed country
LNDC	Lesotho National Development Corporation
MFA	Multi-Fibre Arrangement
MIDA	Mauritius Industrial Development Authority
NAFTA	North American Free Trade Agreement
NASDAQ	National Association of Securities Dealers Automatic Quotation System
PDF	Portable document file
SAARC	South Asian Association for Regional Co-operation
SACU	Southern Africa Customs Union
SAM	Standard allocated minutes
SME	Small and medium-sized enterprise

SMV	Standard minute value
TIFA	Temporary Investment Framework Agreement
UNIDO	United Nations Industrial Development Organisation
UPS	Unit production system
USA-ITA	United States Association of Importers of Textiles and Apparel
WTO	World Trade Organisation
WTO-ATC	World Trade Organisation – Agreement on Textiles and Clothing

1

Introduction

1.1 Context and Purpose of the Study

This study assesses the implications for garment manufacturers in Commonwealth developing countries of the phasing out of the Multi-Fibre Arrangement (MFA), post-2004. The study is motivated by the new multilateral, regional and bilateral trade agreements, and in particular by the situation that will prevail after 2004, when the WTO Agreement on Textiles and Clothing takes full effect. The principal outputs of the study are enterprise-level guidelines suggesting how firms can remain competitive in the face of evolving sourcing policies, technology and practices, complemented by related frameworks at government and institutional levels.

1.2. Background to the Study

While comparative advantage, especially in clothing, has tended to shift from high-wage to low-wage economies, since the 1970s the location of production and the evolution of trade in the industry have been largely shaped by a system of international quotas on developing countries' exports to OECD countries known as the Multi-Fibre Arrangement. *The shift in comparative advantage is likely to accelerate because of the decision – taken in conjunction with the conclusion of the Uruguay Round in December 1993 – to phase out the MFA in 2005* (Navaretti *et al.*, 1995:15). Trade in textiles and apparel has been governed by quantitative restrictions based on the MFA. However, the World Trade Organisation (WTO) ratification of the 1995 Agreement on Textiles and Clothing will phase out the MFA by 2005 and end quantitative restrictions that have historically protected OECD countries' apparel markets.

As quotas cease to be a factor, it is essential to understand the underlying business logic and to encourage manufacturers in Commonwealth developing countries to act accordingly. Mindful of the imminent changes in the industry, this study on changing sourcing practices in the apparel industry and the implications for garment exporters from Commonwealth developing countries was undertaken as a contribution to the emerging debate and to identify and offer some practical approaches that may help to ensure the survival of this thriving sector.

In a large number of Commonwealth developing countries garment manufacturing is the largest employer and possibly the largest earner of foreign exchange. In 2001, for example, Bangladesh earned 77.2 per cent of its foreign exchange from the export of garments, Sri Lanka earned 50.8 per cent and Mauritius 56.5 per cent

The Commonwealth is an association of 53 member states whose 1.5 billion people make up a quarter of the world's population. Many of these countries were former British colonies or dependencies. The vast majority of Commonwealth countries, with the exception of the United Kingdom, Canada, Australia and New Zealand, are what are commonly referred to as developing countries.

The final phase of the removal of quotas established under the MFA will occur in 2005. This poses both opportunities and threats for apparel-producing countries: opportunities, in that they will now have quota free access to lucrative markets in the developed world; threats, in that they will now have to compete in an increasingly unfettered and globalised marketplace.

1.3 Objectives of the Study

This study attempts to develop an understanding of the relative importance of the purchasing criteria of ready-made garment buyers in North America (the largest single market for the global apparel industry) following the demise of the quota system. Secondly, it sets out to translate these into strategies for use by garment manufacturers and export and industrial development officials in Commonwealth developing countries, so that they can both add value to their products and strengthen their position in the market. While the focus of the study is North America, limited reference will be made to the European apparel market, the second largest market for most garment exporters from Commonwealth developing countries.

From the fieldwork undertaken in a sample of Commonwealth developing countries it was evident that many manufacturers are struggling to conform to the evolving requirements of their international clients and that there is intense pressure in many quarters to remain competitive. More critically, it emerged that there is a need to better understand the motivations of the buyers, the forces that are driving their continued demand for change in ways of doing business and how these translate into practical sourcing criteria. The fieldwork showed that there is a strong desire to learn about and implement the production and management processes that will enable manufacturers to respond to these new criteria.

The approach of this study is based on the need for *practical and urgent implementation of strategies for survival*. It focuses on the needs of the manufacturer and ties these needs to a strategic framework that can and should be used by the industry as a whole and by governments to foster the development of the apparel industry in their own countries.

1.4 Conduct of the Research

As part of the study, in 2002 the authors undertook fieldwork and analysis of the garment sectors in a number of Commonwealth developing countries at various stages of development and/or dependence on the ready-made garment industry. The selection of the sample countries was based on the need to have a regional and geographic spread as well as focusing on those economies where the impact of the removal of the MFA could be significant. The countries selected were Mauritius, South Africa, Lesotho, Sri Lanka, Bangladesh and Jamaica.

In October and November 2002, the authors met with top sourcing executives in the United States to survey their strategic sourcing practices and how these might change in the coming years. The meetings were, almost without exception, held with vice-presidents responsible for *strategic sourcing* or, in one or two cases, for *global logistics and supply chain management*. Meetings were also held with representative importers in Canada. To complete the understanding of the issues, senior executives of the Cotton Council, the United States Association of Importers of Textiles and Apparel (USA-ITA) and representatives of the World Bank involved with the apparel industry in Africa were also interviewed.

The preliminary findings of the study were the focus of a presentation at a Commonwealth Secretariat-funded South Asian Association for Regional Co-operation (SAARC) seminar on the impact of the ending of the MFA held in Colombo, Sri Lanka in December 2002. Comments from the participants at this event provided important insights and served to reinforce the orientation of the study. The authors also attended the 14th Annual Textile and Apparel Importers Trade and Transportation Conference in New York organised by USA-ITA and the American Import Shippers Association (AISA). The presentations at that event served to bring the various issues into perspective and to highlight issues of concern to US importers and the US government. (This was particularly important in view of the heightened security concerns since the terrorist attack in the US on 11 September 2001.)

1.5 Structure of the Study

Chapter 2 reviews pertinent literature relating to changing forces in the apparel industry, with particular emphasis on their impact on apparel producing countries and approaches to up-grading production and management capabilities at the enterprise level.

Chapter 3 describes in more detail the context and background in which the research study is set. The position of Commonwealth countries in the global garment apparel trade and an examination of the importance of the garment industry to the exports of these countries are presented in some depth. Export and import statistics are presented showing the relative importance of Commonwealth apparel exports and, more critically, the importance of these exports to the economies of Commonwealth countries. The chapter also looks at various Commonwealth countries' share of the two major export markets – the United States and Europe.

Chapter 4 focuses on the view from the marketplace, garnered during in-depth interviews held with top executives from a cross-section of the leading apparel industry companies in the United States – importers, manufacturers and retailers. The chapter also highlights critical issues of concern to apparel importers in the US that were addressed by industry executives and senior government officials at the 14th Annual Textile and Apparel Importers Trade and Transportation Conference organised by USA-ITA and AISA in November 2002. Findings concerning the nature and structure of the marketplace for garments are presented, together with the central issues concerning buyer/vendor relationships and the balance of power relative to each.

Chapter 5 reports on findings from interviews with executives and top-ranking stakeholders in the apparel sectors of Commonwealth developing countries. This chapter takes a closer look at apparel exports from each of the three regions and presents a review of the business environment and key business issues post–2004. The review focuses on country-level issues but takes a regional perspective where appropriate.

Chapter 6 provides an assessment of the production capabilities and principal technical issues facing the apparel industry in these countries. The assessment is based mainly on interviews with key industry representatives, as well as assessments and observations made during factory visits to a selected sample of firms. A number of the industry representatives interviewed are experts in the field of garment production and design and have been involved in various government and private sector appointed committees in their respective countries to assess the state of their apparel industry. Their insights into the technical aspects of the industry were very useful.

The critical economic, social and political issues facing Commonwealth developing countries are reviewed and analysed. Arising out of this, a detailed examination concerning the impact, implications and options open to governments in light of the phasing out of the MFA is undertaken.

Chapter 7 explores the lessons that can be learned from Commonwealth developing countries about how companies – and national industries – are attempting to move to higher value added products and make innovations to remain competitive. Measures that have been initiated at national and enterprise levels to prepare for and adapt to changes in the apparel industry are summarised; emphasis is placed on the lessons learned in one country that might be applicable elsewhere

Chapter 8 addresses the issue of how to build on the findings of this study and how to move forward to strengthen individual apparel manufacturing companies, as well as the overall apparel industry in Commonwealth developing countries.

Chapter 9 presents the conclusions which have emerged directly from the data. These include recommended next steps towards the adoption of measures which are designed to enable the continued survival and growth of the apparel industry in the specified Commonwealth developing countries. The chapter also reflects on the actual contributions, wider implications and recommendations for industry-government initiatives that are vital for the survival of national industries.

2

Changing Forces in the Apparel Industry

2.1 Introduction

The spread of the apparel industry throughout much of the developing world has been fuelled in part by the desire to reduce product costs through lower labour costs and in part by a quota system established, initially, to protect the domestic apparel manufacturing industries in the major markets. The result is that apparel production is one of the most globalised activities in the world economy (Lee, 2001:1). Whalley (1999) contends that the main trade advantage of the developing country apparel exporters lies in their low wage rates for cutting and sewing rather than in their raw material prices.

Diao and Somwaru (2001) argue that developing countries have a comparative advantage in textiles and apparel trade. This advantage, they point out, allows developing countries to diversify beyond traditional primary commodities, production of which may be restrained by natural resources. The apparel industry, as a leading labour-intensive manufacturing sector, is often thought to represent the first base in economic growth and development in a country. Demand for textiles and apparel commodities, posit Diao and Somwaru, steadily grows in both developed and developing countries as countries become wealthier. This implies that for many developing countries there is room for future expansion of their production and export capacities. The relative importance of apparel exports of Commonwealth developing countries is underscored by the significant foreign exchange earnings this sector has contributed to these economies.

Many of the changes in the ready-made apparel industry are driven by the demands of the competitive retail environment and emphasis on *lean retailing*. Advances in information technology have enabled major retailers to change the ways in which they do business (Abernathy *et al.*, 1999). This in turn has changed the manufacturing rules of the game. Cost considerations have forced buyers to look for an optimal way of executing supply chain transactions and technology has accelerated formation of this global supply chain by ensuring, and enabling, efficient information flow (Tyagi, 2003). Changes, according to Tyagi, include shifting more value-added activities such as cutting and marker making to contractors and speed sourcing (or quick response) and reduction of lead times.

A number of authors also comment on the increasing importance attached to the time factor (Forza and Vinelli, 2000; Spinanger, 1999; Tyagi, 2003). According to Forsa and Vinelli (p.138), '*the way in which the* [supply] *chain works can be greatly altered by speeding up time to market and by the continuous transmission of information from the customers throughout all the links in the chain. On the one hand, this improves the quality of service offered to the customer and, on the other, it reduces overall entrepreneurial risk along the chain.*' Ryan (2003a) reinforces this view and states that *'apparel sourcing is not just about cheap labour anymore'*. Ryan goes on to discuss the drive for shorter lead times as a key element of supply chain efficiency. Tyagi (2003), among others, links this drive for shorter lead times to the benefits of proximity, for example in the case of the Caribbean Basin and the United States or of North Africa and Western Europe.

Another force for change is the proliferation of bilateral and regional trade agreements which grant preferential market access such as the US has granted to sub-Saharan Africa and the Caribbean and the European Union has granted to South Asia. Spinanger (1999) notes this, as do Forza and Vinelli (2000). The intensity with which the US was negotiating free trade agreements in late 2002 and early 2003 is further evidence of this force for change. The emerging role of China is another critical force for change in the light of its entry into the WTO and the related safeguard measures designed to prevent undue perturbation in the marketplace.

These factors are all familiar to anybody who is involved with, or who follows developments in, the apparel industry. But they are known piecemeal and little is known, it appeared from our earlier discussions with manufacturers in Commonwealth developing countries, about what should be done in relation to them. This is the motivation behind this study: to understand the implications of these changing forces, and particularly of the demise of the quota system, for Commonwealth developing countries and to translate this understanding into specific actions that can be taken to mitigate negative impacts.

2.2 Some Initial Viewpoints

Much has been written and is being written about the forces of change in the apparel industry, including the potential impact of the demise of the MFA. We contend, however, that little has been written on what to do about this, at least not at the practical level of the enterprise and those agencies that assist in enterprise development. The following sections present a review of some of the more significant views expressed by observers of the apparel industry. They are grouped as follows:

- impact on apparel producing countries;

- production organisation and value chains;

- full cost frameworks;

- management capabilities;

- up-grading routes;

- de-localisation;

- strategy development.

Impact on apparel-producing countries

There is no consensus on the specific impacts on developing countries of the Agreement on Textiles and Clothing. Kathuria *et al.* (2000) report that modelling results suggest that South Asia as a whole will gain, although there may be different experiences in different countries. Spinanger (1999) offers a different viewpoint. He explored whether there will be increasing concentration of the textile and clothing industry in China. He offers the toy industry, unfettered by quotas, as an example, claiming that it is highly concentrated in China and Hong Kong, with probably over 50 per cent of exports of toys coming from these two economies. Birnbaum (2001) contends that many countries that profited from the quota system will face serious troubles. Birnbaum (2001) foresees a drive for consolidation of sourcing and argues that the countries with smaller market share in the US, say less than 3 per cent, will be particularly at risk. Worse off will be those countries whose exports of apparel approach, or exceed, 50 per cent of total exports. A critical strategy, other than either abandoning the industry or seeking special market access arrangements, is to seek to become a strategic supplier. Birnbaum contends, however, that not all supplying countries, or companies, can possibly achieve this goal.

A key aim of this study is to gain insights from the marketplace perspective into the role of China and the factors that might work in favour of buyers[1] retaining their business links with suppliers in Commonwealth developing countries.

Production organisation and value chains

An accepted approach for enterprise or sector development is to work with the notion of value (or supply) chains. Companies, or countries, can then determine where they are situated in the chain and investigate what additional functions in the chain they could beneficially and feasibly undertake.

A critical distinction between buyer-driven and producer-driven commodity chains is made by Gereffi (1999). Producer-driven chains are tied to technology leadership and capital intensity, as in the automobile industry. Buyer-driven chains are characterised by low capitalisation and occur when design and market access are critical, as in the apparel industry. Gereffi looks at trends in the evolution of the garment industry in East Asia and argues that East Asian manufacturers have evolved to be 'full package' integrators who act as the bridge between the market and lowest-cost producers. Their success, he argues, has been the result of an ability to establish close links with a diverse array of lead firms (primary sources of material inputs, technology transfer and knowledge) in buyer-driven chains. More generally, Gereffi emphasises the need to have both company and country or regional initiatives. He sees networks as a key element. Initially, there are the sub-contract supplier networks of successful lead firms. These networks then serve as a means to 'learn the business' and hence to up-grade. At a later stage, suppliers can create their own networks so as to have more control vis à vis buyers. He notes in this context that buyer companies are growing increasingly larger.

---

[1]The term buyer is used throughout this study as a general reference to the buying companies and their personnel.

Humphrey and Schmitz (2002) address the issue of marrying cluster development, with its local focus, to the global value chains that are key to the apparel industry. They suggest four types of relationship in value chains:

- *Arm's length market relations* – the buyer's requirements (including quality, reliability, etc.) can be met, or assured, by a range of firms;

- *Network relationships* – firms co-operate in a more information-intensive relationship;

- *Quasi-hierarchy relations* – one firm exercises a high degree of control over other firms and processes in the chain;

- *Hierarchical relations* – the lead firm takes direct ownership of some operations in the chain.

Humphrey and Schmitz argue that up-grading prospects of clusters differ according to the type of value chain to which they are linked.

Bovet and Martha's (2000) seminal research on *value nets* focuses on companies that have gone beyond the traditional supply chain to completely redefine their business model to take account of modern enabling technologies such as IT and the internet. The authors contend that value net concepts are highly applicable to the garment industry and provide mini case studies on three leading companies: Zara (an integrated Spanish retailer, designer and manufacturer), The Limited (a major US retailer) and Li & Fung (a leading Hong Kong-based global strategic outsourcer).

The value net concept defines business by five key elements. These are:

- *Value proposition* – what is offered to profitable customers;

- *Scope* – what is done in-house and what is outsourced;

- *Profit capture* – essentially, optimisation of cost activities;

- *Strategic control* – actions to protect the profit stream;

- *Execution* – human capabilities and digital technology that hold all the elements together.

A key issue in terms of the garment industry, and particularly for manufacturers, is the *value proposition*. This consists of three generic elements: *super service, convenient solutions* and *customisation*. Of these, super service is key, as measured by such variables as speed (order cycle time and time to market), reliability (on-time shipment and delivery and stock-out rates). Other measures are inventory, inventory turns and the cash conversion cycle. The convenient solutions factor is important to differentiate the successful company's offer from that of the run-of-the-mill company. Customisation is not really an issue in a traditionally customer-driven value chain business, such as the garment industry.

Full cost framework

Christopher and Towill (2002) call for sourcing strategies based on lowest total supply chain costs. They argue that to use manufacturing or purchase cost, sometimes called 'first cost', as the basis for costing is inadequate since it does not reflect the true total costs attached to the product. They acknowledge, however, that it is still the main driver in many sourcing decisions.

Birnbaum (2000) also addresses the implications as importers move from seeking the lowest direct or manufacturing cost to seeking the lowest total cost – what he terms moving from a buying approach to a sourcing approach. Although Christopher and Towill (2002) identify some of the costing implications of moving to total supply chain costs, it is Birnbaum who offers the most comprehensive proposals. He proposes a model of *full value cost analysis* in which he divides costs into three principal categories: *macro* costs, *indirect* costs and *direct* costs. He argues that in today's apparel industry, quality, delivery and price all come down to questions of cost. The winners will not be those companies with lowest direct costs but rather those that can provide the garment, in the market, at the lowest total cost.

Direct costs are those related to the actual making of stock garments and include material costs (fabric and trim), the actual making costs (cutting, sewing, finishing, pressing and packing, in the case of wovens), factory overheads and agents' commissions. The making cost items, it should be noted, for knitted sweaters are slightly different. Birnbaum explains that at the labour rates prevailing in offshore locations, the potential gains from reduced labour costs are minimal and almost irrelevant when compared to the gains from reduction of macro costs and indirect costs. He also ascribes the continued strength of the apparel industry in many high labour cost countries, such as Italy and Hong Kong, to the very low macro costs and indirect costs that prevail there.

Macro costs, says Birnbaum, are the costs of doing business in one country as opposed to another. Import duties are perhaps the greatest macro cost (frequently 18 per cent or more of Free on Board (FOB) value) and trade agreements that eliminate or reduce such duties are a clear advantage for the beneficiary exporting countries. Quota charges, shipping costs, infrastructure service costs and interest rates can also be described as macro costs. They can also include a range of perhaps less obvious costs related to education, or more properly the lack of it, and to human rights issues, including monitoring of codes of conduct and costs. Macro costs are also those that are related to any negative impacts from trade disputes and to negative reaction in the marketplace to the policies of a specific country. These macro costs are largely in the purview of government and in the case of duties and other costs related to rules of origin are tied to various trade agreements – multilateral, regional or bilateral. Macro costs, Birnbaum contends, are the single most important contributor to total product cost and are a key factor in the decision of an importer to work in a particular country.

Indirect costs are the costs of all operations in the broadly defined manufacturing process other than the actual 'making' charges for the stock garments. They include pre-production expenses for activities such as design, pattern making and sample making, material selection and purchase. Indirect costs also include costs due to high minimums, costs due to returns and cancellations, as well as costs due to delays, late delivery and penalties. In essence, Birnbaum argues, passing many or most of the pre-production activities to offshore operators can lead to substantial cost savings; savings far greater than those related to ever-cheaper labour rates. At the same time, any factory that has the management capability in place to minimise incurring the less tangible costs – due to delays, poor quality, high minimums and so on – can greatly reduce the final costs to the importer, through actual avoidance of these factors or through increased trust leading to less reliance on agents, inspection companies and the like.

Management capabilities

Various authors indicate that plant efficiency is critical and that low wages can only compensate for this to a limited degree. In the final analysis, high-calibre manufacturing management and production planning are critical.

The importance of management is also emphasised by Lee and Chen (1998), who argue that up-grading is not just technical – management is critical. In their book on the impact of lean retailing on apparel manufacturing, Abernathy *et al.* (1999:258) argue that successful response to lean retailing requirements does not result from hardware or software purchases, or from changing production processes, but rather from successful management.

Up-grading routes

Given the current state of the apparel industry a frequent concern is how to up-grade. Kaplinsky and Readman (2001) propose three general routes to up-grading within the value chain. These are:

- become better at what you do – process up-grading;
- take on more functions in the chain, such as pattern making and grading – functional up-grading;
- product up-grading – introduce new products.

Using the terminology developed by Birnbaum (2000), process up-grading addresses direct costs and functional up-grading addresses indirect costs.

Birnbaum classes factories as *zero-service*, *normal-service* and *full-service* as a function of their ability to respond to the requirements of buyers and to thereby reduce the indirect costs. The zero-service company will operate under at most 'cut-make-trim', while the full service company will have the potential to be involved in every step of the manufacturing process. The normal-service company operates within a wide range between the two extremes but is attuned to the goal of reducing indirect cost for its customers – offering at least pattern making, grading and sample making and operating on an FOB basis. Birnbaum recognises, however, the trade-off to be made by the buyer between the cost savings of entrusting various pre-production activities to a vendor as opposed to the risk reduction by doing the tasks in-house or through agents and other intermediaries. On the other hand, Birnbaum points out, the more services that are provided by a vendor, the greater opportunity for the vendor to make profit.

The decision for change depends heavily on the preferences and capabilities of the buying company in relation to the capabilities of the country and its vendors as well as to the size and relative importance of the orders (Gereffi *et al.*, 2003). This is born out by Humphrey and Schmitz (2002:12), who go on to remark: '... *buyers who consider sourcing as their core competence are unlikely to leave the management of the supply chain to their producers. In contrast, buyers who see their core competence in market-ing and branding are less likely to retain this function.*' The attitude, and indeed the *perceived* attitude, of the all-important buyers, can be critical to up-grading. UNIDO (2003:107) cites a paper by Schmitz (2002) on the Sinos Valley footwear cluster in Brazil, in which a collective marketing and up-grading plan was not implemented because a small number of influential export manufacturers feared an adverse reaction from their main foreign buyer.

Humphrey and Schmitz (2002:11) point out, however, that establishing and main-taining quasi-hierarchical governance, which is the most common relationship in apparel value chains, is costly for the lead firm. This provides the leverage for one pro-posed strategy, which is to move into functions that the lead firms governing the chain are willing to relinquish, particularly when they are assured that the risk of failure by the supplier is minimal. This ties in to Birnbaum's (2000) proposition regarding the evolution from zero-service to normal-service or full-service in a drive to reduce indi-rect costs of the product. However, according to Humphrey and Schmitz, up-grading requires a strategic decision to make the necessary investments in equipment, organi-sational arrangements and people.

Gibbon (2000) provides material for reflection on the abilities to move up the value chain in his case study on Mauritius. He argues that attempts by Mauritian-owned enterprises, in the mid-1990s, to move up the value chain by extending their design capacity and launching own brands, private labels and collections were not successful. He notes that most companies in Mauritius returned to a least-cost basic products strategy by de-localising operations to Madagascar where labour costs were substan-tially lower. The issue here is which path to take in expanding the value chain: a key issue for this study.

Up-grading is also related to management capability. Thus Lee and Chen (1998) conclude that in addition to the nature of interdependence between the contract manu-facturer and the buyer, successful up-grading also depends heavily on the managerial capability of the manufacturer.

De-localisation

As discussed above, Mauritius apparel companies used de-localisation to Madagascar as a core strategy. Birnbaum (2000) also offers de-localisation as a viable strategy, par-ticularly as a means to benefit from geographic specific trading bloc benefits. He cites the example of Far East companies setting up operations in Mexico to benefit from the North Atlantic Free Trade Association (NAFTA). The opportunity to benefit from such geographic diversification is also a key issue investigated by this research project.

Strategy development

Much of what has been discussed emerged as the most immediate concern to the executives of individual enterprise, or groups of enterprises interviewed during this study. But, as indicated by Birnbaum (2000), most of the macro costs fall within the purview of government, and it is macro costs that are the most significant contributor to total cost. He concludes that to develop a competitive industry a country must work to reduce the macro costs, particularly through the development and maintenance of capital assets.

At the enterprise level, Birnbaum favours strategic partnerships, recognising that vendors will want to guarantee that the investment in facilities, staff training and machinery will lead to better orders and increased profit. He cautions, however, that some buyers, particularly those catering to the low-end mass market, will continue to focus on minimising direct cost. This points to a need for vendors to seek customers who are susceptible to an increased service offering and also to the probability that many companies will have to continue to deal with the low-end mass merchandisers, for better or for worse.

2.3 Summary

This literature review has indicated that low wages alone are no longer enough to ensure the survival, let alone growth, of an apparel industry. The criteria traditionally used by buyers in major markets are changing and increasingly buyers are moving from seeking the best price from vendors to a structured and highly controlled consideration of minimisation of total costs throughout the supply chain. Such a switch will not, however, remove the requirement for vendors to increase efficiency and strive to reduce direct costs; it will place increased burdens on vendors and require them to undertake additional tasks within the value chain, often requiring considerable investment. And yet it is clear from this study that the buyer still plays a key role in deciding what functions to pass to vendors and to what extent it is in the buyer's interest to give up control.

Some authors (Birnbaum, 2000; Lin *et al.*, 2002) have attempted to associate particular market niches with sourcing patterns and with willingness, or not, to pass responsibilities to vendors. However, given the nature of the business and the range of product handled by any given company, these assertions remain unproven – they may represent general patterns but are they an infallible rule? Further insight into the sourcing strategies foreseen by leading buyers and their assessment of the impact of the demise of the quota system is therefore critical in formulating advice for apparel manufacturers (vendors) and agencies of vendor countries on strategies for survival. The buyer perspective is thus a major element in this study.

3

The Commonwealth and the Global Garment Trade

3.1 Introduction

This chapter presents a review of the position of Commonwealth member countries in the global garment trade. Export and import statistics are presented showing the relative importance of apparel exports to the economies of Commonwealth developing countries. The chapter also looks at various Commonwealth countries' share of the two major export markets – the United States and Europe.

3.2 Relative Importance of Apparel Exports from Commonwealth Countries

Total apparel exports

As indicated in Table 3.1, Commonwealth countries exports of apparel in 2001 were valued at over $25 billion. Of this $25 billion, just over $19.7 billion of exports were from Commonwealth developing countries – that is, excluding the UK, Australia, New Zealand and Canada. The largest exporter by value was Bangladesh, at $5.02 billion, followed by India at $4.97 billion, the UK at $3.4 billion, Sri Lanka at $2.3 billion and Pakistan at $1.8 billion. The other Commonwealth exporters that exceeded or were close to the $1 billion level were Canada at $1.7 billion, Singapore at $1.5 billion, Malaysia at $1.2 billion and Mauritius at $0.9 billion. There was then a significant gap to the next largest exporter, Brunei Darussalam, at $0.4 billion.

Significance of apparel exports

Table 3.2 presents the relative importance of apparel exports in the economies of selected Commonwealth countries, expressed as a percentage of total merchandise exports. Bangladesh was the most dependent on apparel exports, at 77.2 per cent. The next most dependent on apparel exports was Mauritius at 56.5 per cent, followed by Sri Lanka (50.8%), Maldives (42.3%), Fiji (35%), Pakistan (21.53%), Lesotho (19.5%), Jamaica (18%) and India (12.2%) The other countries with apparel exports contributing more than 5 per cent of total merchandise exports were Brunei, Cyprus, Malta, Malawi and Belize.

What the above data shows is that more than a quarter of Commonwealth developing countries rely significantly on the apparel industry as the mainstay of their economies. Any global shift in sourcing patterns by major apparel importers, in particular North America and Europe, will significantly affect the economies of these countries. This is in contrast to major apparel exporting countries such as the United Kingdom, Canada, Singapore and Malaysia where, as a percentage of total exports, the apparel industry is not a significant contributor to foreign exchange earnings.

3.3 United States Apparel Imports from Commonwealth Countries

Total US apparel imports

In 2001, the imports of apparel to the United States reached a value in excess of $58.5 billion. The distribution by region is indicated in Table 3.3 and Chart 3.1. The American Apparel and Footwear Association (2001:1) reports that US imports continued to account for a rapidly growing percentage of the US apparel market in 2001 with imports controlling 96.4 per cent of the US market, increasing from 93.1 per cent in 2000.

Chart 3.1: US Apparel Imports by Region, 2001
(total imports $58.5 billion)

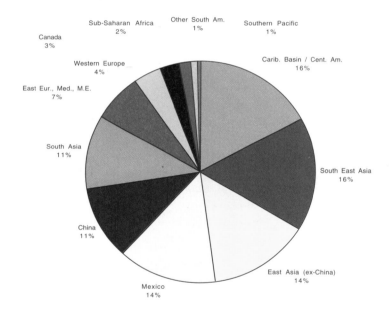

Source: Extracted from US Department of Commerce data for HS61 and HS62 (from www.strategis.ic.gc.ca)

In terms of export of apparel by region, Asia was the most important region, accounting for almost 52.7 per cent of US imports. The other large suppliers were Mexico (13.7%) and the Caribbean Basin/Central America (16.9%). The total from the Americas was 34.2 per cent.

Given the rising interest in sub-Saharan Africa and the Andean region, it is noteworthy that imports from the former accounted only for 1.6 per cent and South America contributed less than 1 per cent.

Top countries exporting to the US

The top apparel exporting countries to the US in 2001 are presented in Table 3.4 and Chart 3.2. Mexico is in premier place, with 13.7 per cent of all imports, followed by

China with 11 per cent. The top ten countries account for 57 per cent of all imports and the next 13 for a further 28.8 per cent. The balance, 14.3 per cent, is divided among all the remainder. Bangladesh, which is ranked eighth with a 3.3 per cent share, is the top exporting country from the Commonwealth. India, although ranked eleventh, is close behind and accounts for 3 per cent of imports. Other Commonwealth countries in the top 23 are Canada (2.7%), Sri Lanka (2.5%), Pakistan (1.6%) and Malaysia (1.3%).

Chart 3.2: US Apparel Imports by Leading Countries, 2001
(total imports $58.5 billion)

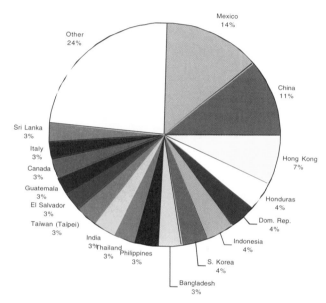

Source: Extracted from US Department of Commerce data for HS61 and HS62 (from www.strategis.ic.gc.ca)

US apparel imports from Commonwealth developing countries

As shown in Table 3.5 and Chart 3.3, US apparel imports from the Commonwealth were valued at $10.7 billion in 2001. Of these, all but $2 billion came from Commonwealth developing countries. Taken as a whole, Commonwealth developing countries supplied almost 15 per cent of all US garment imports. This figure rises to over 18 per cent for Commonwealth countries' market share when Australia, Canada, the UK and New Zealand are included.

The leading exporter to the US from Commonwealth developing countries was Bangladesh, with a 3.3 per cent share valued at $1.9 billion. Jamaica and South Africa were in tenth and eleventh position respectively, with 0.3 per cent market shares. In between, in descending order were India, Sri Lanka, Pakistan, Malaysia, Singapore, Mauritius, Lesotho and Brunei Darussalam.

Chart 3.3: US Apparel Imports from Commonwealth Countries, 2001
(total imports from Commonwealth $10.7 billion)

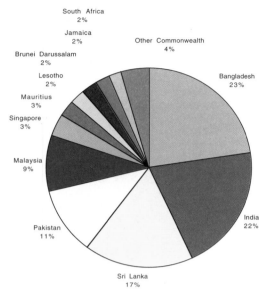

Source: Extracted from US Department of Commerce data for HS61 and HS62 (from www.strategis.ic.gc.ca)

3.4 European Union Apparel Imports from Commonwealth Countries

Total EU apparel imports

In 2001, the imports of apparel to the European Union reached a value of just under €50.4 billion. The distribution by region is shown in Table 3.6 and Chart 3.4.

Asia, taken as a whole, was the most important region, accounting for 47.4 per cent of imports. The other large suppliers were Eastern Europe, the Mediterranean and Middle East, with 47.1 per cent. In contrast, this region only supplied 7.1 per cent of US imports. Again, it is noteworthy that imports from sub-Saharan Africa accounted only for 2.1 per cent. The Americas, again in contrast to the situation for imports by the US, played a very minor role at 1.4 per cent. This figure includes imports to Europe from the US itself.

Top countries exporting to the EU

The top exporting countries to the European Union for apparel in 2001 are shown in Table 3.7 and Chart 3.5. China was in premier place, with 15.8 per cent of all imports, followed by Turkey with 11.5 per cent. The top 18 countries accounted for just under 80 per cent of all imports.

The top Commonwealth exporter was Bangladesh, with a 5.5 per cent share, followed by India with 4.3 per cent of imports. Other Commonwealth countries in the top group were Sri Lanka (1.5%), Mauritius (1.3%) and Pakistan (1.3%).

Chart 3.4: EU Apparel Imports by Region, 2001 (total imports ECU 50.4 billion)

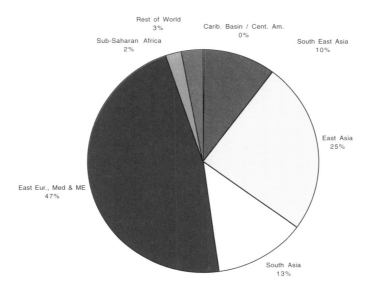

Rest of World
3%

Carib. Basin / Cent. Am.
0%

Sub-Saharan Africa
2%

South East Asia
10%

East Asia
25%

East Eur., Med & ME
47%

South Asia
13%

Source: Extracted from EUROSTAT data for HS61 and HS62

Chart 3.5: EU Apparel Imports by Leading Countries, 2001 (total imports ECU 50.4 billion)

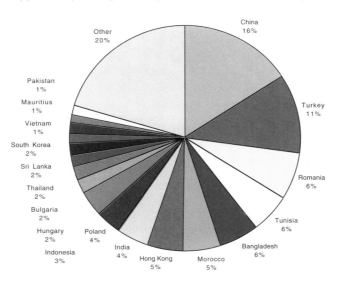

China
16%

Other
20%

Turkey
11%

Pakistan
1%

Mauritius
1%

Vietnam
1%

South Korea
2%

Romania
6%

Sri Lanka
2%

Thailand
2%

Bulgaria
2%

Tunisia
6%

Hungary
2%

Poland
4%

Indonesia
3%

India
4%

Hong Kong
5%

Morocco
5%

Bangladesh
6%

Source: Extracted from EUROSTAT data for HS61 and HS62

EU imports from Commonwealth developing countries

As shown in Table 3.8 and Chart 3.6, EU apparel imports from the Commonwealth were valued at $7.9 billion in 2001. Altogether, Commonwealth developing countries supplied just under 16 per cent of all EU imports.

The leading Commonwealth developing country exporter to the EU was Bangladesh, with a 5.5 per cent share valued at €2.8 billion, followed by India with a 4.3 per cent share valued at €2.2 billion. Jamaica and South Africa were in ninth and tenth place respectively with 0.2 per cent market shares. In between, in descending order were Sri Lanka, Mauritius, Pakistan, Malaysia, Malta and Singapore.

Chart 3.6: EU Apparel Imports from Commonwealth Countries, 2001
(total imports from Commonwealth ECU 7.9 billion)

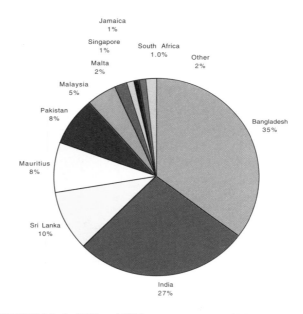

Source: Extracted from EUROSTAT data for HS61 and HS62

3.5 Choice of Countries for Case Studies

The countries selected for field research are from three regions: Southern Africa, Asia and the Caribbean. All three areas include countries in which apparel exports play a significant role in the economy. The market shares of these countries (Jamaica, Bangladesh, Sri Lanka, Mauritius, South Africa and Lesotho) for the US and EU markets are presented in Table 3.9. The contribution of apparel to their exports is also indicated.

These countries were chosen in order to obtain a cross-section of views on the issues pertaining to each region and to the key stakeholders in that region. At the same time, there is a broad cross-section in terms of dependence on apparel exports, ranging from

Bangladesh with apparel representing just under 75 per cent of all exports, to South Africa where the industry accounts for less than 1 per cent of export sales, but is significant in domestic production of apparel. Most of the sample countries are also among the leading Commonwealth exporters in their region.

3.6 Summary

Based on their export performance and as a contributor to foreign exchange earnings, it is clear that the apparel sectors in many Commonwealth developing countries are significant to the economic wellbeing of these economies. Any external threats or global shift in trading patterns in the apparel sector will impact significantly on the economies of these countries. In 2001, Commonwealth countries supplied close to 16 per cent of all EU apparel imports and in excess of 18 per cent of US apparel imports. One Commonwealth country ranked in the top ten for US imports (Bangladesh, in eighth place) and two ranked in the top ten for EU imports (Bangladesh, in fifth place, and India in eighth place).

The data also clearly indicate the impact of proximity, with the United States sourcing 34.2 per cent of its garment imports from the Americas and only 7.1 per cent from Eastern Europe, the Middle East and the Mediterranean. In contrast, this latter region supplied 47.1 per cent to the EU, while the Americas, including the US, only supplied 1.4 per cent of EU imports. The continued strength of Western Europe as an apparel supplier is noteworthy; in 2001 it supplied 3.8 per cent of US imports.

Birnbaum (2001) postulates critical thresholds for identification of countries that are particularly at risk in the changing apparel industry environment – these are market shares of less than 3 per cent and an apparel share of total exports that approaches or exceeds 50 per cent. In this context, it is noted that there were three Commonwealth developing countries with apparel exports exceeding 50 per cent of total exports. These were Bangladesh (77.2%), Mauritius (56.5%) and Sri Lanka (50.8%). Three other countries had apparel exports that accounted for more than 20 per cent of total exports, namely Maldives (42.3%), Fiji (35.0%) and Pakistan (23.1%).

In terms of market share, only Bangladesh and India met or exceeded the 3 per cent threshold in Europe (5.5 per cent and 4.3 per cent, respectively) and in the US (3.3 per cent and 3.0 per cent, respectively). Sri Lanka was relatively close to the threshold for the US with 2.5 per cent.

Table 3.1: Apparel Exports from Commonwealth Countries, 2001 (ranked by value)

Country	Apparel Exports	
	Value (US$ million)	% of Total Exports
Bangladesh	5,016.00	77.2
India	4,976.16	12.2
United Kingdom	3,383.82	1.3
Sri Lanka	2,327.80	50.8
Pakistan	1,830.22	21.53
Canada	1,709.09	0.7
Singapore	1,595.76	1.3
Malaysia	1,194.02	1.4
Mauritius	860.03	56.5
Brunei Darussalam	371.64	10.2
Jamaica	272.44	18.0
South Africa	227.99	0.7
Fiji	172.61	35.0
Australia	165.48	0.3
Malta	135.98	7.7
New Zealand	75.10	0.5
Kenya	71.46	4.8
Botswana	54.62	3.1
Lesotho	50.91	19.5
Maldives	32.41	42.3
Malawi	32.00	7.5
Cyprus	30.50	8.0
Belize	17.28	6.8
Mozambique	14.40	2.1
Swaziland	11.43	1.6
Trinidad and Tobago	10.51	0.2
Sierra Leone	3.42	3.6
Tanzania	2.31	0.5
Barbados	1.71	1.0
Samoa	1.47	2.3
Nigeria	0.61	0.0
Ghana	0.57	0.0
Grenada	0.53	1.0
St Kitts and Nevis	0.45	1.6
St Vincent and the Grenadines	0.15	0.1
Gambia	0.13	0.5
Zambia	0.12	0.0
Antigua and Barbuda	0.06	0.0
Uganda	0.04	0.0
Dominica	0.02	0.1
Cameroon	0.01	0.0
All Commonwealth	25,062.18	
Except UK, Australia, New Zealand and Canada	19,728.69	

Source: Compiled by the International Trade Centre from COMTRADE Database of UNSD

Table 3.2: Apparel Exports from Commonwealth Countries, 2001 (ranked by percentage of total exports)

Country	Apparel Exports	
	Value (US$ million)	% of Total Exports
Bangladesh	5,016.00	77.2
Mauritius	860.03	56.5
Sri Lanka	2,327.80	50.8
Maldives	32.41	42.3
Fiji	172.61	35.0
Pakistan	1,830.22	21.53
Lesotho	50.91	19.5
Jamaica	272.44	18.0
India	4,976.16	12.2
Brunei Darussalam	371.64	10.2
Cyprus	30.50	8.0
Malta	135.98	7.7
Malawi	32.00	7.5
Belize	17.28	6.8
Kenya	71.46	4.8
Sierra Leone	3.42	3.6
Botswana	54.62	3.1
Samoa	1.47	2.3
Mozambique	14.40	2.1
Swaziland	11.43	1.6
St Kitts and Nevis	0.45	1.6
Malaysia	1,194.02	1.4
United Kingdom	3,383.82	1.3
Singapore	1,595.76	1.3
Barbados	1.71	1.0
Grenada	0.53	1.0
Canada	1,709.09	0.7
South Africa	227.99	0.7
New Zealand	75.10	0.5
Tanzania	2.31	0.5
Gambia	0.13	0.5
Australia	165.48	0.3
Trinidad and Tobago	10.51	0.2
St Vincent-Grenadines	0.15	0.1
Dominica	0.02	0.1
Nigeria	0.61	0.0
Ghana	0.57	0.0
Zambia	0.12	0.0
Antigua and Barbuda	0.06	0.0
Uganda	0.04	0.0
Cameroon	0.01	0.0
All Commonwealth	25,062.18	
Except UK, Australia, New Zealand and Canada	19,728.69	

Source: Compiled by the International Trade Centre from COMTRADE Database of UNSD

Table 3.3: US Apparel Imports by Region, 2001

Region/Country	% of Total	Value (US$ million)
Caribbean Basin/ Central America	16.9	9,868.0
South East Asia	16.7	9,788.9
East Asia (excluding China)	14.3	8,348.6
Mexico	13.7	8,027.5
China	11.0	6,429.7
South Asia	10.7	6,282.2
East Europe, Mediterranean, Middle East	7.1	4,159.3
Western Europe	3.8	2,237.9
Canada	2.7	1,573.3
Sub-Saharan Africa	1.6	949.6
Other South America	0.9	544.1
Southern Pacific	0.6	340.6
Total	**100.0**	**58,549.6**

Source: Calculations based on US Department of Commerce data for HS 61 and HS 62 (from www.strategis.ic.gc.ca)

Table 3.4: US Apparel Imports from Top 23 Countries, 2001

Rank	Country	% of Total Imports	Value (US$ million)
1	Mexico	13.7	8,028
2	China	11.0	6,430
3	Hong Kong	7.2	4,202
4	Honduras	4.2	2,438
5	Dominican Republic	3.8	2,226
6	Indonesia	3.8	2,215
7	South Korea	3.7	2,172
8	Bangladesh	3.3	1,930
9	Philippines	3.2	1,877
10	Thailand	3.1	1,840
	Top 10	57.0	33,358
11	India	3.0	1,781
12	Taiwan	2.9	1,699
13	El Salvador	2.8	1,633
14	Guatemala	2.8	1,612
15	Canada	2.7	1,573
16	Italy	2.6	1,516
17	Sri Lanka	2.5	1,486
18	Macau	1.9	1,085
19	Turkey	1.8	1,045
20	Pakistan	1.6	935
21	Cambodia	1.6	920
22	Malaysia	1.3	785
23	Costa Rica	1.3	771
	Nos. 11–23	28.8	16841
	Total: top 23	85.8	50,199
	Total: others	14.2	8,350
	Overall total	**100.0**	**58,550**

Source: Calculations based on US Department of Commerce data for HS 61 and HS 62
(from www.strategis.ic.gc.ca)

Table 3.5: US Apparel Imports from Commonwealth Countries, 2001

Rank	Country	% of US Total Imports	Value (US$ million)
1	Bangladesh	3.3	1,930.2
2	India	3.0	1,781.4
3	Sri Lanka	2.5	1,486.3
4	Pakistan	1.6	934.8
5	Malaysia	1.3	785.3
6	Singapore	0.5	298.5
7	Mauritius	0.4	238.2
8	Lesotho	0.4	214.8
9	Brunei Darussalam	0.4	212.4
10	Jamaica	0.3	187.5
11	South Africa	0.3	173.3
	Other developing Commonwealth	0.6	373.6
	Total: Developing Commonwealth	14.7	8,616.4
	Australia, Canada, New Zealand, UK	3.5	2,046.7
	Total Commonwealth	**18.2**	**10,663.1**

Source: Calculations based on US Department of Commerce data for HS 61 and HS 62
(from www.strategis.ic.gc.ca)

Table 3.6: EU Apparel Imports by Region, 2001

Region/Country	% of Total	Value (ECU million)
Caribbean Basin/Central America	0.3	166.0
South East Asia	10.0	5,013.4
East Asia	24.7	12,427.5
South Asia	12.7	6,412.1
East Europe, Mediterranean, Middle East	47.1	23,696.4
Sub-Saharan Africa	2.1	1,072.6
Rest of world	3.1	1,564.1
Top 6	96.9	48787.9
Other South America	0.2	112.6
US, Canada, Mexico	0.9	465.8
Southern Pacific	0.7	350.6
Other Western Europe	1.3	635.1
Total	100.0	50,352.0

Source: Calculations based on EUROSTAT data for HS 61 and HS 62

Table 3.7: EU Apparel Imports from Top 18 Countries, 2001

Rank	Country	% of Total	Value (ECU million)
1	China	15.8	7,977.9
2	Turkey	11.5	5,775.5
3	Romania	6.5	3,257.5
4	Tunisia	5.7	2,866.9
5	Bangladesh	5.5	2,794.5
6	Morocco	5.2	2,625.2
7	Hong Kong	5.1	2,552.6
8	India	4.3	2,162.5
9	Poland	3.8	1,921.6
10	Indonesia	3.5	1,759.6
11	Hungary	2.1	1,047.9
12	Bulgaria	2.0	986.4
13	Thailand	1.7	839.8
14	Sri Lanka	1.5	763.2
15	South Korea	1.5	755.9
16	Vietnam	1.5	738.3
17	Mauritius	1.3	666.8
18	Pakistan	1.3	645.5
	Total: top 18	79.7	40,137.5
	Others	20.3	10,214.5
	Total	**100.0**	**50,352.1**

Source: Calculations based on EUROSTAT data for HS 61 and HS 62

Table 3.8: EU Apparel Imports from Commonwealth Countries, 2001

Rank	Country	% of Total	Value (ECU million)
1	Bangladesh	5.5	2,794.5
2	India	4.3	2,162.5
3	Sri Lanka	1.5	763.2
4	Mauritius	1.3	666.8
5	Pakistan	1.3	645.5
6	Malaysia	0.7	371.4
7	Malta	0.3	137.6
8	Singapore	0.2	88.7
9	Jamaica	0.2	84.3
10	South Africa	0.2	77.9
	Other	0.3	133.9
	Top 10	15.5	7,792.4
	Total Commonwealth	**15.7**	**7926.3**

Source: Calculations based on EUROSTAT data for HS 61 and HS 62

Table 3.9: Market Shares of Countries Selected for Case Studies

	Country Data	US Market		EU Market	
	Apparel as Share of Exports (%)	Share in Region (%)	Share of US Imports (%)	Share in Region (%)	Share of EU Imports (%)
Jamaica	19.0	2	0.3	51	0.2
Bangladesh	77.2	6	3.3	12	5.5
Sri Lanka	50.3	5	2.5	3	1.5
Mauritius	56.5	25	0.4	62	1.3
South Africa	0.7	18	0.3	7	0.2
Lesotho	19.5	23	0.4	0.4	–

Source: Calculations based on previous tables

Kankakee Community College

4

Survey of Sourcing Practices

4.1 Introduction

The discussion of changing forces in the apparel industry presented in Chapter 2 emphasises that the buyers control the value chain and that vendors must strive to develop the capability to carry out as many functions as the buyers wish to pass on. It also emphasises, however, that not all buyers have the same expectations of, or care to place the same burdens on, their suppliers. Insight into the sourcing strategies and selection criteria of leading buyers and their assessment of the impact of the demise of the quota system is therefore critical in formulating advice to apparel manufacturers (vendors) and support agencies in Commonwealth developing countries. The views of leading sourcing executives surveyed during research for this study are the focus of this chapter.

Meetings were held in February 2001 with a number of leading European importers and the European Apparel Importers Association. The principal research activity, however, consisted of face-to-face interviews in October and November 2002 in North America with industry association representatives and top sourcing executives of 15 companies – 13 in the US and two in Canada. These were complemented by participation in the 14th Annual Textile and Apparel Importers Trade and Transportation Conference organised by USA-ITA and the American Import Shippers Association in November 2002. This conference provided viewpoints on key issues of concern to importers from very senior government and industry representatives.

In preparing the survey of sourcing executives, the major companies in each of the five principal industry categories were identified. A shortlist was then compiled of suitable companies in each of these five categories, taking account of available time and travel constraints. Appointments were then requested and an appointment schedule developed. Table 4.1 presents the companies which participated in the survey and the general category into which they are best classified. It should be noted that there is growing overlap in categories as traditional retailers develop internet sales and as direct merchants and branded apparel companies open shop front operations. Table 4.2 lists the institutions and associations that were interviewed.

The 15 companies included in this survey represent a broad cross-section of apparel importing organisations, be they retailers, wholesalers, importers or branded merchandisers. Most companies are leaders in their category and many of the importing companies, while leaders in their field, also sell to the leading retailers. The FOB value of apparel imports of the companies included in the survey ranged from $100 million to $3 billion. Taken as a whole, the 13 US companies are estimated to account for approximately 25 per cent of US apparel imports in 2001.

More specifically, the US survey sample included two of the leaders in branded goods, three of the top ten department stores, two of the leading specialty retailers, two of the top independent import houses and three of the top direct marketers. Three smaller companies were also interviewed, one in the US and two in Canada, to ensure that the viewpoints of firms other than the giants of the industry were also taken into account.

Meetings were conducted in a discussion format, using an interview guide to keep the discussion on track. The focus of the meetings was to review the following:

- current patterns of sourcing (countries, market segments and product types);

- criteria for selection of countries and vendors within these countries;

- the extent to which current patterns are, or were, dependent on quota availability;

- how these patterns and selection criteria might change following full integration of the WTO Agreement on Textiles and Clothing in January 2005, and with the accession of China to the WTO;

- changes in sourcing practices for competitive reasons and how vendors could respond to these.

The interviews provided a wealth of information on sourcing practices, criteria and trends that should provide valuable input to the discussion of implications for Commonwealth apparel manufacturers. Interviewees suggested strategies for moving forward. Matching existing knowledge of the industries in Commonwealth developing countries with interviewees' comments confirms that much information needs to be appropriately conveyed to, and adopted by, the various stakeholders in the apparel industry.

The findings are presented under the following three general headings:

- Driving Forces in the Apparel Market

- The Post-quota World

- The Way Forward

The priority attributes and issues identified by respondents are presented in the text and summarised in tabular form.

4.2 Driving Forces in the Apparel Market

The responses of sourcing executives concerning the forces that shape the apparel business and the sourcing decisions fall into three main categories:

- trade policies and politics;

- changing market environment;

- supply chain management.

Trade policies and politics

As pointed out in Chapter 1, and according to Birnbaum (2000), trade policies are the major contributor to macro costs which, in turn, are the major contributors to total product cost. Sourcing executives interviewed in the course of the survey made it very clear that trade politics and the resultant trade policies within which industry personnel have to work have been a key determinant of their choice of supplier country. They also state that this will be at least as true, and perhaps more true, following the demise of quotas.

> *If you are a sourcing director you need to be a student of United States trade policy, and you need to act on that information.*
> Chairman of the USA-ITA and a senior vice president of J.C. Penney, USA-ITA
> and AISA Trade and Transportation Conference
> *Author's note:* It could be argued that the same applies if you are an apparel exporter.

Of the 15 companies included in the survey of sourcing executives, representatives of nine companies identified trade policy issues as critical. The data presented in Table 4.3 highlight the key trade policy-related issues of concern to respondents and the number of companies whose representatives raised these issues as being important to their company. The principal issues are:

- the uncertainty created by the demise of the MFA;

- trade agreements;

- social impact on Least Developed Countries (LDCs) post-2004;

- lobbying effectiveness;

- other issues in strategy development.

The issues identified with an asterisk (*) in Table 4.3 were also discussed at the 2002 annual meeting of the USA-ITA, a sign of the importance attached to these issues by the apparel importing community. The impact and importance of these concerns are discussed below.

The uncertainty created by the demise of the MFA

Regardless of opinions and expectations about the impact of the final phase of removal of the MFA provisions at the end of 2004, there is a strong consensus that the apparel import industry is about to enter a period of great uncertainty. The uncertainty arises because the relatively stable and forecastable quota system has been replaced by a number of wild cards that are outside the control of the established negotiating and management mechanisms. Anti-dumping and countervail, for example, are in the hands of the US domestic textile and apparel industry, often referred to as the *textile lobby* – the timing and scope are largely in their hands, not those of government. The safeguard provisions established in connection with China's entry to the WTO are also in the forefront of the concerns of sourcing strategy makers.

As a result of this uncertainty, importers realise that it is essential to hedge their bets in order to avoid getting caught up in any anti-dumping, countervail or safeguard disputes. It is also worth noting that the increased likelihood of such anti-dumping and countervail measures makes it even more important that vendors maintain proper costing and records in order to respond to any such allegations.

Trade agreements

Respondents followed closely the evolution of trade agreements that give or will give preferential access on regional and national bases. These include the key regional agreements for sub-Saharan Africa, the Caribbean and the Andean region. In addition, at the time of the study, a number of new free trade agreements were being negotiated.

The countries/regions for which agreements and potential agreements were in various stages of negotiation in November 2002 were reported by the office of the US Trade Representative to include Singapore, Chile, Central America, Morocco, the Southern Africa Customs Union and Australia. There were no public signs of regional free trade agreements in the near term with South Asia or with individual countries in South Asia. It is noted, however, that Sri Lanka has a Temporary Investment Framework Agreement (TIFA) with the US.

Social impact on Least Developed Countries post-2004

Several sourcing executives expressed awareness of and sympathy for the plight of many countries that are heavily dependent on apparel exports. Executives were aware of the potential social and economic impact that could result if these countries are faced with significant job losses. However, the executives saw no mechanism through which they could act on these concerns.

More generally, there is a view among many of the sourcing executives interviewed in the US that developing country issues are not on the trade politics radar screen. The possible exception is sub-Saharan Africa, as a result of AGOA (African Growth and Opportunities Act) (see Chapter 5 for a description of the terms of the Act). Those who did express concern believe that more effective lobbying is necessary to address these issues with key opinion leaders and decision makers, for example in the US Congress.

> *WTO-ATC abandonment of quota is misguided in terms of social issues* [in apparel exporting developing countries]. *People need a chance to participate* [in economic development] *otherwise there will be problems.*
>
> Vice-President, Worldwide Operations
> *Author's note:* Asked if this was an issue the Vice-President responded: 'We hope that this is an issue.'

Lobbying effectiveness

A number of those interviewed for this survey were of the opinion that the effectiveness of measures to intervene or lobby in the US decision-making and legislative process should be reviewed by exporting countries. Some of the hot button issues that can help or hinder such lobbying efforts are set out in the following paragraph.

Transhipment is a critical issue with customs and apparently has resonance in the US textile lobby. Third-country fabric arrangements, for example as under AGOA, also present difficulties because third-country fabric tends to be identified as fabric from China, and so leads to strong resistance from the US textile lobby. Third-country fabric provisions are also viewed as a block to development of the regional textile industry.

> *Most Asian countries are not lobbying effectively. They should plug their issues harder. They should work for safeguards; tell a better story.*
>
> Vice-President, Worldwide Operations

Other issues in strategy development

A number of other trade policy issues are reported to be factored into the sourcing strategies of major US buying companies. These include the issues presented in the following quotations. They reinforce the notion that for US buying companies, apparel is a global business and that the sourcing decisions are both complex and dynamic.

> *Some 'what-ifs' in our strategy development: changes in the applicable rules of origin; agreement by China to an extension on quota rather than face the uncertainty of safeguards and anti-dumping.*
>
> Vice-President, Strategic Sourcing

> *We are looking at possible developments concerning what happens with Vietnam, Andean region, Cuba, Syria, Africa; plus what happens if North Korea opens up and links for textile supply from South Korea*
>
> Vice-President, Sourcing

Changing market environment

The data presented in Table 4.4 highlight the key issues in the changing market environment that were of concern to interviewees and the number of companies whose representatives expressed such concerns. Of the 15 companies surveyed, representatives of 11 companies identified one or more of the issues listed in the table as being important to their company. The issues identified by respondents and discussed below are:

- price deflation;

- the way in which requirements differ by market segment;

- security and customs compliance;
- shareholder profit, customer value and consolidation;
- changes in the US textile industry;
- values and ethical standards.

The impact and importance of these concerns are discussed below. The issues identified with an asterisk (*) in the tables were also discussed at the 2002 annual USA-ITA and AISA Trade and Transportation Conference, a sign of the significance the importing community attach to them.

Price deflation

There is a general expectation that there will be price deflation in the market due to the removal of quotas, and therefore removal of quota rents, and also as a result of increased competition among suppliers. An exacerbating factor is that it is widely believed that there is over-capacity worldwide in apparel manufacturing. The precise level is open to question, but this situation will certainly contribute to the downward pressure on prices. Thus there will be competition both within and between countries.

The way in which requirements differ by market segment

Survey respondents indicated that the sourcing requirements in terms of price, quality, lead time, involvement in the design process and other key factors differ as a function of market segment. Thus a mass market discount retailer will tend towards longer lead times and large orders of basic items, whereas a fashion retailer will have many more styles, small orders and shorter lead times. Respondents stated that fashion retailers are continually changing styles and operate on at least four seasons, whereas catalogue merchants have two basic seasons and much more consistent styles and product lines. As a result, catalogue (or direct) merchants can be more flexible in lead time and can forecast longer in advance. They are thus less driven to seek in-country or vertical fabric supply.

These differing practices have a direct impact on apparel manufacturers (vendors). Despite these general tendencies, it was clear from the survey that companies in a given segment do not all follow the same practices. This underscores the importance of understanding the requirements of individual customers, and of deciding whether such customers can make suitable business partners.

Security and customs compliance

It was evident from the survey findings and from the attention paid to security issues at the USA-ITA and AISA Trade and Transportation Conference that security concerns are of prime importance to US government officials, and therefore to US importers. By extension these issues must also be of concern to apparel manufacturers (vendors) in developing countries.

The critical development was the introduction by the US government in April 2002 of the United States Customs Trade Partnership Against Terrorism (CTPAT). This is a joint initiative between government and business as a response to the terrorist attacks of 11 September 2001. It requires business and government to develop and maintain security measures from factory to port, and involves buyers, vendors, government and all other logistics players (US Customs Service, 2002).

As a result of this agreement, security compliance will become as, or more, critical than compliance with codes of conduct. In addition, there will be an increased burden on vendors in terms of documentation and paperwork resulting from increased security measures, including 24-hour advance shipment notice, requiring increased record keeping and data transmission capabilities.

The motivations behind these issues, the attention that should be paid to them and the benefits that will result from their stringent implementation are indicated in the following quotations from key speakers on the subject of security at the November 2002 USA-ITA and AISA Trade and Transportation Conference.

> *Container security initiatives will result in greater port competitiveness. This requires the support of all stakeholders in the supply chain.*
>
> Deputy Commissioner, Hong Kong Customs

> *The result will be tangible benefits through reduced inspections.*
>
> US Commissioner of Customs

> *Factory level security checklists and security certification will be handled in the same way as the HR compliance.*
>
> Logistics Director, J.C. Penney, Inc.

> *Do you know who your vendor is, who is working for him, who runs his trucks, repairs his equipment, etc, etc? You must be proactive.*
>
> US security consultant

Coupled with increased security concerns are the ongoing requirements of US Customs for compliance with documentation procedures and rules of origin. These concerns were frequently raised by survey respondents and were a focus of presentations at the USA-ITA & AISA Trade and Transportation Conference. Several survey respondents alluded to the data burden placed on importers and their vendors as a result of customs compliance requirements, and viewed a vendor's ability to provide adequate and timely documentation as an increasingly important selection criterion.

Shareholder profit, customer value and consolidation

Many respondents referred to the fact that the US apparel industry functions in a very competitive environment and in a business climate driven by a demand for shareholder profit. This is also borne out in the literature (Abernathy *et al.*, 1999). The bankruptcy of a number of major importers and retailers was a result of this competition, according to several respondents. Consolidation in the industry was another result – horizontally, between retailers and between brands and vertically, between retailers and importers or buying houses.

Respondents also emphasised that, to stay in business, retailers must meet the competition from price leaders in the marketplace, either by directly cutting their prices or by providing a better 'value package' combining price, fashion, style and quality. Many buying operations have, in turn, to satisfy their immediate customers: the merchandisers and retail stores. As intermediaries in the supply chain, they also have to face the risks and the penalties inherent in dealing with merchandisers and retailers.

As a result of the highly competitive environment, respondents reported that they had had to refine their sourcing practices so as to lower costs. This can result in increased demands on apparel manufacturers (vendors), lower prices and less and less time allowed from time of order to delivery of goods to the stores. It is important that apparel manufacturers (vendors) in Commonwealth developing countries understand that these changing requirements are not whims of fancy but are brought about by constant changes in the marketplace. Examples of how these factors influence the sourcing environment are highlighted in the following quotations.

Cost reduction measures pay for increasing demands by retailers.

Logistics Manager

Sales are down but profits are up. This reflects the overall approach of the company.

Logistics Manager

A key issue is what we tell our shareholders. Our products must sell!

Vice-President, Worldwide Operations

Vendors must understand that we exist for our customers, so that they can make money

Chief Executive Officer

Our policy is to provide as compelling a value as our competitor but at a better quality.

Senior Vice-President

Changes in the US textile industry

There are some indications that the US textile industry may be moving towards acceptance of what some would claim is the inevitable, and begin to internationalise. This would mean transferring its expertise to the developing world so that US-owned or allied companies can continue to supply fabric for the US apparel market, even though such apparel would now be made outside the United States. This possibility was raised by speakers at the USA-ITA and AISA Trade and Transportation Conference and was echoed by sourcing executives interviewed during the survey. Such a change of strategy could present opportunities for countries seeking to up-grade their textile production.

Values and ethical standards

Several respondents referred to issues of values and ethical standards – indeed, they identified their values as being defining elements of their companies. Consumers have pushed buyers into this increasing awareness of and respect for values and ethical standards (Abernathy et al., 1999: 271–72) which has led to the requirement for respect for codes of conduct and to the fact that some companies will not do business in certain countries.

It is speculation, but this is surely a first step in laying the groundwork for the establishment of equitable or fair trade in the apparel industry – as is increasingly happening, for example, in the coffee industry.

Supply chain management

As noted in the literature review, the advent of lean retailing has been closely tied to advances in information technology that have enabled major retailers to change the ways in which they do business (Abernathy et al., 1999). This, in turn, has forced buyers to look for an optimal way of executing supply chain transactions (Tyagi, 2003). As a result, it was expected that logistics and supply chain management would be of paramount concern to the sourcing executives interviewed during the survey.

The data presented in Table 4.5 highlight the issues that were of concern to respondents and the number of companies whose representatives expressed such concerns. Of the 15 companies surveyed, representatives of 13 firms identified one or more issues as being important to their company. The issues are:

- advent of the strategic sourcing function;
- supply chain management and optimisation;
- reduction of lead time to market;
- total systems cost, not just first cost;
- push functions and costs to vendors;
- reduction in span of control and vendor base.

The impact and importance of these concerns are discussed in the following sections.

Advent of the strategic sourcing function

At least five of the 13 companies interviewed in the US have established their strategic sourcing function within the past five years or more recently. They reported moving from a first cost or manufacturing cost point of view to consideration of all costs (see the quotation below). This confirms Birnbaum's (2000) assertions regarding the impor-tance of total costs: macro, indirect and direct.

> *The Sourcing Department was only established four years ago: strategic sourcing is a new science in the apparel business.* Vice-President, Sourcing

Supply chain management and optimisation

The need for supply chain management and optimisation was raised by more than the five companies that had formally created supply chain management functions. This reinforces the conclusion that ways of doing business are changing and that vendors must be prepared to adapt, as discussed above, and to be able to interact profession-ally on supply chain issues.

Reduction of lead time to market

Many respondents identified speed to market, and the resultant reduction in lead time from inception to receipt of shipment, as an over-riding factor driving their sourcing decisions. As will be seen in the sections on specific selection criteria, speed to market is almost more important than price. It is a critical element of lean retailing, and such practices are not limited to the apparel industry. Abernathy *et al.* (1999:259) state that suppliers in most consumer industries now face such pressures.

Based on the survey results, the key observation is that pressure to reduce lead time is growing, and that lead times have been reduced in response to market pressures. Respondents indicated that much of the expected shake-out and rationalisation of the supply base which will follow the end of quotas will be the result of pressures to increase speed to market. Respondents emphasised that countries with long lead times will be at a distinct disadvantage post-2004. One major buying company reported that their average lead time was reduced from 21 weeks in 2000 to 18 weeks in 2001 and 14 weeks in 2002; the target for 2003 was set at 12 weeks.

Some of the benefits to be gained from reduced lead time, and the motivation behind the drive to reduce these times, are illustrated in the following quotations.

> *Buyers try to wait as long as possible. Buyers do not want to be pinned down.* Director, Imports

> *Three years ago most fabric for our Bangladesh operations came from China. Now there is a big shift to Bangladesh fabric and regional fabric. We have reduced the lead time for fabric from 30 days to two weeks.* Vice-President, Sourcing

Total systems cost, not just first cost

One of the core functions of the supply chain optimisation process, as identified in the literature review, is to take into account total system cost. Respondents to the survey confirmed that the days of negotiating the lowest price and hoping that it would meet targets once delivered to the distribution centre are over. Respondents reported that they increasingly include inspections, cost of time delays and penalties in the cost equation in deciding where to place an order, and that they work hard at reducing more transparent costs such as shipping and duties (see the quotations below). The implication is that apparel manufacturers in developing countries must take on increasing responsibility. In this environment they must take account of the total cost approach and be able to intervene to contribute to cost reduction.

> We have moved from a first cost viewpoint to a total cost. Thus vendors must be aware of invisible costs, such as that they need 40–45 ft containers, not 20ft ones.
>
> Vice-President, Worldwide Operations

> We work out the total cost. Five years ago sourcing was a question of negotiation by the product department. It has evolved from meeting a selling price to getting the best value.
>
> Vice-President, Sourcing

Push functions and costs to vendors

Many company representatives interviewed during the survey referred to the increasing role played by apparel manufacturers (vendors). In essence, the buyers have realised that by requiring vendors to do more they can also pass costs, and the capital requirements, on to them. This confirms the observations in the literature review about the reduction of indirect costs by transferring activities to vendors (Birnbaum, 2000). Respondents to the survey provided a number of indicators of an enhanced role for apparel manufacturers from developing countries. These include a move from working on a cut, make and trim (CMT) basis to a full package basis, increased requirements for fabric in inventory, a trend to landed duty paid (LDP) terms rather than FOB and a trend to credit terms rather than letters of credit.

The implication is that apparel manufacturers from developing countries must be able to respond to these demands. They must be able to take on new functions. They must also be able to raise the required capital for the necessary investments or to carry increased costs, for example, for inventory. The increased capitalisation may in turn require consolidation or collaboration in order to reach critical mass.

Reduction in span of control and vendor base

According to respondents, a critical issue in management of the vendor base is the *span of control*. Respondents frequently stated that their companies were sourcing in anything from 20 to 40 or more countries, with up to ten or more factories per country. This is a vast number, particularly when compared to the concentration in most other industries. Thus respondents indicated that there is a natural drive to reduce the number of countries, and perhaps more critically, the number of factories in each country from which they source – in management terms, to reduce the span of control. The result is a strong intent, once no longer constrained by quota, to move towards a reduction in the number of countries and factories. The views of respondents from four major US companies illustrate this point.

> *We are always trying to reduce the vendor matrix.*
> Vice-President, Planning and Inventory
>
> *We need to shrink the supply chain; we need flexibility in the supply chain.*
> Vice-President, Sourcing
>
> *In 1995 we sourced 65 million units from 500 factories in 38 countries. In 2002 we sourced 160 million units from only 280 factories in 32 countries. Our target is to get this down to 16 countries. At present, probably 40 per cent of [vendors] are selected because of quota and some 20 countries account for 80 per cent of product.* Vice-President, Worldwide Operations
>
> *In 2002 we are sourcing from 280 factories in 36 countries. Our target is 160 factories in 20 countries.* Vice-President, Sourcing and Operations

4.3 The Post-quota World

Respondents to the survey provided significant insights into their expectations for the evolution of sourcing practices following the demise of the quota system at the end of 2004. The critical factors identified are presented in Table 4.6. All 15 companies surveyed contributed to the formulation of the expected outcomes and strategies set out in the table. The principal expectations and strategies are discussed in the following sections.

Two complementary visions

There was a general consensus from respondents that simply on the basis of good supply chain management, companies will be under pressure to consolidate their sourcing. There was also consensus that China will be a net beneficiary and that some countries will lose business, particularly where quota availability is the principal motivating factor.

It was also clear from the survey, however, that companies intend to resist the temptation to rapidly reduce their sourcing base to a minimum. That is, they will spread their business, and any risk, through more countries than might otherwise be indicated. As a result, it is expected that there will continue to be a broad base of significant supplying countries. Once the uncertainties surrounding anti-dumping, countervails and safeguard measures have dissipated, however, it would appear that the extent of risk-spreading will be re-examined and further reductions might occur.

Forces for buyer retention

As discussed in the preceding paragraphs, survey findings indicate that there are a number of factors that will have the net effect of continuing to spread business among a relatively broad base of countries and suppliers. This being said, it is expected that the supplier base for any one company will be substantially reduced from 2002 levels. Key factors that are expected to keep business with the better prepared companies and in the better prepared and/or more favoured countries are discussed below. They are:

- spreading risk;

- concerns about China;

- the benefit of strong relationships;

- the impact of trade agreements;

- opportunities in other countries.

Spreading risk

On account of the uncertainties related to safeguard provisions and to the expected launch of anti-dumping and countervail proceedings by US industry, most survey respondents indicated that their buyers would hedge their bets and retain a supplier base that is wider than might otherwise be expected. Furthermore, most interviewees stated that putting all their eggs in one basket was not an option, not only for fear of safeguard, anti-dumping and countervail actions but, more basically, as prudent risk management.

Concerns about China

A further factor that emerged from the survey is that some respondent companies have concerns about China that go beyond safeguards and anti-dumping. They foresee the possibility of rising costs in China and are uncertain about the ability of suppliers to maintain prices, quality and service as business moves inland. These possibilities are further factors that encourage companies to retain a broad supplier base. An additional factor is the growing domestic market for apparel and a consequent impact on prices.

> *Chinese domestic consumption in apparel is rising and for the first time the increase in consumption is greater than the increase in production capacity. Therefore prices will rise.*
>
> Vice-President, Sourcing

Strong relationships

Several respondents stated that their companies had established strong relationships with some suppliers and/or had made substantial investments in time and money in suppliers. They expressed the view that in these cases they intended to continue to do business with these countries and companies.

Impact of trade agreements

The benefits for buyers stemming from trade agreements, such as those for sub-Saharan Africa, the Caribbean and the Andean region, were cited as factors that would influence location. The African Growth and Opportunity Act was of particular interest in this connection, especially for synthetic fabrics where there is a substantial duty advantage.

Opportunities in other countries

A further stabilising factor referred to by respondents is opportunities in other markets. They expressed the belief that opportunities would arise in the global market and that too heavy concentration in one region or country would limit their ability to capitalise on them.

Winners and losers

In terms of winners, there appears to be consensus among respondents that China will become the standard in the apparel industry and that it will gain business. The strength of this belief is perhaps best illustrated by the overt extent to which respondents emphasise their search for alternative strategies so as to spread risk. There will, however, be other beneficiaries, particularly those countries that are already competitive and can attain rapid turn-around times for fabric, either because of local production or through excellent supply arrangements. The following quotation illustrates this more optimistic view.

> *Low labour cost countries with good infrastructure will probably be beneficiaries; particularly if they have yarn, fabric and trim supply.*
> Chairman of the USA-ITA at USA-ITA and AISA Trade and Transportation Conference

Respondents also indicated examples of situations where country exports were constrained by quota limits. In such situations, exports will be expected to grow post-2004.

In terms of losers, there is consensus that not all buying companies will leave the same countries, so the impact will probably be diffused. This will particularly be the case until the China safeguard period draws to a close. Some countries are, however, clearly more threatened than others, as indicated by the following quotation.

> *Problem countries: where there is not enough velocity; for example, if we are only working with one factory in a country. It becomes too costly to get QC people there.*
> Vice-President, Sourcing

Another factor referred to by several respondents was the need for a country to retain a critical mass of business and of potential suppliers – it has to be worthwhile for buyers to visit the country, for example. A further factor could be the impact of a reduction in sourcing from a particular country. Shipping frequency could drop or indirect routings might result, leading to longer shipment time. Another concern of some respondents was that where fabric has to be imported, fabric suppliers in those fabric-producing countries might choose to favour domestic apparel manufacturers. Other factors raised during the survey and indicated in Table 4.6 are discussed below are:

- role of textile mills;
- niche opportunities;
- strength of relationships.

Role of textile mills

Several respondents foresaw a growing role for textile mills as key players. The importance of locally produced fabric as one way of reducing lead time and so increase the opportunity for a country to retain its apparel business underscores this potential. Conversely, several respondents remarked that, due to the importance of fabric quality and availability, textile mills might be expected to play a proactive role in structuring and marketing a country's apparel manufacturing capability.

Niche opportunities

There is a general belief among respondents that countries and companies have to establish reputations for particular types of product. One respondent also pointed out that there is a need to find sources for all products at all price points, and that this is a motivation to spread the business.

The survey also found that some types of buyer have more flexibility than others with regard to the availability of local fabric as opposed to having to import fabric. This indicates a strategy for countries where fabric production is limited to focus on market and product niches that can better accommodate imported fabric.

Strength of relationships

The relationship between vendor and buyer is mentioned again because, in the final analysis, this is the *critical factor*. Vendors do not sell to niches – they sell to people. And people buy from people, people whom they trust and in whom they have confidence to deliver what they want, on time, all the time.

Several respondents indicated that while they were pleased with many of their relationships with vendors, they would not be actively looking to establish new partnerships. The implication of this is that, given the short deadlines remaining, the winners will be those companies that have already attained this strong-relationship status. There is then clearly a challenge for those suppliers who do not yet have strong relationships with their customers.

4.4 The Way Forward

This section reports on survey responses that addressed the issues related to country selection, to selection of vendors and to a more detailed discussion of how buying companies manage the process. The findings have been grouped under seven headings:

- attributes sought in a supplier country;
- attributes sought in a vendor – the basics;
- attributes sought in a vendor – pre-production and financing capabilities;
- attributes sought in a vendor – quality of vendor management;
- sourcing structure;
- supply chain management practices;
- factory size.

The details are presented in the following subsections.

Attributes sought in a supplier country

In the course of the survey, respondents were asked about the criteria used in selecting countries in which to do business and then in selecting the vendors in those countries. The conciseness of the response depended upon the individual and their relative viewpoints and many respondents tended to address both country and vendor criteria together. Sufficient distinction can be made, however, to discuss the two issues separately.

Of the 15 company representatives interviewed, 14 identified one or more of the attributes listed in Table 4.7 as important to their companies when deciding on countries from which to source apparel. The importance attached to these attributes varied from company to company and an attempt has thus been made to categorise the responses in terms of the degree to which attributes are deemed to be critical, to be preferred, where there is scope for adjustment/adaptation or where the attribute is not required. Some companies, for example, require more stringent criteria (for example for speed to market, availability of local fabric and shipment time) for some products than for others and are willing to seek an accommodation. In the case of design capability, two companies stated categorically that this was not required and none of the executives interviewed identified this as a critical requirement.

The responses from the survey indicate that the following issues, discussed below, are of concern:

- human rights and labour codes;
- local raw material supply;
- good business climate;
- security and customs conformity;
- country reputation and capability appropriate for product;
- trade and investment agreements;
- design capability.

Human rights and labour codes

There are two forces at work here: first, that the countries have established labour codes and human rights codes that meet the requirements of the consumer community and of the US companies; second, that these codes are enforced. The forces behind the development and assessment of these standards are complex; but suffice it to say that this is what the market requires and companies have little choice but to insist on compliance. Some companies are more sensitive than others, and some will source from certain countries while others will not. The following quotations illustrate these points.

> *Our approach is that we try to live our values and we ask that you respect your law not our law.* [For these reasons] *we do not work in* [certain countries].
> Executive Vice-President, Production and Sourcing

> *We avoid* [a certain country] *because of issues of collective bargaining in the* [export processing zone]
> Vice-President, Worldwide Operations

Local raw material supply

The issue of raw material supply, and particularly of fabric supply, is intimately tied to the speed of response to an order. There was considerable variation in respondents' concerns regarding local fabric supply, as illustrated by the diversity of views on the fabric issue in the following quotations.

> *Raw materials that are indigenous to country of manufacture is key. This could be 40–45 per cent of the sourcing decision*
> Vice-President, Worldwide Operations

> *Some orders can be handled to minimise the impact of lack of fabric. An option is to keep fabric in stock, to use a programme of intelligent buying; or to position fabric in terms of greige fabric, dyed fabric and/or yarn*
> Vice-President. Planning and Inventory

> *Vertical [fabric and production] is better but you pay more. So you can look at how to solve getting all the bits together*
> Vice-President, Planning and Inventory

As indicated in Table 4.7, local fabric was critical for one company and preferred by two others, but six companies indicated a willingness to work out alternative solutions such as stocking of fabric. This can be done either as griege fabric or as finished but uncut fabric. One option discussed by respondents is for fabric processing to be undertaken in-country, including dying, printing and finishing. Another is simply to set in place the procedures to allow for fast, efficient import from the chosen fabric suppliers. The issue of alternative means of fabric supply is addressed in more detail in Chapter 7.

Good business climate

As indicated in Table 4.7, three respondents formally identified this attribute but it was clear from the tenor of the interviews with other respondents that many other factors fall within this broad category. These include lack of bureaucracy and regulation, ease of importation and exportation of goods, port and transportation efficacy, quality of communications systems, and openness and efficiency of the banking system. In addition, respondents interviewed at the World Bank stated that their research had underscored the importance to the textile and apparel industry of a good business climate. These conclusions are aligned with those of Birnbaum (2000) concerning macro costs and the elements that constitute such costs. The following quotations illustrate the nature of the business climate issue.

Import policies are an issue. It is essential to implement measures to help non-textile producers to get fabrics faster; to help to reduce lead-time. Waiting 90–120 days for fabric is too much when China can ship within this time period.

Vice-President, Imports

The country must gear up to give the entrepreneur the tools; to help them to manage on their own

Vice-President, Imports

The really crucial/key factors are the investment climate and the business climate. Problems arise all too often with delays to load/unload containers or with the permitting process, all contributing to unreliability.

Economist, World Bank

Security and customs conformity

A related issue to respect of codes of conduct is that of conformity to customs requirements, such as measures to prevent illegal transhipment designed to by-pass the rules of origin. More critical still is compliance with security requirements (see the following quotations).

In 2001, US Customs visited 1800 factories worldwide. In the future these visits will also look at, and help to verify, security.

US Customs official at USA-ITA and AISA Trade and Transportation Conference

A key issue for us is to conform to US Customs requirements. We cannot afford for something to go wrong, such as transhipment. Then we would be targets.

Executive Vice-President, Production and Sourcing

The importance and sensitivity of these issues to the importing industry are underscored by the fact that security and customs compliance were key topics at the USA-ITA and AISA Trade and Transportation Conference. Respondents to the survey also indicated that security will become increasingly critical and that if a country has a reputation for problems with shipments then buyers will hesitate to do business with them.

Country reputation and capability appropriate for product

Many respondents stated that their starting point is to ask the question: Where could this product be made, taking account of price, quality and market positioning? They will look at general rules of thumb for acquisition of fabric, making of garments, shipping, quality, price and, more generally, best value. They will consider the general image of the country with respect to performance; the potential benefits from duty waiver or preference as a function of trade agreements will also be an issue.

Critical here is the reputation of the country, which may differ from the reality and from the performance of an individual vendor or group of vendors. This underscores the importance of government and industry being mindful of reputation and image, and taking measures to convey the desired and correct information to the marketplace. The following quotations illustrate the process of seeking a supplier country and particularly the importance of country reputation in the marketplace.

Our first questions are: Where can we go to get that product made and where is the right place to make the product?
Director, Sourcing

We do not shop fifty countries. We start off focusing on 3–4 countries where we could place the business,
Vice-President, Imports

Trade and investment agreements

As mentioned above, respondents confirmed that the existence of favourable trade agreements plays a big factor in calculating price advantage and therefore in selecting a country from which to source apparel. In addition, respondents also indicated that the existence and nature of investment agreements can be important in cases where the buying company is seeking to establish longer-term relationships – particularly where such relationships require investment by the buying company or other foreign companies.

Design capability

As indicated in Table 4.7, the importance of design capability varies from buyer to buyer. Some respondents stated that they were open to ideas; others that they actively sought new ideas and design capability; and some stated that they merely wanted a manufacturer to execute a given order. The issue of design capability, and more generally of pre-production capability, is addressed more fully in the next section, concerning attributes sought in a vendor. In the context of country selection, the issue is primarily one of country reputation and of national level capability.

Basic vendor attributes sought

Respondents were also asked about the criteria they used in selecting individual vendors or factories with which to do business. There is some overlap with country selection, which is addressed in the preceding section, but the responses largely concern enterprise level issues. The conciseness of the response depended upon the individual and their relative viewpoints. Many respondents used the terms vendor and factory interchangeably, but more generally *vendor* refers to a multi-factory corporate entity. A vendor is to be distinguished from a buying house or agent by the fact that the vendor owns and operates factories.

Of the 15 company representatives interviewed, 11 discussed one or more attributes that were important to their companies when deciding on vendors from whom to source apparel. These are presented in Table 4.8, together with the number of companies whose representatives indicated that such attributes were important.

The responses from the survey indicate that the following issues are of concern:

- price, quality and speed to market define value;
- code and security compliance are pre-requisites;
- consistent quality;
- speed to market;
- references and reputation;
- service.

Price, quality and speed to market define value

The three standard criteria identified by respondents are price, quality and speed to market. These criteria, however, cannot be viewed in isolation – rather they come together as an indicator of *value*. Most respondents spoke of *competitive pricing*, and went on to clarify that this did not necessarily mean the lowest price because other factors also contribute to the final cost of doing business (Birnbaum, 2000).

Code and security compliance are pre-requisites

The issues of compliance with codes of conduct and security are fundamental. The important issue to remember is that these requirements are imposed externally, by the market and by US Customs. Respondents did state, however, that they are willing to work with some factories to seek improvement, to help them reach the required levels.

Consistent quality

The key word here is *consistency*. Buyers want consistency. They trade off price, quality and speed to market – but they want these parameters to remain constant throughout their experience of working with a vendor on a particular programme.

Speed to market

Speed to market is both a country and a vendor criterion, as was discussed in the previous section on country attributes. The following quotations apply to the individual vendor–buyer transaction and underscore the motivations behind this issue.

Moving the textiles is really not on any more. We buy packages: flexibility in manufacturing, multidimensional and lastly indigenous raw materials.

Vice-President, Worldwide Operations

As a part of speed to market and changing standards, the ability to hold cut tickets for an additional three weeks can be critical. This yields maximum flexibility in deciding what to make and in being able to sell it.

Vice-President, Worldwide Operations

We have lots of categories and products: some need shorter lead times, others are not so critical. The higher the fashion, the more critical the lead time.

Senior-Vice-President

References and reputation

The reputation of a company plays an important role in the buyer's decision-making process. Many respondents stated that when seeking a new vendor they place considerable weight on references and reputation in terms of past clients and past performance (see the quotation below).

Reputation is key. There must be a reason to have you in our portfolio.

Executive Vice-President, Production and Sourcing

Service

Service was used in this portion of the survey as a surrogate for explaining the overall ease, reliability and consistency of doing business with a vendor, including such specifics as on-time delivery and completeness of orders.

Respondents indicate that there are variations from company to company regarding expectations for level of service and in terms of imposing penalties or cancelling orders in cases of late delivery. They emphasise that it is essential for the vendor to understand their expectations in terms of level of service – and to meet these expectations.

Pre-production and financing capabilities sought

Most respondents elaborated on what they seek in terms of pre-production activities such as inputs to the design, sample making and pattern making and fabric sourcing, as well as financial capability. Almost without exception, they emphasised the abundance of choice and that they need strong reasons to retain suppliers, let alone seek new ones (as illustrated by the following quotation).

Production capability is much greater than needs; so being a good factory is not enough. We need a compelling reason to look at a new supplier.

Vice-President, Sourcing

Of the 15 company representatives interviewed, 14 identified one or more of the pre-production and financial capabilities listed in Table 4.9 as important to their companies when selecting vendors from whom to source apparel. The importance attached to these attributes varied from company to company. An attempt has therefore been made to categorise the responses in terms of the degree to which attributes are deemed to be most important, are needed for some markets/are a possible trend or, finally, are not required/not favoured.

The principal findings from this component of the survey, as discussed below, concern:

- Full package as opposed to CMT;
- LDP as opposed to FOB;
- vendor financial capability;
- product development;
- partnerships;
- fabric inventory.

Full package as opposed to CMT

It was clear from the interviews that almost all respondents are moving towards a full package capability in the selection of vendors. This places the onus of obtaining and financing the procurement of fabric on the vendor. In some instances respondents indicated that they would specify where fabric should come from and might even use their stronger bargaining power to negotiate a price and terms, but increasingly vendors are expected to be able to locate and source fabric.

This being said, some buyers will continue to work on a cut and make (C and M) or cut, make and trim basis, particularly for highly valued fabric. Several respondents also indicated that their systems are set up for these processes and that, for the moment, they are reluctant to change. However, change is expected to come. Respondents also indicated that there is a natural reluctance to give up the control that would result under a full package scenario. There are many indications, however, that the more a vendor can offer, the greater their chance of doing business, even if the CMT scenario is retained, at least initially. The following quotations illustrate these viewpoints.

Vendors have to be more proactive. Not simply CMT but bring product ideas and capability. CMT is not really the right mentality. It is no longer adequate to say 'I do great CMT, please come to me.'

Vice-President. Planning and Inventory

We aim for more turns, smaller runs. Therefore modular sewing, smaller factories, good links to fabric suppliers. [Local fabric] *preferred but not essential.*

Vice-President, Sourcing and Operations

Landed Duty Paid as opposed to Free On Board

An increasing trend was observed of buyers operating under terms of LDP; that is, for the vendor to price the goods on the basis of having landed in the US and cleared customs, maybe even including delivery to the buyer's distribution centre. The more traditional FOB usually means, in practice, delivering to a consolidator at or close to the port in the country of manufacture. LDP is currently most frequently applied to products sourced in Mexico and, more generally, in the Caribbean region. Instances were cited, however, of LDP being offered from Chinese vendors. It should also be noted that there is a growing movement to go to standard credit terms (such as 30 days from shipment) rather than negotiating letters of credit.

The primary benefit of LDP is that the vendor carries the costs until delivery to the buyer, thus reducing the buyer's costs and, more importantly, the buyer's capital tied up in in-transit inventory. An additional benefit, cited by respondents, related to possible anti-dumping cases. In the event of an anti-dumping case, the vendor would be the Importer of Record and would be responsible for defending against the allegations. The factor most frequently cited against LDP is that buyers often have more bargaining power with shippers and can negotiate a better price. This suggests a potential avenue for gaining competitive advantage for vendors – working together to negotiate the lowest shipping rates.

The following quotations underscore the debate.

We buy FOB. This enables (the company) to use its negotiating power with consolidation, shipment and process management.
Vice-President, Planning and Inventory

We work with Full Package and some LDP. We get some LDP from Asia, but we compare shipping rates
Director of Sourcing

We are not doing much LDP. Our resources are geared for FOB and so we would need to reposition [to do otherwise]. Also we would lose control.
Vice-President, Sourcing

From CBI and NAFTA we ship under LDP. LDP from Asia could work, we have looked at it but most (vendors) cannot do this at less cost than [our company].
Vice-President, Sourcing and Operations

Vendor financial capability

The trend of buyers to seek vendors offering full package capability and operating on LDP terms, as well as the requirement that they stock fabric and play a larger role in pre-production activities, all point to the need for vendors to be financially strong. This, in turn, respondents indicated, points to a need for an adaptable banking system that understands the apparel industry and for consolidation within the industry in vendor countries.

Respondents also point out that it is partially to overcome the lack of financial capability of vendors that they work with intermediaries such as importers and buying houses that are prepared to provide this capability.

Product development

More than half the company representatives interviewed during the course of the survey stated that they wanted their vendors to offer product development and design services. This is partly a cost and speed to market issue; but respondents indicated that it is also an issue of buyers sincerely seeking new ideas and wanting to work with professionals who can contribute to the product development process.

Some respondents, however, saw their core capability as design and were not prepared to give this function over to vendors. The range of views, and motivations driving these views, are indicated in the following quotations.

Vendors must have a taste level, an eye for what will sell and what will not, must be able to turn samples fast, and must have awareness of global fashion trends. We want our vendors to be a part of the design and product development process, and to understand this process. They must present as first sample products that are desirable. Vice-President, Worldwide Operations

We need a range of active vendors offering creative input. They must travel, know what's happening in Milan and London, do their own store checking, come to us with solutions, Vice-President, Planning and Inventory

Vendors need to keep up with what is happening in fashion. Director of Imports

Grading and pattern making are done in [our head office]; *but, for basic items we rely more and more on vendor input.* Vice-President, Sourcing and Operations

We do not want R&D and design, we want people to execute what we have already established. We are not looking for value added at the front end. Executive Vice-President, Production and Sourcing

Partnerships

Many respondents referred indirectly to the benefits and importance of partnerships and two company representatives addressed the partnership issue explicitly. One representative stated that an important criterion in vendor selection was the suitability of the vendor to be a partner and the vendor's attitude towards such longer-term relationships. The other representative, from a company with an existing and extensive partnership network, stated that, although such relationships were at the core of their approach to business, they did not need any more partners. He added that the time for the formation of such relationships had passed.

Fabric inventory

Six company representatives referred to the importance of vendors being willing and able to hold fabric in inventory. This assumes that buyers can predict their fabric requirements and applies particularly to repeat orders, after the basic order. The aim, of course, is to reduce lead time. The issue of collaborative financing of such inventory by vendor and buyer is discussed in the section on supply chain management practices.

Quality of vendor management sought

The 'soft' issues, as represented by the general term *quality of vendor management*, were raised by most respondents. The specifics to which they referred varied, but they all point to a growing requirement for strong, capably managed vendors. The specific items are discussed in the following paragraphs, with illustrative quotations.

Of the 15 company representatives interviewed, ten identified one or more of the management attributes listed in Table 4.10 as important to their companies when selecting vendors from whom to source apparel. The principal findings from this component of the survey, as discussed below, concern:

- management professionalism;
- continuous improvement;
- communications;
- understanding of market and customers;
- integrity, trust and attitude.

Management professionalism

Increasingly, US apparel companies are part of the major league of corporate America and they are managed accordingly. Smaller, owner-managed import companies do still exist, but the bulk of the business is now done by major corporations, with corporate systems and procedures. As the survey has indicated, and the following quotations reinforce, buying companies want their opposite numbers in the vendor organisations to be equally professional.

We want to deal with factories that are businesses. With progressive manufacturers that have earned the right to be at the table.

Vice-President, Worldwide Operations

Mauritius and South Africa can leverage their people [to manage activities through-out the region]. *They can engage with us: thanks to the training from* [the local retailers].

Executive Vice-President, Production and Sourcing

Continuous improvement

Several respondents stated that one of the important management attributes that they sought from vendors was the willingness and ability to implement continuous improvement. That is, to up-grade work methods, collaborate on solutions to reduce response times, improve quality and, inevitably, to reduce costs.

Communications

Respondents also equated management professionalism with the ability, and more critically the willingness, to communicate effectively. This goes beyond infrastructure issues to the nature and timeliness of communication with a buyer, as illustrated by the following quotations.

Communication and exchange between vendor and buyer is essential: sometimes it can lead to a solution ... but not always. Senior Vice-President

We try to train vendors to be open in communication and to do this up front. Don't wait till the end [when it is too late]. *For example with certain issues we can adjust the size scale* [if we know early enough]. Vice-President, Sourcing

Understanding of market and customers

A frequent comment from company representatives was that all too often vendors did not really understand the market, their customer or, more critically, the position of their customer in terms of the market. The following quotations illustrate this point.

Vendors must understand what we want in terms of quality and price.
Chief Executive Officer

Vendors must understand that our primary role is as merchandisers. They must understand our market and the market trends. Senior Vice-President

Integrity, trust and attitude

Further surrogates used as attributes of management professionalism by company representatives interviewed for the survey were integrity, trust and attitude. Many respondents referred to instances where they relaxed their quality control procedures as integrity and trust were proven and partnerships developed.

Attitude is perhaps the most nebulous and difficult concept to define, but it would appear to be a very critical element in establishing a meaningful business relationship.

> *We look at how you do the process. Not necessarily the stuff that is written down. How you approach issues. How QC engage with factory management.*
> Executive Vice-President, Production and Sourcing

> *Show stoppers are management attitude in regard to change, to growth and to flexibility.*
> Vice-President, Sourcing

Sourcing structure

Executives interviewed provided considerable insights into the overseas sourcing structures that they use and the factors that influence their choice of structure. The variety of options used by buying companies is illustrated in Table 4.11, which outlines the extent to which 13 of the 15 companies reported making use of one or more of the options to help manage their supply chain.

The table shows the variety of means used by buying companies to manage the sourcing process. Further responses, as discussed below, provide insights into the decision process of buying companies as they decide on the structures most appropriate for them.

That many companies have one or more regional offices, in Hong Kong for example, with broad responsibilities throughout the region is well known and was confirmed in the survey. It is also evident, from the survey and from observation in the vendor countries, that the larger buyers also sometimes have their own offices in other supplier countries. Many of the functions of a local office can also be carried out by an agent, who may either be local or from a larger company based elsewhere. The complexity of the issue can be illustrated by the following quotation from a major retailer concerning his vendor structure and functioning of the buyer's offices.

> *We work through offices which are sourcing hubs and have key account teams. We also have a [three tier] vendor structure. Tier A are strategic partners with sales of $10 m plus, Tier B would have sales of $3–4 million and Tier C would be new or occasional vendors. Our business would be distributed among the vendors as follows: 50–60 per cent to Tier A, 30 per cent to Tier B and the balance to Tier C.*
> Vice-President, Sourcing and Operations

On the importance of having one's own offices, one respondent summed it up very well:

> *Our view of the marketplace is through our offices.*
> Senior Vice-President

The roles and functions of agents are illustrated by the following quotations.

We will try to cut out as many non-value added people as possible.
Vice-President, Sourcing

We work with agents but know the factories.   Vice-President, Sourcing

We tried dealing directly with a factory in India: it was a disaster. You need a contact to help keep open the lines of communication.   Director of Imports

Although three companies explicitly reported a preference for dealing with multi-factory vendors as opposed to individual companies, there is clearly a debate about this. Many of the issues are indicated in the following comment from a vice president of a major US retailer:

Holding companies, as opposed to individual factories, are of interest only where they add value: finance equipment, buy or source fabric and trims, assist in merchandising. Otherwise we prefer to work at the factory level. Often all factories in a group will have the same overhead applied. This will be a problem with anti-dumping where specific costs are required.   Vice-President, Sourcing

The use of trading companies or large buying houses is favoured by some companies since they are willing to take a large measure of responsibility for sourcing fabric, managing the manufacturer and organising product development and so on. At least two companies reported working with such operations. The line between more limited agent functions, buying houses and these trading companies was not always clear, however. The key point is that their services add value, and in the end reduce costs, for buyers.

It was consistently mentioned during the course of the survey that outside quality control (QC) is almost always necessary. Two companies reported using third-party expertise. Other options include a company's own QC personnel or QC personnel from the agent or trading company involved in the transaction

The representatives of two retailers interviewed during the survey indicated that in addition to sourcing directly they also work with import houses. This is particularly so for smaller and more complicated orders. Respondents also reported using importers, as well as other intermediaries, when vendors were not able to handle financing or such technicalities as full package. A related finding was that importers report that they are often in a competitive position on orders and that they need rapid response from their vendors in order to be able to bid successfully. In other cases they take product ideas, obtain samples and sell the concept to a major retailer, from whom they obtain an order.

Supply chain management practices

The use of selected supply chain management practices was a topic of enquiry with all company representatives interviewed during the survey. The details of their responses varied, since such issues encroach on confidential corporate strategy and in some cases were outside the domain of the respondent. The data and the quotations that follow do, however, indicate the range of alternatives and some of the motivating factors in choosing how to manage the supply chain

Of the 15 company representatives interviewed, 14 reported using one or more of the supply chain management practices listed in Table 4.12. The extent to which these practices are used varied from company to company and an attempt has therefore been made to characterise use under the following categories: used regularly; used sometimes; planned or under study; not needed.

The principal findings from this component of the survey, as discussed below, concern:

- on-line tracking and electronic data interchange;

- electronic auctions;

- US-based vendor representatives;

- assistance in setting up fabric inventory;

- use of sub-contractors.

On-line tracking and electronic data interchange

As indicated in Table 4.12, there was a range of responses concerning the use of EDI and of on-line tracking. Respondents point to a tendency at present to go slowly and to limit the implementation of such technology to the consolidator or local office level. A frequent comment by respondents was that much can be accomplished with e-mail and meaningful, timely communications. As a result of this, these respondents had resisted imposing EDI capability on the factory floor. However, in some cases, buyers do require or are planning to require EDI capability of vendors, even at factory-floor level. It therefore seems reasonable to assume that such capability will eventually be required more widely at factory level in Commonwealth developing countries.

Respondents did report that even if they do not use EDI, they send purchase orders and product specifications by e-mail using the Adobe portable document format (PDF) application. Use of product data management tools such as Gerber's web PDM and other devices were indicated by at least one respondent. A prevailing view, however, was that they preferred to restrict electronic transfer of colour and pattern information to the level of their offices. Several respondents stated that they were not convinced that courier service with real swatches is not more effective.

The following quotations help to illustrate these issues and how they are addressed by buying companies.

Technology is not a driving consideration: you can do a lot with e-mail. It takes time to be sure about a factory and the justification for an e-investment. Feel comfortable first and get things right on delivery, price and quality.

President, Sourcing

We use EDI in the US and some in Central America but we still have to get Asia to sign-up to the paperless order system. We will not insist on EDI initially but rather after a couple of seasons.

Director, Sourcing

Most vendors are too small for EDI and they can be handled through agents; but in China every factory seems to have direct EDI.

Vice-President, Sourcing

Electronic auctions

The use of electronic auctions was discussed in some depth by three of the company representatives interviewed during the survey. Two of these companies organised them for some programmes with approved vendors. One was very firmly against electronic auctions, for the reasons explained in the following quotation.

We don't need to auction. Our manufacturing professionals know the price. We need executors and consistency!

Executive Vice-President, Production and Sourcing

US-based vendor representatives

Three company representatives addressed this issue explicitly. One was against having vendor representatives in the US on the basis that it only creates one more layer for communication. The other two believed that this was the way to develop and ensure good relationships with vendors; although they also raised the option of vendors travelling more often to the marketplace. The following quotes illustrate some of the benefits.

Through co-operation we arrive at a better product; they should have some presence in the US or travel often to the US. This eases logistics of sending our staff to the East.

Senior Vice-President

[A vendor of sweaters] has a New York office. This helps drive the process because [as a vendor] you must be in the buyer's face.

Vice-President, Sourcing

Assist in setting up fabric inventory

During the interviews four respondents stated a willingness to share the cost and risk of the vendor establishing a fabric inventory. This was particularly so with, but not limited to, direct merchandisers who work on a two-season rather than a four-season system and whose requirements are thus more predictable. The following quotes provide indicators to how such systems could function to the benefit of all.

> *We will work with vendors to build raw material inventory.* Director of Sourcing
>
> *Some orders can be handled to minimise the impact of lack of local fabric production. Where there are similar fabrics but maybe 20–30 styles we can hold dyed fabric as back-up, awaiting style decision. This can be referred to as strategic standardisation. An option is to keep fabric in stock, to use a program of intelligent buying. An example: position fabric in terms of griege, dyed and/or yarn. We never burden the vendor 100 per cent; we will share costs and risk.*
> Vice-President, Planning and Inventory

Use of sub-contractors

The use of sub-contractors was an issue that was raised during the interviews. Respondents were generally not in favour of this practice but were not necessarily specific in the reasons for their objections. The quotation below reflects the views of most respondents.

> *We do not go into sub-contract agreements. We have to put too much energy into human rights and quality control. With small sewing shops we have too much exposure to the downside. Also we have no muscle in terms of vendor loyalty. We need to be able to exercise our will.* Vice-President, Sourcing

Factory size

The issues of factory size and the related issue of numbers of customers and the relative importance of the order were frequently discussed during the survey. While no hard and fast rules emerged, the following quotations serve to indicate some general patterns.

> *A minimum level of business per factory would be US$10 m FOB and this should represent 30–40 per cent of your [the vendor's] business.*
> Executive Vice-President, Production and Sourcing
>
> *Our relationship must be important to the vendor, and vice versa. We do not have a fixed percentage of business. Sometimes 60–70 per cent, sometimes only 10 per cent. It depends on how they [the vendors] treat you.* Director of Imports
>
> *We want to be important to our vendors: maybe 20 per cent to 40 per cent of their capacity; not 5 per cent and not 70 per cent. This [70 per cent] would be bad for both.* Senior Vice-President

Plant size would typically be 1500–2000 workers; but we look at ratios – typically 60 per cent in sewing.   Vice-President, Sourcing

We would want 40–50 per cent of a factory's business; for outerwear maybe 50 per cent and no more than four or five clients per factory.
                                                  Vice-President, Sourcing and Operations

4.5 Summary

There is a general consensus that on a company-by-company basis there will be significant shrinkage of the vendor base following removal of quotas. The extent and scale of this remains to be seen; but the most severely hit will be those suppliers with whom buying companies have been dealing primarily through quota availability. This will be particularly so where they have had few programmes in a country or have been dealing with a very limited number of companies in that country. China is expected to gain because it meets most of the criteria sought by buyers, including vertical supply of fabric and trims and, through Hong Kong or directly, an increasing capability in pre-production activities.

It would appear, however, that at least for the next few years, buyers will retain a significantly diversified position as a hedge against implementation of safeguard provisions against China and anti-dumping measures. In addition, and more importantly, is the fact that where good business relationships have been developed with competitive suppliers, buyers will retain these links. Buyers have enhanced their supply chain management capabilities, however, and expect that vendors will also become increasingly professional in the interface with sophisticated supply chain management practices.

Almost without exception, buying companies report that they seek more than the lowest price for garment manufacturing. There is a growing recognition that their survival depends on recognising all costs associated with developing, making, shipping and marketing the product and delivering lower costs for the total package from idea to market. They thus specify speed to market, price and quality as basic selection criteria and they increasingly want vendors to take on some of the pre-production activities and to carry a greater share of the costs of holding raw materials and finished product. This change in thinking is perhaps best illustrated by the observation that one-third of the representatives of the major corporations interviewed indicated that their company's strategic sourcing unit had been established within the past five years.

The findings of this survey have many important messages for owners and operators of apparel factories in Commonwealth developing countries. The most critical is the need for professional management that will both undertake the internally oriented continuous improvement that is required and that will relate with the increasing professionalism of the representatives of the buying companies. Factories will increasingly have to operate in a manner that requires access to adequate financing and will have to take on more of the pre-production activities.

A new and critical element in the equation is the concern about security, imposed as part of anti-terrorism procedures in the United States. The need for enhanced security, together with the associated drive to on-line reporting, will place additional cost burdens on factories. There was a widespread belief among respondents that these requirements for more and better financing, professional management, security and pre-production capabilities would inevitably lead to corporate consolidation among garment manufacturers.

Availability of textiles will increasingly become an issue, but a number of alternatives to the major investment implied by in-country fabric production and textile self-sufficiency have been identified. In this context, textile companies are expected by some respondents to play an increasing role and there could be some interesting openings for greater involvement with US textile companies.

Finally, the findings from the survey make it abundantly clear that the first decision by most buying companies is to select countries with which to work. Business climate and infrastructure are key and critical factors, as are trade agreements. These, as explained by Birnbaum (2000), are macro-level costs that fall within the purview of government.

Table 4.1: Sourcing Survey – Corporate Meetings

United States

Department stores	J.C. Penney Private Brands Inc. Nordstrom May Department Stores
Speciality retailers	The Limited Ann Taylor
Direct merchants	Speigle Land's End Eddie Bauer
Branded apparel	VF Corporation Liz Claiborne
Importers	E.S. Sutton Inc. Donnkenny Apparel Inc. RK Industries Inc.

Canada

Importer	Canada Sportswear Corp.
Retailer	Reitmans Ltd.

Table 4.2: Sourcing Survey – Institutional Meetings

Meetings were held with representatives from:	Cotton Council World Bank United States Association of Importers of Textiles and Apparel (USAITA)
Speakers at the USA-ITA and AISA Trade and Transportation Conference included representatives of:	United States Customs Hong Kong Customs US Trade Representative's Office Trade Sub-committee of House Ways and Means Committee Cotton Inc. US Department of State

Table 4.3: Principal Trade Policy Issues of Concern to Responding Companies

Issue	Number of Companies
Uncertainty, caused by:	
China safeguards*	7
Anti-dumping*	6
Political risk	5
Trade agreements and other preferences*	4
Social impact on LDCs	3
LDC lobbying effectiveness*	1

*Issues addressed at the USA-ITA and AISA Trade and Transportation Conference

Table 4.4: Principal Market Environment Issues of Concern to Responding Companies

Issue	Number of Companies
Price deflation*	4
Requirements differ by market segment	6
Security and customs compliance**	3
Shareholder profit; customer value	5
Consolidation in US market*	2
Changes in US textile industry*	1
Market is changing: styles, collections	3
Values and ethical standards are issues	2
Over capacity in supply*	2

*Issues addressed at the USA-ITA and AISA Trade and Transportation Conference

Table 4.5: Supply Chain Management Issues of Concern to Responding Companies

Issue	Number of Companies
Advent of strategic sourcing function	5
Supply chain management and optimisation	7
Reduction of lead time to market*	6
Total systems cost, not just first cost	4
Push functions and costs to vendors	6
Reduction in span of control and vendor base*	6

*Issues addressed at the USA-ITA and AISA Trade and Transportation Conference

Table 4.6: Views of the Post-quota World from Responding Companies

Outcomes/strategies	Number of Companies
Some countries will lose business	9
China set to gain business	8
Spread business in view of unknown impact of restraints and other factors	7
Expect potential benefits in AGOA	7
Opportunities in other countries expected	6
Other trade agreements will also influence country choice	5
Potential key role for textile companies	4
If strong relationships: will retain business	3
Specialise, find niche	3
Some concerns with China prices/quality	1

Table 4.7: Attributes Sought in a Supplier Country

Attributes sought	Number of Companies for which the Attribute was Identified as:			
	Critical	Preferred	Open to negotiation	Not required
Respect of human rights and labour codes	9			
Local raw material supply	1	2	6	
Good business climate	3			
Security and customs conformity	1			
Country reputation and capability appropriate for product	2	7		
Trade and investment agreements		4		
Design capability		3	1	2

Table 4.8: Basic Vendor Attributes Sought

Attributes Sought	Number of Companies
Competitive pricing (not necessarily lowest)	8
Code compliance and security	7
Consistent quality	7
Speed to market	5
References/reputation	4
On time delivery	3
Service	3
Completeness of orders	1

Table 4.9: Pre-production and Financing Capabilities Sought

Capability	Number of Companies for which the Capability was Identified as:		
	Most important	Needed markets/ for some possible trend	Not require/ Not favoured
Full package as opposed to CMT	6	1	
LDP as opposed to FOB		7	3
Strong vendor financial capability	3		
Product development/design capability	7	2	2
Partnerships: willingness and ability	1		1
Hold fabric in inventory: ability and willingness	5	1	

Table 4.10: Quality of Vendor Management

Attributes sought	Number of Companies
Management professionalism	4
Continuous improvement: ability and willingness	3
Communications: ability and willingness	3
Understanding of market and customers	3
Integrity, trust and attitude	5
Delivery of proper documentation	3

Table 4.11: Sourcing Structure

Type of overseas structure	Number of companies
Their own offices	6
Agents	7
Multi-factory vendors	3
Trading companies	2
Purchasing agents	2
US-based importers	2

Table 4.12: Supply Chain Management Practices

Supply chain practice/ standard	Number of companies for which the practice was explicitly identified as:			
	Used regularly	Used sometimes	Planned/ studied	Not needed
Online tracking and EDI				
Online tracking from consolidator	3	1		
Require online tracking in plants	1	1		2
Require EDI at factory level			1	2
Electronic auctions	2			1
Colour approval by scanning	1			
Work with US-based vendor representatives	2			1
Purchase orders and specs: e-mailed in PDF	3			
Assist in setting up fabric inventory	4			
Use of sub-contractors				1

5

The Apparel Industry Business Environment in Selected Commonwealth Developing Countries

5.1 Introduction

The role of Commonwealth developing countries in the global apparel industry and the relative importance of apparel exports in their economies were reviewed in Chapter 3. Six countries in three regions were selected for field research: Mauritius, South Africa and Lesotho in Southern Africa; Sri Lanka and Bangladesh in South Asia; and Jamaica in the Caribbean. Meetings were held with senior representatives of 45 apparel factories or factory groups and with 25 representatives of government agencies and departments, industry associations, training establishments and other private sector organisations. These included representatives of industry associations and government agencies working with the apparel industry. The aim was to select a cross-section of companies that had substantial export business and would give a valid view of the issues facing the industry. In general, the selection of companies involved a mix of some of the major players plus a number of smaller but innovative companies.

A further step in the research was the hosting of a seminar for South Asia Association of Regional Cooperation (SAARC) member countries in December 2002 on issues relating to the demise of the Multi-Fibre Arrangement. This seminar was organised by the Commonwealth Secretariat in collaboration with the SAARC Secretariat and hosted by the Government of Sri Lanka. The participating countries were Bangladesh, Bhutan, India, Maldives, Nepal, Pakistan and Sri Lanka. Representatives of each country presented one or more position papers on the profile of the apparel and textile industry in their country, summarising the threats and outlining proposed strategies to address them. Key comments are incorporated in the research.

This chapter takes a closer look at the apparel exports from each of the three regions and then presents a review of the business environment and key issues post-2004. The review focuses on country-level issues, but takes a regional perspective where this is more appropriate. The chapter concludes with a comparative assessment of the relative positioning of the six Commonwealth developing countries with respect to macro-cost factors. An assessment of technical issues facing the apparel industry in the selected countries is presented in Chapter 6. This is followed, in Chapter 7 by a review of up-grading measures being implemented to address these issues at the national and enterprise level.

5.2 Southern Africa: Regional Overview

Market share for apparel

United States imports from sub-Saharan Africa

Apparel imports to the United States in 2001 from sub-Saharan Africa were valued at $950 million, as indicated in Table 3.3. This was equivalent to 1.6 per cent of total apparel imports in that year. All but one of the top exporting countries, Madagascar, as listed in Table 5.1, were from the Commonwealth. The top exporters from the region and their relative share, as indicated in Table 5.1 and in Chart 5.1, were Mauritius (25%), Lesotho (23%), Madagascar (19%) and South Africa (18%). Other ranking countries were Kenya (7%), Swaziland (5%), Zimbabwe (2 %) and Malawi (1%).

Chart 5.1: US Apparel Imports from Sub-Saharan Africa, 2001
(total imports from region $0.95 billion)

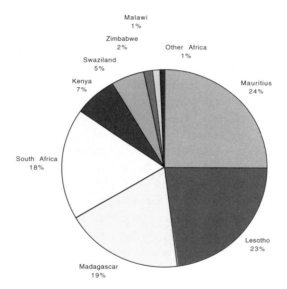

Source: Calculated from US Department of Commerce data for HS61 and HS62 (from www.strategis.ic.gc.ca)

Although not shown in the table, Nigeria, Ghana and Cameroon each had exports worth $250,000. Tanzania and The Gambia had exports valued at $20,000 and $10,000, respectively.

European Union Imports from sub-Saharan Africa

Apparel imports to the European Union in 2001 from sub-Saharan Africa were valued at ECU 1,072.6 million as indicated in Table 3.6. This amounts to 2.1 per cent of EU apparel imports. The majority of these countries were from the Commonwealth.

The top exporters from the region and their market shares, as indicated in Table 5.2 and Chart 5.2, were Mauritius (62.2%), Madagascar (24.8%) and South Africa (7.3%).

Other ranking countries were Zimbabwe (2%), Botswana (1.8%), Lesotho (0.4%), Tanzania (0.2%), Kenya (0.2%) and Mozambique (0.1%).

Chart 5.2: EU Apparel Imports from Sub-Saharan Africa, 2001
(total imports from region ECU1.1 billion)

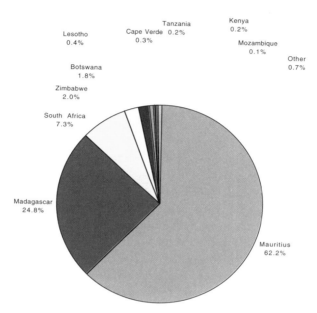

Source: Calculated from EUROSTAT data for HS61 and HS62

African Growth and Opportunities Act

One of the principal factors affecting the development of the industry in Southern Africa, and indeed throughout sub-Saharan Africa, is the US African Growth and Opportunities Act. This Act came into force in May 2000 and governs almost all imports from the region to the US.

Under AGOA, market access is both duty and quota free provided that fabric and yarn are produced in the region. Certain provisions of the original version of AGOA, particularly regarding admissibility of apparel 'knit-to-shape' were clarified in an amended version of the agreement, known as AGOA II. This was signed into law in July 2002 as part of the Trade Act of 2002. The basic provisions of AGOA are summarised in Table 5.3.

Under AGOA I, Least Developed Countries in Africa, including Madagascar and Lesotho, but excluding South Africa and Mauritius, were eligible for duty and quota free access, regardless of fabric source. Under AGOA II, this LDC provision has been extended to Namibia and Botswana. It must be noted, however, that the LDC provisions were set to expire in September 2004.

5.3 Mauritius

Industry overview

The export-oriented apparel industry in Mauritius originated in the 1970s when Hong Kong companies established operations to benefit from cheap labour and the favourable quota environment. Until the mid-1980s the textile scene was dominated by Hong Kong companies with, it is reported, an almost mono-product orientation in knitting of T-shirts and pullovers. The key institutional engine for development was the Export Processing Zone (EPZ) legislation that granted favourable tax and duty treatment, among other benefits, to companies engaged primarily in export-oriented processing or manufacture. This legislation did not tie such companies to specific industrial parks. Most of the companies benefiting from EPZ status were in the textile or apparel industry and support services from government were mainly focused on worker training.

The EPZ Development Authority (EPZDA, 2001:3) reports that the industry reached a peak of 591 firms and 89,080 people employed in 1988. Investors saw Mauritius as a platform for preferential access into European markets. By 1990, competitiveness was down and companies began to diversify into other apparel products. There was, as a result, a reduction in the number of knitwear companies. By June 2000, the textile and apparel industry in Mauritius together accounted for some 80,000 jobs out of a total of 90,700 (EPZDA, 2002). These were distributed between 45 textile and 240 apparel companies. By December 2001, total employment had fallen to 87,600, of which 77,000 were in the textile and apparel industry. The number of companies remained essentially the same.

The distribution of employment from 1999–2001 is presented in Table 5.4. Employment was divided in a ratio of approximately 2:1 between women and men (EPZDA, 2002). Foreign labour plays a significant role in the apparel and textile industries. In 2000 the number of foreign workers was estimated at 13,451, or some 17.5 per cent of the total workforce (EPZDA, 2001). Informal discussions within the industry yield a higher estimate of some 18,000–20,000 foreign labourers working in the textile and apparel industry on up to three-year contracts. Many industry representatives interviewed during the research in Mauritius indicated that labour availability was a problem. There is a pool of unemployed Mauritians, but they are reportedly not interested in employment in the apparel industry.

Two of the most significant developments in the industry in Mauritius were an attempt in the mid-1990s to move up the value chain and the later move to transfer much of the lower valued activity from Mauritius to Madagascar, and now to other countries in Southern Africa. In the mid 1990s:

> ... a number of Mauritian-owned enterprises made concerted attempts to 'move up the value-chain', by extending their design capacity and launching own brands, private labels and collections. The objective was to achieve a dramatic expansion of margins, and in the process shift Mauritius's position in the GCC (global commodity chain) decisively inwards from the outer ring. The outcome of these efforts was

disappointing, and for the enterprises concerned financially costly. Mauritian com-
panies and groups proved to be too financially and managerially weak, too physi-
cally and socially remote from end markets and too internally inflexible to manage
this form of functional up-grading. Their generally successful experience of manag-
ing backward integration in order to meet EU/Lomé Rules of Origin was not trans-
ferable to a process of forward integration.   Gibbon, 2000:43

The movement to Madagascar during the late 1990s through early 2000 was motivated in large measure by the issue of labour availability and the resultant relatively
high wages in Mauritius. Since 2000, a further motivation was that apparel sewn in
Madagascar can benefit from the LDC provisions of AGOA. Most observers report
that Madagascar is a natural partner for Mauritius. It is a little over an hour's flying
time away, has low labour rates and abundant workers. Combined with this are the
LDC provisions of AGOA that allow the use of fabric irrespective of origin. According
to Gibbon (op. cit.: 44): '... *the move "back to the basics" and toward higher volumes*
is certainly not one all the way to the bottom, for it is not (mainly) directed at the dis-
count store market segment. It is more in line with the focus on becoming high-volume
suppliers to the mid-market, pioneered by the major Hong Kong manufacturers in rela-
tion to US brands.'

Most of the major Mauritian companies are reported to have made substantial
investments in Madagascar and it is understood from the interviews undertaken in
Mauritius that by 2001 some groups had up to 70 per cent of their operations there.
At the peak, probably in mid to late 2001, there were 80,000–100,000 workers in the
apparel and textile industry in that country. Due to the political troubles and unrest of
late 2001 through to mid-2002, transportation and basic services were severely dis-
rupted and this forced the closure of plants and withdrawal of Mauritian management
and technical support. The result was a dramatic loss of customers, particularly in the
US market, which had been a focus of the move. It is understood that most Mauritian
companies had to write down these investments and to find alternative production
strategies in order to continue in business. In some cases the financial shocks were too
great and the Madagascar losses, combined with growing lack of competitiveness in
Mauritius and the weakening of the US and EU markets in 2001, precipitated bankruptcy.

This was the situation that prevailed at the time of the field research in June 2002.
It is understood that the situation in Madagascar has since normalised, and that as of
early 2003 business was again picking up. In the final analysis, industry observers did not
believe that the Madagascar crisis would have a terminal effect on Mauritian industry.

Markets

The local and tourist markets are not a significant factor in the apparel industry at
present and thus there is an almost total reliance on exports. Textile and apparel industry exports increased from 22.2 billion rupees (US$0.87 billion at a nominal 25.5
rupees/$) in 1999 to an estimated 27.4 billion rupees (US$0.98 billion at a nominal
28.0 rupees/$) in 2001, as summarised in Table 5.5. Of these, just over 70 per cent

went to the UK, France and US, as indicated in Table 5.6. Based on anecdotal evidence regarding patterns of trade, it is likely that a significant portion of the balance was for textile exports to Madagascar and other countries benefiting from AGOA.

Institutional framework

Trade regimes

Mauritius has benefited historically from the favourable treatment afforded by the European Union and the United States. Exports to the EU were, by 2002, duty and quota free. Until 2000, exports to the US were under quota but there were no rigorous rules of origin for fabric. Then, in May 2000, AGOA came into force. This is one of the key factors affecting development of the industry today in Mauritius. It is worth noting that the negotiations for AGOA took from 1995 to 2000 to finalise and that Mauritius was a leader in the lobbying efforts both for the original Act and for the 2002 amendments. Mauritius was also very active in the subsequent endeavours to explain the Act and its opportunities to eligible countries in Africa.

Industry support

The garment sector has considerable institutional support to sustain its development and progress. Support institutions such as the Clothing Technology Centre (CTC) and the Industrial Vocational Training Board (IVTB) provide short-term training. Longer-term training is available through the University of Mauritius or various vocational training schools. They have been instrumental in consolidating technology and skills and in assisting factories to develop their performance and their market.

The CTC has become a centre of excellence for the industry and the cluster development initiative is centred here, as discussed later in this chapter and in Chapter 7.

Industry structure

Apparel

There were 239 apparel companies in Mauritius in 2001, as indicated in Table 5.7. The interviews revealed that there are 50–70 larger-sized companies, of which six or seven are vertically integrated and account for approximately 40 per cent of capacity. Another source estimates that 80 per cent of the business is with some 20 companies. Most investment in the sector is reported to be from Mauritius and/or Hong Kong. It is understood that while there are some US buying agents in Mauritius, there is no US investment as such in apparel or textile production.

There is some debate, as was clear from discussions with industry representatives and observers, as to whether, under present circumstances, the industry is profitable. A number of major factories are reported to have closed, with job losses of perhaps between 3000–4000 people. This is reportedly due to the pricing squeeze over the past five years, plus the difficulties with Madagascar. Generally, the discussions conclude that while there are profit and loss issues for the larger companies, the weakest companies went under in 2001 and the smaller companies remain profitable.

Yarn and textiles

In the textile, yarn and fabric segment there are 47 companies, as shown in Table 5.7. According to the interviews, there are two major textile firms, SOCOTA and Consolidated Fabrics. These companies are similar in size and together account for some 80 per cent of production. Expansion plans included spinning in Mauritius and new weaving facilities in Madagascar.

Buying houses and agencies

For the past 15 years at least, Mauritius has been the regional centre of activity for a number of major buying houses, including MAST, Gap, Eddie Bauer, William O'Connor and Lee & Fung. There are indications, however, that on the strength of AGOA-related opportunities, at least some companies are moving their regional operations to South Africa. It is clearly easier to visit countries around the sub-region from either Cape Town or Johannesburg, and Madagascar is essentially as close to South Africa as to Mauritius.

Positioning for the future

Apparel remains important

Despite a national effort and will to diversify into Information and Communication Technology (ICT) and other industrial sectors, it would appear that the garment industry will remain a mainstay of the economy for at least another decade. As one interlocutor stated: *'There are very few alternatives to or for the garment industry.'*

Three main avenues have been adopted for future development of the industry. These are:

- move to lower volume, higher margin, product niches;

- leverage the knowledge and market credibility through establishment of operations in other countries within the region;

- develop co-operation networks (or clusters) among Mauritian companies to enable them to better compete globally

Industry development

At the time this study was conducted, industry development was primarily the responsibility of the Mauritius Industry Development Agency (MIDA), which is also responsible for export promotion. In addition, an investment promotion agency was created in 2001. On account of the growing importance of the US market, MIDA has recently opened a liaison office in New York for marketing purposes. Prior to this, it was claimed during interviews, there had been little direct marketing to the US market, except through major retail buyers such as Gap. It was reported that many major US stores do not travel to Mauritius and thus most products are sold through buying offices only.

The necessity of a move to lower volume, higher margin, product niches appears to be widely accepted. As an example, at least three of the Mauritian manufacturers interviewed are moving away from mass production and trying to diversify their production lines and flexibility so as to compete in high value added market niches. A further avenue, particularly in the context of AGOA and the requirement for AGOA-conforming yarn for the knitting industry, is to market the stability of Mauritius for major capital investment. Investment in spinning is now, therefore, a major challenge.

Regional diversification

There is recognition that Mauritius has considerable apparel manufacturing, procurement and product development capability that can be used to advantage. There is thus a sense among industry stakeholders that Mauritius can leverage its reputation for stability and its credibility as a supplier to play a leading role in the development of the textile and apparel industry in Southern Africa. It is also realised, however, that it is a challenge to get, and then keep, Mauritius on the map, in terms of US buyer trips.

The move to find lower-cost production bases resulted in Mauritian investment in Madagascar, as described earlier, and more recently in investment elsewhere in Southern Africa and even further afield. Mauritian apparel manufacturers have started to develop linkages and undertake investments in South Africa and in nearby countries such as Lesotho. During the interviews, some respondents expressed interest in expanding their operations to Ghana and Senegal due to their proximity to markets, but little has developed as yet.

This delocalisation appears to have the support of the Mauritian government. The implication of this is that there is some recognition that it is better to maintain head office and other higher valued functions in the country than to see the entire industry migrate.

Clusters

Since the late 1990s key stakeholders in the apparel industry and its supporting institutions have reportedly discussed the benefits of some form of enhanced collaboration in order to strengthen their chances of survival. The challenge has been how to collaborate in practice and this has led to the concept of clusters. A key factor in formulating this plan was the dominance of the few – but big – apparel groups that were vertically integrated. This vertical integration had removed much of the incentive to outsource and sub-contract, thus preventing the ability to develop collaborative clusters. It was reported, however, that in the early days of the industry companies did some sub-contracting.

The cluster development initiative is centred on the Clothing Technology Centre, designed to provide technical capabilities to small and medium-sized enterprises (SMEs). Its facilities include computer-aided design (CAD) and an electronic/electric spreader for the cutting room. It also offers courses and cutting facilities. It has ten regular users who use the facilities to carry out prototyping. Technical assistance with implementation of the collaborative cluster concept began in June 2002, with consultants from France.

Challenges

At the time of the fieldwork in June 2002 it was clear that Mauritian industry and support institutions were, of necessity, casting around for new strategies following the failure of their ventures in delocalisation in Madagascar. Despite the re-opening of Madagascar, the challenges that drive the industry remain. These can be summarised as follows:

- Mauritius must move to higher value and leave cheaper ranges to delocalised plants.

- The industry must look for alternatives to Madagascar; a logical possibility is South Africa and more generally all the LDC-eligible countries in Southern Africa. West Africa presents possibilities in the longer term.

- A key provision of AGOA is that apparel sewn in selected LDCs from any fabric (not necessarily from the region) has duty and quota free access to the US, under certain up-side limits. This, although beneficial to the countries concerned, is a constraint on investment in fabric and yarn production.

- There is at present a fabric and yarn gap in AGOA-eligible countries. Supply is inadequate to meet demand under AGOA-compliant terms.

- Concerns were expressed that education levels are reported to be slipping.

- A critical mass in textiles and garments is required in order to maintain Mauritius as a place that buyers visit, or from which they operate. This is important if Mauritian companies hope to lever their expertise and credibility as reliable, quality suppliers. The alternative, clearly, is that the centre of operations in the region migrates to South Africa. One source places this critical level at 40,000–45,000 workers.

- Perhaps the biggest challenge is summarised by the following comment from one observer: 'shareholders are reticent; therefore banks are reticent'.

5.4 South Africa

Industry overview

A strong domestic market in South Africa, coupled with the necessity for self-reliance during the apartheid years, led to the development of a substantial textile and apparel industry. Adapting to the global market environment, major retailers have imposed on their suppliers many of the practices prevalent in the North American market. As a result, the industry features a high degree of state of the art equipment and systems (CLOFED, 2000:63). In addition, many industry leaders interviewed during the fieldwork pointed to the strong links between manufacturers and retailers.

Output from the clothing industry in 1998 was estimated at close to US$2 billion (op. cit.:62) and to have remained around that level through 2000. It is estimated that 80–90 per cent of production is for the domestic market; but this proportion is changing rapidly with the advent of AGOA and a drive for export markets in both the traditional European market, particularly the UK, and in the US. Exports reached US$150 million in 2000, split approximately 60:40 per cent between woven and knitted fabric. In 1998, locally produced textiles accounted for just over 75 per cent of local clothing production. An overview of the evolution of the textile and apparel industries is presented in Table 5.8.

CLOFED (2000) reports that approximately 1,400–1,500 firms are officially recognised in the clothing industry, but that there are probably twice as many when the less formal sector is considered. CLOFED (op. cit.:62) also estimates that annual sales could reach $3 billion when the informal sector is included. The textile industry consists of 31 weaving mills, 27 spinning mills and 16 dyeing plants, according to data obtained from the Textile Federation of South Africa. Employment is estimated to be about 130,000 in the formal apparel industry and some 60,000 in the textile industry, according to the Clothing Export Council. The main clothes producing regions are Cape Town, Johannesburg, Durban and Port Elizabeth. There is, however, increasing production in rural and decentralised areas, including Newcastle, Ladysmith and the former 'homelands' such as Kwazulu. Companies tend to be relatively small. The largest company in Johannesburg has 600 employees, according to one industry player interviewed, but there are apparently some large Chinese-owned plants in the decentralised regions. The largest plant in the country, at the time of the study, is reported to have approximately 1,000 employees.

Many of the apparel industry executives interviewed have a pessimistic outlook concerning future sales and profitability. Several factors were cited, including pricing of regionally produced AGOA-eligible fabric, factory inefficiency and relatively high labour costs. Imported fabric is also often less expensive than purchasing locally. There is a general consensus that exports to the US would be extremely difficult without the benefits accorded by AGOA.

Markets

Domestic market

The retail market has been a key factor in the development of the South African clothing industry. More critically, for the potential export success of the clothing industry, the reported adoption of many of the supply chain practices of US retailers has required manufacturers to perform to these requirements. Indeed, retailers in South Africa who have traditionally operated on a cut, make and trim basis have had close links with clothing manufacturers.

Imported goods play an increasing role in South African retail, although domestic production is still protected by high tariff barriers of up to 40 per cent. According to some apparel executives interviewed there is uncertainty as to whether the tariff barriers are high enough to protect the domestic market.

Exports

Traditionally, exports have focused on the UK, but attention has now shifted to the US with the advent of AGOA; exports have also become an increasingly significant part of overall production.

There are a number of reasons for this change in focus. Roberts and Thoburn (2000), for example, are of the view that competitive pressures from imports have led firms to increase their exports; this has been accompanied by much up-grading of equipment and by increased specialisation in order to develop competitive niches despite South Africa's high manufacturing wage levels. Industry representatives interviewed during the survey point out that various entities in the industry and government have been trying for approximately ten years to encourage members to develop an export focus. They claim that it was the advent of AGOA that helped to stimulate interest in exports.

Regardless of the cause, there is now a strong desire and capability to export, but also a widespread belief that in the established production areas such as Johannesburg and Cape Town wages are too high to pursue the high volume mass market segment. Most respondents indicated that they are looking for small and specialised market segments and are focusing on higher-valued products, including suits and jackets.

A number of apparel industry representatives expressed a belief that textile companies in South Africa were exporting part of their production in addition to serving the local market. This is viewed unfavourably by local clothing manufacturers struggling to meet AGOA-compatible origin requirements and underscores an often mentioned shortfall in available textiles from the region.

Marketing and business development

Interest on the part of US buyers is growing, and representatives of many of the significant US companies have apparently visited South Africa and established sourcing channels. Proactive marketing, however, on the part of South African producers has been slow to materialise. In addition, many South African factories feel more comfortable working for the local market and they are still finding it tough to compete for high-volume, low-value items, because cost remains the driving factor in purchasing decisions. These companies prefer to stay away from mass production due to the lack of production capacity. Their interest in the export market is also shaded by the dramatic fluctuations in the value of the South African rand compared to the US dollar.

Larger companies are reported to be fairly comfortable with their traditional domestic market but they realise that they need to export and have begun to do so. These companies constitute the core of the export council and many claim to have contacts in the US market. Another example of the new interest in exports is demonstrated by the collaborative efforts of the Fashion Designers' Association and the South African Fashion Council to organise an export-oriented show together with leading apparel manufacturers.

Institutional framework

Trade regimes

The advent of preferential access to the US under AGOA has been an incentive to the clothing industry to attempt to increase exports to that market. In principle, South Africa is well placed to benefit substantially from these access provisions. The duty free preference is particularly important, giving an advantage of as much as 19–27 per cent on some products using synthetic materials.

In Europe, market access is assured through a bilateral trade and cooperation agreement (TDCA) with the European Union. The sub-regional Southern Africa Customs Union is also important, particularly in the context of goods shipped for further production within the region.

Support by government

The government provides support for overseas travel aimed at market development and various programmes are available for up-grading production capability. Programmes also exist to foster the development of smaller enterprises in the apparel sector.

In terms of export development activity, the key organisation is the Clothing Industry Export Council, an industry-driven body which acts as the prime link to government action in support of exports. This organisation is discussed in more detail below.

The government has developed various grant programmes to encourage the growth of domestic manufacturing in terms of hiring new labour and increasing exports. As an example, programmes assist businesses with travel expenses to meet buyers; they also support on-the-job training programmes for sewing operators by paying 100 per cent of their wages for a period of three months during the training. Funding is also available for technology upgrading projects. Another programme is a duty credit scheme covering imported materials used for export. The credits can either be used directly or traded.

The government is also reported to be assisting in the development of local apparel clusters involving the smaller companies in the industry and aimed particularly at the local market.

Industry structure

Apparel

As indicated above, the apparel industry is estimated to consist of some 1,400–1,500 firms. Many of these are small, as indicated by the following data from the *Clothing Federation Handbook 2000/01*, based on 1993 data. At that time, there were 1,389 apparel manufacturers, of which 1,310 had less than 300 employees, 51 had between 300 and 800 employees and 18 had more than 800. Seven of these had in excess of 1,000 employees. Many of the companies with less than 200 employees were working proprietorships. The top 21 companies reported sales in excess of R40 million; 31 companies had sales of between R20–40 million. Only 25 of the clothing companies were foreign owned or joint ventures.

Most locally owned factories concentrate primarily on the local market, whereas foreign factories from Hong Kong and Taiwan, located in the decentralised areas, are reported to export 80 per cent of their production to the US. Despite the number of companies in the industry, industry sources estimate that the top ten firms account for 85 per cent of exports and the top 20 account for 95 per cent. Small to medium-sized enterprises (50 employees or less, or with a turnover of less than R2.4 million) are generally considered too small to produce goods for export. There are, therefore, various schemes designed to encourage SMEs to form co-operatives. Such schemes are reported to have been particularly active in the townships.

Yarn and textiles

In the textile industry, about 60 per cent of the enterprises are domestically owned and 40 per cent have at least some foreign ownership holding. There is some cross-ownership between manufacturers and retailers. The textile industry is divided approximately one-third each in technical fabrics, apparel and household fabrics.

Buying houses and agencies

Foreign buying houses are estimated by some sources to account for 25 per cent of export sales, but their role and presence is still limited. There are indications, however, that this is changing as AGOA-driven business rolls into high gear.

At the time of the survey, a major US buying house was reportedly shifting its regional office from Mauritius to South Africa in order to take better advantage of the business flowing from the AGOA preferences. This could provide advantages for local manufacturers in South Africa and underscores the potential for South Africa to become a regional sourcing hub.

Positioning for the future

The established and demanding domestic client base, combined with the established fabric and yarn suppliers, all work to the benefit of the South African industry and are critical for early success. In addition there is the fact that seasonal production is out of sync with that in the northern hemisphere. This means that there is an opportunity for year-round production, serving both local and export markets, with a resulting drop in production costs. Other factors that benefit South African industry include:

- excellence of infrastructure;
- the educated work force;
- design capabilities;
- capability in all the steps of the process, including communicating with clients and flexibility in terms of production.

Clothing Industry Export Council

Founded in 1999 at the behest of the Minister of Industry, the Export Council is, according to its executive director, an industry-led body whose role is to be the independent collective voice to government on the 'what, where, when and how' required to drive exports. The organisation is member led, member funded and member driven and is focused on the creation of a successful export environment. Similar organisations exist for other industries including, for example, the textile industry. Membership is by invitation and is not compulsory. Members sign a pledge relating to maintenance of the image of the country – recognising that this image is as good as that of any individual company. Growth must be within this constraint of maintaining a positive reputation.

The Clothing Industry Export Council has been at the forefront of export development. The Council has encouraged companies to take the plunge into exports, despite the challenges of breaking away from the comfort of the domestic market. They have instigated a number of targeted marketing initiatives to France, UK and Ireland, for example, as well as to the east coast of the United States.

Decentralised regions and surrounding nations

The wage levels in the decentralised regions are approximately half those that prevail in the urban centres around Johannesburg, Cape Town and Durban. This has led to the establishment of much of the larger commodity production in these areas. And, more critically, firms based in the traditional centres have factories, joint ventures or contract arrangements that allow them to undertake much of their production in these decentralised areas.

As a further extension of this practice, a number of firms contract work to companies in the LDC-eligible countries of the region such as Lesotho and Swaziland. Through this arrangement they can benefit from the AGOA provisions allowing for use of non-regional fabric.

Challenges

Despite the evident success in certain niches, such as formal wear, a number of critical challenges were identified by respondents. These include:

- Current competition from other Southern African countries able to benefit from the LDC privileges under AGOA. The key, of course, as has been shown by a number of companies, is to leverage this benefit by outsourcing to those countries. This happens, however, at the expense of local employment.

- Fabric and yarn supply that is AGOA-eligible is as much of an issue in South Africa as elsewhere in the region. One of the challenges will be for the two industries (textiles and clothing) to better harmonise their development and investment efforts. The apparent uncertainty regarding the fate of the LDC provisions under AGOA after 2004 was also mentioned by some as a constraint to the development of the textile industry.

- Although many long-standing manufacturers have benefited from the demanding performance requirements of South African retailers, the traditional industry had declined considerably prior to AGOA, with a resultant thinning out of middle management ranks. This dearth of middle management is viewed as a critical constraint.

- There is a general belief that the clothing and textile industry needs a critical mass that is greater than the current numbers of 60,000 in textiles and 130,000 in the apparel industry. One source (the Export Council) stated that this needs to be 400,000–500,000 in combined textile and apparel industries before the industry will be taken seriously and that the country had four to five years to reach this critical mass. Without this there would be no sustained interest on the part of buyers.

- Although a few companies have established seemingly strong linkages to the US and European markets, it would appear that these need to be expanded and deepened. There is a strong reliance, at present, on US buying houses that have established offices in the region.

- A limiting factor to the growth of the industry is relatively high labour costs, although this is mitigated by lower cost production in decentralised zones.

- Economic stability and security were also cited by many as a cause for concern.

5.5 Lesotho

Industry overview

The garment manufacturing industry in Lesotho was established in the 1980s due to constraints at that time on exporting from South Africa. It became significant in the early 1990s on the strength of active promotion by the Lesotho National Development Corporation (LNDC) and a special derogation within the Lomé Convention. This derogation, which lasted until 1996, avoided yarn-forward rules of origin, thus allowing duty free shipment of garments to Europe as long as 30 per cent of value was added in Lesotho (Rubin, 2001: 3). The focus shifted to the US market with the advent of AGOA and, indeed, as a positioning move before AGOA came into force.

Lesotho received its certification for LDC status under AGOA in 2001. Under these provisions, Lesotho and other LDC-eligible countries have duty and quota free access to the US but are exempt from the constraints requiring local AGOA-eligible fabric. Thus these benefits can be obtained with fabric imported from, for example, China and Taiwan. These benefits expire in late 2004 under current provisions.

Employment in Lesotho's clothing industry almost doubled from 2000 to 2002, from 19,000 in April 2000 to 29,000 in March 2001 and 34,300 in April 2002. The value of exports in F/Y 2001–2002 was estimated by LNDC at 2.2 billion rand, equivalent to some US$240 million (LNDC, 2000).

Companies in the garment manufacturing industry are mainly Taiwanese-owned. As a result of the short-term benefits under AGOA, however, other countries, particularly South Africa, are reported to be interested.

Markets

Established foreign vendors own almost all the companies in the apparel industry. These vendors handle all marketing and business development activities. Thus local companies rarely, if ever, participate in auctions or deal with buying houses, other than on quality issues.

Institutional framework

Lesotho benefits from the same access to the major markets as do the other Southern Africa countries eligible both for Lomé and AGOA provisions, but with one important difference. This is that Lesotho qualifies under AGOA for the LDC provision that allows duty and quota free access until late 2004 for third-party fabric. This has, it would appear, been the major factor that has drawn Taiwanese and other apparel companies to the country.

The key player in the development of the apparel industry in Lesotho has been the LNDC. It initially undertook an active promotional campaign and offered factory shells and other incentives, including a training scheme for potential investors. Most of this funding had been supported by a World Bank project, but this is reported to have ended.

Industry structure

Apparel

A summary of the scale and structure of the apparel industry in Lesotho is presented in Table 5.9. Twenty-four companies were identified by LDNC, with an estimated combined output value of $240 million. Most of these are Taiwanese owned. With a total workforce of 34,300 in the clothing sector, the top three companies account for 50 per cent of exports and the top ten for 80 per cent. Distribution of employment is less concentrated, which perhaps indicates that in some cases companies collaborate, or sub-contract, on export orders, with only one becoming the exporter of record. According to calculations from LNDC-supplied data, the top eight firms account for 50 per cent of employment and the top 18 for 80 per cent.

The countries of origin of these companies and the principal products that were identified in their applications for investment approval by LNDC are indicated in Tables 5.10 and 5.11. Of the 33 companies for which data are available, 26 are from Taiwan and account for 91 per cent of the workforce. Three are from South Africa and four from other countries, accounting for 3 per cent and 6 per cent of the workforce, respectively. In terms of products, nine companies with 35 per cent of workers produce jeans and 20 companies with 59 per cent of workers produce T-shirts. Four companies, with 6 per cent of the workforce produce other products or a mix of products, sometimes including T-shirts. A further four companies nominally employ some 5,200 workers.

Yarn and textiles

Most textiles and yarn are imported from the Far East, but an increasing quantity is reported to come from sub-Saharan Africa in order to qualify under AGOA. In June 2001, construction began on a denim mill for integration with the new jeans manufacturing operations of one of the largest investors from Taiwan.

Positioning for the future

The success of employment creation in the apparel industry in Lesotho has been due in no small part to the proactive investment attraction programme run by the LNDC. It is also understood that the initial Taiwanese companies came into the country at a time (the early 1990s) of formal diplomatic relations with Taiwan. In any event, the fact of having attracted some significant early investment clearly provided encouragement to other Taiwanese firms to follow. A further factor is the availability of ample electricity – Lesotho is a major exporter of electricity to South Africa.

The sustained success of the Lesotho apparel manufacturing industry depends on the ability to develop AGOA-eligible sources of fabric.

Challenges

The fabric issue is critical to the future success of Lesotho in a post-quota world. The country is landlocked and dependent on the South African rail, road and port systems for all supplies. According to company managers interviewed, capacity constraints on these cause difficulties. A further factor is the increased competition, at least until 2005, as a result of the admission of Botswana and Namibia to the LDC benefits of AGOA.

5.6 South Asia: Regional Overview

Market share for apparel in the United States

The Asian region supplied 53 per cent of all US apparel imports in 2001, valued at $30.8 billion. The two leading exporters were China and Hong Kong, accounting for 21 and 14 per cent, respectively, as indicated in Table 5.12 and Chart 5.3. South Asian countries accounted for just under 21 per cent of US imports sourced from Asia, valued at $6.3 billion. Commonwealth exporters were Bangladesh, with $1.9 billion (6.3%), India with $1.8 billion (5.8%), Sri Lanka with $1.5 billion (4.8%), Pakistan with $0.9 billion (3%) and Maldives with $97 million (0.3%).

Chart 5.3: US Apparel Imports from Asia, 2001 (total imports from region $30.8 billion)

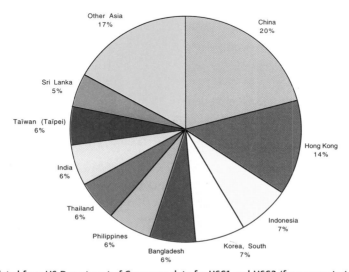

Source: Calculated from US Department of Commerce data for HS61 and HS62 (from www.strategis.ic.gc.ca)

Market share for apparel in Europe

The Asian region supplied 47.4 per cent of all EU apparel imports in 2001, valued at ECU 23.9 billion. The leading exporter was China, accounting for 33.5 per cent of imports from Asia. Bangladesh, Hong Kong and India ranked second, third and fourth with 11.7, 10.7 and 9.1 per cent, respectively, as indicated in Table 5.13 and Chart 5.4. In total, South Asian countries accounted for just under 27 per cent of EU imports sourced from Asia, valued at ECU 6.4 billion. Commonwealth exporters were Bangladesh, with ECU 2.8 billion (11.7 per cent), India with ECU 2.2 billion (9.1 per cent), Sri Lanka with ECU 0.77 billion (3.2 per cent) and Pakistan with ECU 0.65 billion (2.7 per cent).

Chart 5.4: EU Apparel Imports from Asia, 2001 (total imports from region ECU 23.9 billion)

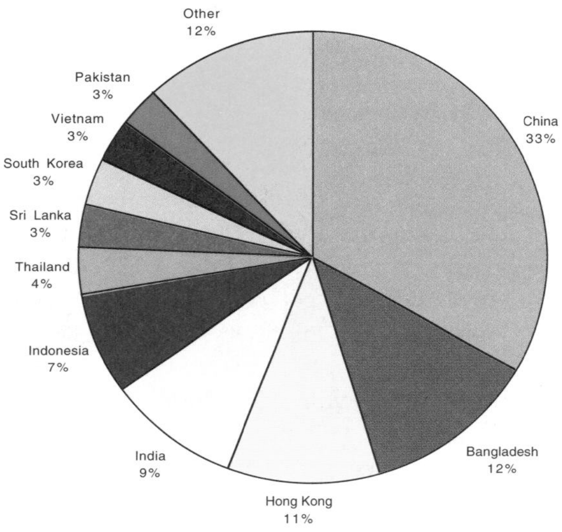

Other 12%
Pakistan 3%
Vietnam 3%
South Korea 3%
Sri Lanka 3%
Thailand 4%
Indonesia 7%
India 9%
Hong Kong 11%
Bangladesh 12%
China 33%

Source: Calculated from EUROSTAT data for HS61 and HS62

Trade agreements

There are no regional trade agreements between the countries of the region and the US that offer anything approaching the market access privileges of the AGOA agreement. The EU has eliminated quotas and allowed the Generalised System of Preferences (GSP) tariff rate for apparel from the region, subject to rules of origin on yarn and fabric. Specifically, the rule of origin criteria for the EU initially required at least two stage transformation within the country, meaning that only a garment product made of locally produced fabric out of locally produced yarn could qualify for GSP. The requirement has now been relaxed to a minimum of one stage transformation for regional LDCs, so that garments produced out of locally made fabric alone will now qualify for GSP, regardless of whether the yarn is manufactured locally or imported.

Third party fabric has not been allowed, however. Locally produced fabric, particularly for woven products, is limited. In Bangladesh, for example, only 30–35 per cent of the requirement is locally produced. The EU thus offered a regional cumulation option to the member countries of SAARC. Under this arrangement, garments made from fabric/yarn produced in the region would have been eligible. Given the relatively high levels of availability of fabric and yarn from India and Pakistan, this could be a potentially interesting option. Implementation, however, requires adoption by all member countries and this had not happened as of early 2003.

5.7 Sri Lanka

Industry overview

The value of exports of the ready-made garment industry was US$ 2.3 billion in 2001. This represents 50.3 per cent of export revenue as indicated in Table 3.1. The industry developed in the mid to late 1980s largely as a result of quota issues (Government Sponsored Committee, 2000:26).

The apparel industry is the largest employer in the country and total employment in the industry is reported to be just under 340,000 (ibid.:8). The size of the apparel industry is variously estimated at between 830 and 860 companies. More critically, it is estimated that 12 per cent of these companies accounted for 72 per cent of export revenue and that the top 22 per cent contributed for 85 per cent in 2000 (ibid.:2). Many of the larger companies have foreign investment or partnerships and many of these are located in free trade zones (FTZs), particularly in two large FTZs near Colombo.

In an effort to decentralise the industry away from Colombo and Gampaha districts, which account for about 60 per cent of employment in the apparel industry, the government launched what was known as the 200-Garment Factory Programme. This generated significant employment in so called 'remote areas' (ibid.:8).

Approximately 60 per cent of the apparel manufactured in Sri Lanka uses woven fabric, most of which is imported (ibid.:11). Despite a growing textile segment, most raw materials are imported. This reliance on imported fabric is viewed as a major constraint to the development of the industry.

Markets

It is estimated that 95 per cent of production from the apparel industry is exported (ibid.:6). The local market is thus not significant.

From 1989 to 2000, the value of exports rose from US$468.7 million to US$2,710 million, and in 2001 dropped to US$2,337 million (ibid.:6). The principal export market has traditionally been the US – accounting for 65 per cent of exports in 2002. Other significant markets are the EU (30%) and Canada (2%). It is worth noting that in 2001 all EU exports were quota free and all exports to Canada were under quota. Of the exports to the EU, approximately 64 per cent go to the UK, 12 per cent to the Benelux countries and 10 per cent to Germany. Most of the latter is from German-owned investment in Sri Lanka (ibid.:7).

The top exports to the US and the UK are presented in Tables 5.14 and 5.15.

Institutional framework

Trade regimes

Since 2001, Sri Lanka has benefited from quota-free access to the European Union. There are no special access agreements with the US, either regionally or bilaterally, although there is talk in Sri Lanka of a free trade agreement. There is, however, a Temporary Investment Framework Agreement that has been helpful to some of the US companies with investment or joint ventures in the country.

Given the strength of both India and Pakistan in the production of cotton and its transformation into yarn and fabric, it could potentially be beneficial to Sri Lanka to import fabric from these countries; particularly if a South Asian regional preference agreement similar to AGOA could be negotiated with the US. Unfortunately, as of early 2003, this was not on the horizon.

Industry support

The principal organisations supporting the apparel and textile industry are the Board of Investment, the Export Development Board and the Clothing Industry Training Institute. The roles of each are discussed below, starting with the Board of Investment.

The numerous textile and apparel factories in the FTZs, and the decentralised factories established under the 200-Garment Factory Programme, enjoy many benefits deriving from their status as Board of Investment (BOI) approved ventures. These benefits include simplified customs and import-export procedures and preferential access to credit, including foreign currency loans. Non-BOI manufacturers, mainly smaller older Sri Lankan-owned factories located in the vicinity of Colombo, have recently scored gains, which have helped to level the playing field.

The apparel export companies have had strong support throughout their development from the Export Development Board. This agency has been instrumental in organising many market development initiatives and has played a leading role in the recent strategic plan developments together with members of the textile and clothing industry associations.

The training institute provides wide support to the industry and runs a textile training and services centre. While basic training is adequate, there is reportedly a need for enhanced production management and marketing training.

Industry structure

Apparel

There are between 830 and 890 registered apparel manufacturers in Sri Lanka. Total employment in the industry is just under 340,000 and if indirect jobs are included is estimated to involve one million persons. It is estimated that 87 per cent of the total workforce is female (Government Sponsored Committee, 2002: 8). Industry sources estimates that 72 per cent of exports come from 12 per cent of the companies. The dominance of the large players is further indicated by the data presented in Table 5.16 on the distribution of exports by size and number of companies.

As a result of government policies, particularly the creation of FTZs and the provisions of the 200-Garment Factory Programme, the industry is reasonably geographically dispersed, with 29 per cent in Colombo and 31 per cent in Gampatha districts.

Based on the findings of the fieldwork undertaken in Sri Lanka, it would appear that well over half of all garment firms have either foreign equity participation or long-term supply relationships with foreign buyers and customers. These foreign buyers represent many leading brand names and department stores in the US and Europe.

Yarn and textiles

Local production of export-quality fabric is limited, and it is estimated that Sri Lanka imported over 80–90 per cent of fabric inputs and 70–90 per cent of trims (Government Sponsored Committee, 2002: 19). Hong Kong, South Korea, Taiwan and India are the major exporters of textile fabric to Sri Lanka.

There is some local textile production but, with one exception, these facilities are understood to be in difficulty, according to views expressed at the SAARC–Commonwealth Secretariat conference. The one operation that is understood to be a success story is closely tied through ownership and partnerships to a major integrated apparel vendor, MAS Holdings.

Although virtually all inputs, particularly fabric, are imported, efforts are being made to develop some backward integration in a variety of areas. Packaging, hangers and tags are increasingly sourced locally. Another area with potential is fabric finishing – more dying is being done locally, as is stone washing treatment (in collaboration with a German company). Kuruwita Manchester, a joint venture between a local firm and a US-owned company, processes (dyes and prints) grey fabric. This venture hopes to triple the factory's daily capacity of 4,800 kg through an expansion that was underway at the time of this study. Local production in the accessories area is more mixed: good quality elastic, thread, buttons and trims are being made in foreign joint ventures, but in limited quantities and often with imported inputs and the vast majority of zippers and padding continue to be imported. Designs, on the other hand, continue to be brought in from the US and UK.

Buying houses and agencies

Many garment manufacturers in Sri Lanka have relied on dealing with local buying houses and agents and have not established direct links with major retailers. This has left them somewhat remote from the marketplace.

Positioning for the future

The focus on product quality remains a major success story for both individual factories and for the industry as a whole. Other positive factors are compliance with international labour regulations, reputed international customer base, good price and quality and on-time delivery of standard all-season products (EDB, 2002). Quota free access to Europe since 2001 is another positive factor even though duties must still be paid.

Aware of the potential fragility of the industry, the government and stakeholders in the apparel industry have undertaken a number of joint initiatives. In 2000, a master plan study was commissioned and in 2002 a five-year strategy for the apparel industry was developed by a committee of leading industry stakeholders and support agencies.

The output of the strategy was the identification of priority issues, including training, textile supply and support services. Follow-up on this action agenda was underway as of late 2002 under the direction of leading industry representatives. The involvement of these representatives is seen as one of the first indications of members of the industry working together for the betterment of the industry as a whole, as opposed to remaining focused on their individual companies.

Factors facilitating the collaboration include a general desire to further the development of backward linkages to yarn and fabric, and the realisation that there is a danger of losing the critical mass that has driven the development of relatively good shipping links to major markets. If business drops, the whole industry is in danger of embarking on a downward spiral.

The industry is working to address and improve a range of macro issues such as those related to utility rates, port efficacy, labour laws and infrastructure. Initiatives have also been launched to enhance market intelligence and market development, to train marketing professionals for the industry, and to increase productivity and technology at the enterprise level.

Challenges

Many stakeholders in Sri Lanka's apparel industry are acutely aware of the potential difficulties with which they will be faced when the quota system is dismantled. They have begun to take steps to meet evolving buyer requirements but there is much uncertainty. The fear is that the Sri Lankan apparel industry will survive for a few years and then start to lose critical mass. The challenge faced by the industry is to overcome a number of critical weaknesses, which include:

- inadequate yarn, fabric and trim supply;

- low productivity of labour and inefficient use of machinery and manufacturing processes;

- inadequate production management and industrial engineering capability;

- lack of strong presence in the marketplace, although this is not easy in a buyer-driven environment;

- lack of design and creativity ability;

- weaknesses in infrastructure, including communications and the high cost of utilities;

- lack of awareness on the part of manufacturers about the need for compliance with codes of conduct and the related difficulty of maintaining these standards.

5.8 Bangladesh

Industry overview

Over the past 20 years, the ready-made garment industry has grown from virtually nothing to account, in 2001–2002, for over 76 per cent of Bangladesh's exports. The industry today employs close to 1.8 million people, of whom 1.5 million are women. Exports were valued at US$4.8 billion in 2000–2001.

The Bangladesh Garment Manufacturers and Exporters Association (BGMEA) had 3,304 members in 2000. Approximately 2,200 of these companies are located in Dhaka, with most of the rest in Chittagong. The Bangladesh Knitwear Manufacturers and Exporters Association (BKMEA) had 586 full members in 2000, mostly located in Narayanganj, approximately 75 of which are members both of the BKMEA and BGMEA, making a total of around 3,800 companies in the ready-made garment sector (Ministry of Commerce, 2001:35).

Despite this growth, the product range manufactured by the industry is relatively narrow, concentrating on basic low-cost, low-margin garments such as T-shirts, polo shirts, pajamas, woven shirts, trousers, shorts, undergarments, anoraks and parkas, although some higher value items have been introduced. A recent development for the industry has been the increase in the production of knitted garments as a result of the demand from the EU because of the GSP. Value added is greater than for woven garments due to higher prices and because yarn dyeing and knitting are often done locally. Many knitwear manufacturers also knit the fabric, and an increasing number have their own dyeing and finishing plants (ibid.: 35). A further characteristic of the industry is the heavy concentration in urban areas of facilities that are not necessarily suitable for manufacturing activity.

Markets

Ready-made garment exports rose from US$32.6 million in 1983–84, representing 4 per cent of national exports, to US$4.9 billion in 2000–2001, representing 75.2 per cent of national exports. Although exports dropped in 2001–2002 to US$4.6 billion, the share of exports actually rose, to 76.6 per cent. The principal markets are the US and Europe, accounting for 45.3 and 50.5 per cent, respectively, in 2000–2001. Canada holds a very distant third place. In terms of market share, Bangladesh supplies just over 3 per cent of the apparel imports of each of these three markets.

In 2001–2002, Bangladesh faced quotas only with the US (20 items) and Canada (9 items). Quota utilisation has risen substantially in the past few years, from 85 per cent in 1997 to 99 per cent in 2001 (Hassan, 2002). This full utilisation of quotas is also reflected in data on the growth of imports to the US from Bangladesh. It is noteworthy that, as of January 2003, Bangladesh had duty and quota free access to the Canadian market.

With a population of 130 million, there is also a substantial local demand but this is not very significant for the largely export-oriented apparel manufacturers.

Institutional framework

While the two key factors in the success of the sector have been low labour costs and the dynamic role of the private sector, other institutional factors have been important. These include the continuity of policies in successive governments, decontrol of the reserve sector, abolition of the ceiling on private investment, the structural adjustment policies of government and the introduction of back-to-back letters of credit and of bonded warehouse facilities. The Multi-Fibre Arrangement quota system and Bangladesh's LDC status under the GSP have been contributory factors in the rapid growth of ready-made garment exports, particularly to the EU and US (Ministry of Commerce, 2001: 36).

The industry is represented by the BGMEA and BKMEA. Due to its much larger number of members, the former plays a key role in development of the industry and as an interface with government. The BGMEA has played a key role in the establishment of the Fashion Institute and, latterly, in the initiation and partial funding of a strategy study for the sector. The textile industry is represented by the Bangladesh Textile Manufacturers Association (BTMA) which, it would appear, is not necessarily in favour of encouraging measures to facilitate use of regional, as opposed to domestic, textiles.

The Export Promotion Bureau (EPB) is the focal point of promotion efforts for the sector and has played a key role over the years in its development. The Bureau also allocates quotas and administers the visa system for the US and issues certificates of origin for GSP for Canada and GSP supported by export licence for the EU. The EPB has semi-autonomous status and its affairs are managed by a governing body consisting of members from both public and private sectors and headed by the Minister of Commerce as chairperson.

Industry structure

Apparel

The structure of the ready-made garment industry is described by the Bangladesh Ministry of Commerce (2001: 35–36) as consisting of four groups of companies:

- Approximately 15 companies or groups owning a total of approximately 220 manufacturing units each, with a capacity of 10,000 dozen pieces or more per month. These groups are well established and mostly source their own fabrics. Most have merchandising offices in the US, Europe and/or Hong Kong. Approximately 60 per cent of all quota is controlled by this group.

- Approximately 550 production units with a capacity of 5,000 to 10,000 dozen pieces per month. These companies mainly work for importers or agents, approximately 60 per cent on a cut and make basis, and 40 per cent on an FOB basis. Some sub-contracting for Group 1 companies is also done.

- Seven to eight hundred companies owning an estimated 1,993 production units each with a capacity of up to 5,000 dozen pieces per month which mainly do sub-contracting.

- Approximately 200 companies which are classified as in financial difficulties and are not currently operating. The number of such sick and non-functional units has significantly increased in recent times, in the opinion of the BGMEA, and may be as high as 1,500.

Most foreign investment in the industry is located in the EPZs in Chittagong and Dhaka. In the context of total investment in the apparel industry, this foreign investment is no longer a substantial portion.

Yarn and textiles

There are some 20 composite mills in Bangladesh producing export quality fabric and some 170 spinning mills. It was estimated for 2000–2001 that 80–85 per cent of woven fabric for ready-made garment exports was imported and that 20 per cent of knit fabric was also imported (Hassan, 2002: 5). In the case of knitwear, it is estimated that the production of yarn is now 70 per cent domestic. The domestic share of fabric and yarn has, nonetheless, increased substantially in relative and absolute terms since 1995–1996, when local fabric accounted for only 12 per cent. However, according to industry stakeholders interviewed during the course of this survey, domestically produced fabric is more costly than imported product. Trims and packaging are also increasingly available locally.

Buying houses and agencies

Many of the major European and US buying houses and retailers operate out of Bangladesh, in addition to independent buying houses and agents. Some act as full buying and sourcing departments of the parent company and some as regional quality assurance offices. (Ministry of Commerce, 2001: 36). These play a key role as an interface between client and manufacturer. It is estimated that 90 per cent of companies are tied to buying agents. As a result there is a dependency on such buying agents and no direct relationship with buyers, so little knowledge about trends is developed.

Positioning for the future

The rapid growth of Bangladesh's apparel exports has been due, in addition to quota and GSP advantages, to the low cost of production. The decision of successive governments to play a relatively hands-off role, while facilitating exports, is also cited as a significant success factor. Where government has intervened, for example with letters of credit, this has contributed to success. Significant actions taken by government and industry to position the industry for the future include the issues discussed below.

Strategy study

The principal industry-wide response has been to commission, in 2002, a strategy study funded jointly by industry, working through the BGMEA, government and a World Bank export diversification project. This strategy study, combined with a host of other efforts, will hopefully serve as the focal point for action.

Encouragement of backward linkages

Since signing the WTO's Agreement on Textiles and Clothing, the government of Bangladesh has also encouraged development of backward linkages to spinning and weaving plants. It has assisted in this process through provision of compensation for the higher cost of local product. This cash incentive scheme is scheduled to end by 2004. Despite these measures, however, it is clear that while yarn spinning capacity is reasonable, there is no realistic way that the weaving capacity can be significantly altered in the immediate future: the investment needed is too large and the timeframe too short. Quality and competition issues are also relevant.

Bonded warehouses

Given the constraints on local fabric production, the industry is looking at options for central bonded warehouses able to stock large quantities of yarn, grey fabric and finished fabric. At the same time, fabric processing and finishing facilities are encouraged.

The warehouse will allow for the import of duty free man-made finished and grey fabrics for supply to garments and dyeing and printing factories, respectively, as and when needed. A separate central bonded warehouse will also be allowed for duty free import of chemicals for timely supply to dyeing and finishing mills. These central bonded warehouses will be operated and managed in the private sector and a task force was constituted in late 2002 with the Commerce Minister as its chairperson to prepare guidelines and implementation procedures of such facilities. It is hoped, according to interviews with industry players, that some multinational firms might also be interested in investing in this operation.

Textile villages

The government has also agreed in principle to develop *cluster areas* for garment industries, so that common facilities, including waste water treatment, can be created centrally and compliance requirements easily met. It is also hoped that locating these outside the heavily urbanised areas will provide a generally improved working environment.

The government will acquire land and build up infrastructure under the project, while BGMEA will take care of administration and management. The complete implementation may take time and, as such, it may be considered a medium-term measure. Long-term support to encourage the setting up of more textile units, as well as dyeing and printing mills, will continue simultaneously.

Enhanced training

A training facility to develop a critical mass of trained workers for the textile and garment sector is under consideration by government. With this objective in view, the Ministry of Textiles has already taken a decision to up-grade its Textile Diploma College to a world-class institution to impart training on fabric processing, fabric use, design development and other related matters. BGMEA is also expected to strengthen its Fashion Institute to develop required human resources. In this area also donor support and technical assistance from international agencies could play a crucial role.

Trade agreements

Bilateral and multilateral agreements, particularly those between major buying countries and some supply countries, might put Bangladesh into a disadvantageous situation. To combat this, Bangladesh has strengthened its lobbying efforts for duty free market access as an LDC. This has succeeded to some extent and Bangladesh, together with other LDCs, has been given duty and quota free market access to Canada. Similar treatment from the US is also hoped for. Efforts are also underway to diversify the export market to East European, South-East Asian, East Asian and Middle Eastern countries.

Challenges

The main issues with regard to the implementation of the WTO Agreement on Textiles and Clothing are whether Bangladesh can remain competitive and whether the existing garment industries can face the challenge. The outcome, as of early 2003, was uncertain. The small firms cannot survive, it is believed, under the changed circumstances, as they do not have economic scale of operation. But if they undergo a process of merger and integration they are likely to be viable. There is, therefore, a belief that the big firms working with big buyers in overseas markets can face the post-MFA challenge. Despite this, problems are expected in the transition and some downsizing is expected. This problem may be more acute in the woven sector than the knit sector. If this transitional impact becomes significant, the resultant unemployment will have particular impact on women as most of the workers in the woven sector are female.

More generally, there are a number of constraints on the development of the ready-made garment sector, some of which are specific to ready-made garments and others which affect all manufacturing and commercial activities. According to the Ministry of Commerce (2001:37), they include:

- poor management and technical skills;
- low level of productivity, over-manning, and poor quality control;
- little use of IT and CAD/CAM;
- insufficient investment;
- long lead times due to delays in port, interruption of power supply and frequent strikes;
- poor security and theft;
- corruption in public services;
- lack of design and product development.

Bangladesh is currently dependent for fabric on suppliers in countries such as China, India, Thailand and Pakistan. A challenge is to maintain competitiveness as garment manufacturers in those countries attempt, in a no-quota world, to capture market share. One immediate issue is to obtain internal agreement between the textile industry and the garment industry on the acceptance of regional cumulation rules that would allow for garments made in Bangladesh with Indian or Pakistani fabric, for example, to access the European Union duty free.

5.9 The Caribbean: Regional Overview

Market share for apparel in the United States

As indicated in Table 3.3, imports from the Caribbean and Central America accounted for 17 per cent of all imports to the US, with a further 1 per cent from other South American countries. These data exclude Mexico. The top apparel exporting countries to the US in 2001 from the Latin America and Caribbean region are presented in Table 5.17 and Chart 5.5. The value of exports totalled $10.4 billion, with the major shares coming from Honduras (23.4%), Dominican Republic (21.4%), El Salvador (15.7%), Guatemala (15.5%) and Costa Rica (7.4%).

Jamaica is the only Commonwealth country in the top 11, with a market share of 1.8 per cent, valued at $187 million. The other Commonwealth exporters in the region include Belize, with $15 million (0.2%), Guyana with $10 million (0.1%) and Saint Lucia with $6 million (0.1%); also St Kitts and Nevis, Trinidad and Tobago, and Barbados, each valued at $2 million. Although insignificant for the US, the exports from these small states are important for the respective countries and manufacturers.

Market share for apparel in Europe

As indicated in Table 3.6, European Union imports from the Americas, including from the US and Canada, totalled only 1.2 per cent. Of these, imports from the Caribbean and Central America came to 0.3 per cent. The top apparel exporting countries to the EU in 2001 from the Latin American and Caribbean region are presented in Table 5.18 and Chart 5.6. The value of exports totalled ECU 166 million, with the major shares coming from Jamaica (50.8%) and Colombia (18.8%). The remaining eight countries have shares ranging from Honduras with 10.2 per cent to Belize with 0.5 per cent. Jamaica and Belize are the only Commonwealth countries in the top ten.

Caribbean Basin Trade Development Act

Since 1 October 2000, exports of apparel to the US from countries in the Caribbean Basin, including Jamaica, have been governed by the Caribbean Basin Trade Development Act. Under the Act, duty and quota free preferences are extended from apparel exclusively cut in the US, from US fabric and yarn, to a somewhat broader range of product. In essence, the Act allows for cutting in the region provided that US fabric and yarn are used; it also allows apparel knit-to-shape in the region from US yarns. In addition, there is a provision for T-shirts and underwear that are made from fabric formed in one or more beneficiary countries. There are restraint levels and caps on the quantities involved. It is claimed that, under the Act, Caribbean Basin Initiative (CBI) countries will be given duty and quota free access to the US on a par with levels enjoyed by Mexico (Black, 2000).

Chart 5.5: US Apparel Imports from Latin America and the Caribbean, 2001
(total imports from region $10.4 billion)

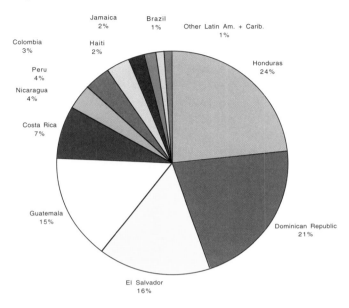

Jamaica
2%

Brazil
1%

Other Latin Am. + Carib.
1%

Colombia
3%

Haiti
2%

Honduras
24%

Peru
4%

Nicaragua
4%

Costa Rica
7%

Guatemala
15%

Dominican Republic
21%

El Salvador
16%

Source: Calculated from US Department of Commerce data for HS61 and HS62 (from www.strategis.ic.gc.ca)

Chart 5.6: EU Apparel Imports from Latin America and the Caribbean, 2001
(total imports from region ECU 166 million)

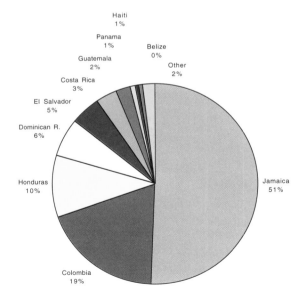

Haiti
1%

Panama
1%

Belize
0%

Guatemala
2%

Other
2%

Costa Rica
3%

El Salvador
5%

Dominican R.
6%

Honduras
10%

Jamaica
51%

Colombia
19%

Source: Calculated from EUROSTAT data for HS61 and HS62

5.10 Jamaica

Industry overview

The export-oriented garment industry in Jamaica got a boost in 1983–85 with the advent of the US provisions for duty and quota free import of garments assembled in the Caribbean from US parts – known colloquially as the 807 provision, after the pertinent section of the Act. Prior to that time a relatively modest but successful garment manufacturing industry had existed in Jamaica. Operating under high tariff barriers, the focus of the industry were the local and Caribbean Community (Caricom) markets.

According to industry players and observers interviewed during the course of this study, 4,000 people were employed in the apparel industry in the mid-1980s. Employment in this sector grew rapidly with the advent of the US-oriented export business, and by the mid-1990s was in excess of 35,000 workers. By early 2002, however, it had fallen back to the pre-boom levels and was estimated at perhaps 6,000–7,000 workers.

Markets

Domestic market

The industry began behind tariff barriers, serving the local and Caricom markets. Since the late 1990s, however, the share of the domestic market share has fallen dramatically due to imports, particularly from Asia. Industry sources estimate that whereas local producers used to have 70 per cent of the Jamaican market, this has fallen to 40 per cent due to extra-regional imports.

One factor behind this are the ties developed by local retailers and wholesalers with suppliers in South Asia and the Far East. They are reported to effectively control the lower end of the market. For example, T-shirts from Pakistan are reportedly sold for less than one local Jamaican manufacturer's cost of material. The same manufacturer had found in the past that a good segment was company work uniforms, for example for banks, but they are now imported. Another company, which focuses on embroidery and printing, has abandoned most locally manufactured apparel in favour of sourcing finished goods from China, albeit largely to their own designs. They then complete the garment with embroidery and printing.

Tourist market

One market that remains significant for some local companies is tourism, both resort and cruise ship visitors. This market also represents excellent opportunities for export within the region, according to industry sources. One company, which is frequently cited as a success, exports about 30 per cent of its production, primarily within the region. Of the 70 per cent for the local market, a further 70 per cent or more goes to tourists. Several apparel industry stakeholders see the tourism industry as a critical avenue to development of a 'full package' capability. Such a capability is seen as the way forward, given the evident difficulty for Jamaica in competing in the low-end 807 segment of the market.

Export market

Apparel exports doubled from US$279.0 million in 1990 to US$579.4 million in 1995 (Chart 5.7). From this point they began to decline dramatically and were at US$363.3 million by 2000. This decline was due to a fall off in business with the US, which, by and large, was either moved to cheaper production areas in the Americas or dried up as a result of corporate consolidation/bankruptcy in the US. The growth and decline in the apparel export business is illustrated in Charts 5.7–5.9. During this same period, however, there was steady growth in business with the rest of the world, but not enough to really compensate for the loss of US markets. As illustrated in Chart 5.8, most of this growth came from exports to Europe. This business was reportedly related to strong in-market connections. At the peak, over 70 per cent of exports were done under 807 and a total of 90 per cent of exports had been for the US. In 2000, this had fallen to just over 65 per cent under 807 (66.3 per cent) and a total of 73.5 per cent for the US, with a solid 25 per cent destined for Europe.

Chart 5.7: Jamaica Apparel Exports, 1990–2000 (US$ million)

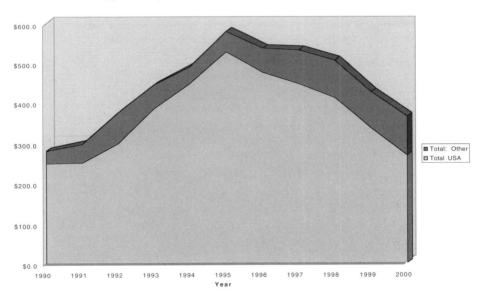

Source: Trade Board Ltd, Kingston

An additional factor, also illustrated in Chart 5.8, is the demise of the CMT business with the US. Until the mid-1990s, this had been running steadily at around US$100 million annually, but has now declined to about a quarter of this – US$26.4 million in 2000. Value added on the 807 work ranged from a low of 14 per cent in the peak years to 16 per cent at the beginning and end of the period. On non-807 work, value added can range from 25 per cent under CMT to as high as 60–70 per cent if fabric printing and design is done in Jamaica, according to a senior official of the Caribbean Textiles and Apparel Institute.

Chart 5.8: Jamaica Apparel Exports by Region, 1990–2000

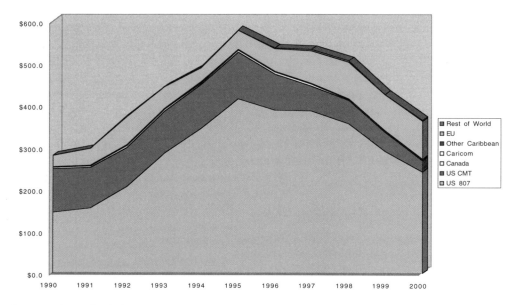

Source: Trade Board Ltd, Kingston

Chart 5.9: Jamaica Exports to the US, 1990–2000

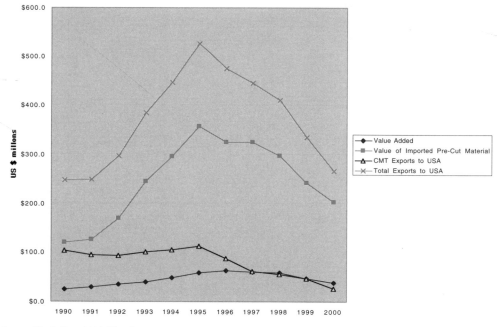

Source: Trade Board Ltd, Kingston

SOURCING PRACTICES IN THE APPAREL INDUSTRY

Institutional framework

Three primary trade regimes have shaped the garment industry: the Caricom agreement, opening up regional markets; the ACP, opening up opportunities in Europe; and the Caribbean Basin Initiative, which opened up the US market. This latter has since been updated and expanded in the Caribbean Basin Partnership Act of 2000. Companies can either locate in a designated free zone where benefits are available in perpetuity, or can locate elsewhere and obtain special incentives for a five-year period. The access agreements with the US have been the most significant. Jamaica had very early success in capitalising on the 807 provisions, as indicated by the growth from 1990 through 1995–96. These provisions provided duty and quota free access to the US market for garments assembled, in eligible Caribbean Basin countries, from parts cut in the US from US-made fabric. Indeed, Jamaica was a leader in such business, setting up industrial free zone facilities, export incentives and strongly targeting this segment of the garment industry.

This success was supported further by the development of training courses for machine operators and other personnel. Additional support for the industry was provided through the Jamaican Business Development Centre, formerly the Design Centre.

Industry structure

The apparel industry in Jamaica consisted in early 2002 of some 80 companies, of which 50 were formal manufacturers and the remainder dressmakers/tailor shops. Approximately two-thirds of the 50 companies, however, were focused regionally and locally and were locally owned. Thus, by early 2002 there were perhaps 15 export-oriented companies, although it was reported by industry players and observers that this number was decreasing almost weekly. The plants that remained were approximately divided between the free zones in Montego Bay and in Kingston, as well as a few factories outside the zones. It is estimated that about 60 per cent of the factories, including most of the large ones, were operating under the 807 programme and that the rest were on CMT.

A number of major US manufacturers have opened manufacturing operations in Jamaica, including Sara Lee and Jockey. The industry ownership of the export-oriented companies was and is a mix of US companies, Jamaican-owned companies and other foreign entrepreneurs. Sara Lee has since pulled out but still sources significant volumes through sub-contracting.

There are no spinning or weaving operations in Jamaica, underscoring the dependence on 807 parts assembly type work and yielding a competitive disadvantage due to the time penalty for fabric delivery.

Positioning for the future

Faced with the dramatic decline in garment industry employment in the past year or so, two government appointed committees were established: one to look at re-structuring issues and the other concerned particularly with how to get more value added from the industry.

One outcome has been the recognition of the need for transition of the industry beyond assembly of imported parts, and of incentives in terms of costs and tax concessions in order to make this happen. As an example, faced with bank loan interest rates of 25 per cent, the government is supporting the industry's full package companies with loans at 12 per cent interest. The other major step is to articulate how the industry can transform itself, placing emphasis on full package work, and with a primary focus on the tourist market and particularly the cruise ship market, as well as local and regional fashion markets. This has resulted in a Fashion Industry Modernisation Action Plan co-ordinated by Jamaica Business Development Centre. It has also been reported that the development of Sea Island cotton on former sugar cane lands is being considered. Caribbean Fashion Week, a series of major shows featuring local designers, is one venture designed to put Jamaica on the regional and tourism fashion maps.

The strategic plan of the Business Development Centre (BDC), formerly known as the Design Centre, focuses on using the tourism business as a driver for such leisure wear products as lingerie, swimwear, pants and shorts. These types of product could use the current industry machinery, with an additional 20 per cent equipment for some special operations. The direction of the strategy can be summed up by the change in the name and the focus of the industry from the garment industry to the fashion industry. BDC's staff are working on selecting ten factories in a pilot project to up-grade the infrastructure according to the new market niche, provide technical support and up-grade labour skills at all levels. They offer some programmes in developing design capabilities and also offer technical support to the industry. As a first priority their focus will be the local market. The centre has a staff of professional engineers and production managers and is fully equipped with state of the art equipment for digitalised printing and for designing.

Challenges

Jamaica was an inadvertent victim of a declining US market in 2001, compounded by changes in the ways that US companies do business, and indeed in the nature of the industry. These include a trend away from company-owned manufacturing facilities (known as de-verticalisation), consolidation and downsizing of the US industry and thus a loss of corporate contacts, and reduction in the number of vendors. This has pushed Jamaica into direct competition with other countries in the region.

Despite these difficulties there is a desire to do better. The focus on more fashion-oriented garments aimed at the tourist and cruise ship industry plays to the strong suit of the Caribbean, and particularly Jamaica – not only design capability but also a proven track record in efficient garment production. A number of industry stakeholders interviewed during the survey commented on Jamaican workers' quality and productivity. This applies to the dexterity and skills base as well as to overall productivity. Many of the companies that remain in operation appear to be highly efficient and to have adopted many of the advanced management and communications packages of their US-based partners. They could, therefore, be well positioned for the more complex CMT and full package operations once they can acquire the missing skills. There is an overriding impression, however, that, with exceptions, companies are barely hanging on financially.

The challenge is to move at the industrial scale from 807 parts assembly to CMT and progressively to full package, including development of styles and sourcing of material. To better assess fashion trends in market niche, factories must develop marketing and merchandising intelligence and activities that reflect the current fashion environment, rather than simply relying on the buyer. Apparel manufacturers must learn about developing specification details about the product and the fabric source. They have to concentrate on developing a proactive market research programme. These skills are available in Jamaica but only on a limited basis.

5.11 Summary

The apparel sourcing survey conducted in North America has clearly established that the overall business-oriented attributes of a country are of critical concern to buyers in deciding where to source product. As discussed in Chapter 2 and confirmed during the sourcing survey, buyers are increasingly moving from a consideration of FOB cost to a *full value cost* or total cost basis. Full value considers all the costs involved in the process and separates these into three principal categories: *macro* costs, *indirect* costs and *direct* costs. Macro costs, as noted in Chapter 2, are the costs of doing business in one country as opposed to another.

Perhaps the greatest contributor to macro cost item is import duties. Thus it is advantageous to have preferential trade agreements with the major importing countries, such as the US, that eliminate or reduce such duties. Macro costs include shipping costs and infrastructure service costs as well as the less transparent costs related to the level of human resource development and to any negative impacts of trade disputes. These macro costs fall largely within the purview of government. An assessment of the relative positioning of the six Commonwealth developing countries in respect of the major macro-cost factors is presented in Chart 5.10. Each country is assigned a rating in terms of whether it is advantaged, disadvantaged or neutral in relation to overall competition. This assessment is not intended as a definitive appraisal, but rather to reflect the general findings of the study and to put the situation reported in a given country into a wider context. As discussed in Chapter 2 and supported by Birnbaum (2000), the factors that are considered in this assessment are trade preferences, shipping, infrastructure, human resource development and risk of trade disputes. The overall positioning of the countries in terms of macro cost is then presented, based on these factors.

In terms of trade preferences, with respect to the EU all six countries are on the same footing, although Bangladesh and Sri Lanka would be able to make better use of provisions if regional cumulation were allowed. With respect to the US, Jamaica benefits from 807-preferences and the countries of Southern Africa benefit from AGOA. Lesotho is rated as neutral, however, since if the LDC provisions are not extended, adjustments will have to be made to the source of fabric supply in order for it to continue to benefit under AGOA. Bangladesh and Sri Lanka have no special trade privileges for the US market. They are not penalised, however, although in practice their fabric costs are higher since fabric has to be imported.

Chart 5.10: Comparison of Selected Macro Cost Factors						
Factors	Degree of Country Advantage					
	Jamaica	RSA	Lesotho	Mauritius	Sri Lanka	Bangladesh
Trade preferences: EU	⊘ Neutral	⊘ Neutral	⊘ Neutral	⊘ Neutral	⊘ Neutral	⊘ Neutral
Trade preferences: USA	● Advantaged	● Advantaged	⊘ Neutral	● Advantaged	⊘ Neutral	⊘ Neutral
Shipping time/costs	● Advantaged	⊘ Neutral	○ Disadvantaged	○ Disadvantaged	⊘ Neutral	○ Disadvantaged
Infrastructure and services	⊘ Neutral	● Advantaged	⊘ Neutral	● Advantaged	⊘ Neutral	○ Disadvantaged
Human resource and social issues	⊘ Neutral	⊘ Neutral	○ Disadvantaged	⊘ Neutral	⊘ Neutral	○ Disadvantaged
Risk of trade or other market-related disputes	⊘ Neutral	● Advantaged	○ Disadvantaged	● Advantaged	● Advantaged	⊘ Neutral
Overall macro cost level	● Advantaged	● Advantaged	○ Disadvantaged	⊘ Neutral	⊘ Neutral	○ Disadvantaged

○ Disadvantaged: Issue needs to be addressed on priority basis
⊘ Neutral: Minor up-grade or initiatives are required
● Advantaged: Continued monitoring and fine-tuning are required

With respect to shipping and related costs, Jamaica is considered advantaged due to its proximity to its major customers in the US. South Africa and Sri Lanka are rated neutral, whereas the others are rated disadvantaged. Lesotho is disadvantaged because it depends on overland transport by train or truck both to bring in raw materials and to ship product, which has to pass through South African ports. Bangladesh has issues relating to its deep water port and transhipment. Mauritius is well equipped but there is, particularly vis à vis the US, an issue of additional distance and time.

In terms of quality of infrastructure and services, South Africa and Mauritius are considered advantaged whereas Bangladesh is disadvantaged. The other countries are neutrally positioned, although each has specific issues. The particular advantage for Lesotho is that it produces abundant electricity and is an exporter of electricity to South Africa).

Lesotho and Bangladesh are disadvantaged with respect to human resource development. Lesotho is the least developed in terms of training programmes and autonomous production capability, with major dependence on foreign investors. Bangladesh has addressed many of the issues but still faces major challenges, although ways forward have been identified by the relevant industry and government bodies. The other countries, however, are rated as neutral, being no more advantaged or disadvantaged than most other apparel-producing countries.

The risk of trade disputes is another element that is important to potential buyers. While these risks are difficult to assess, some indicators were obtained during the research. These relate to the perceptions of the Customs and other authorities in the importing countries whether real or unreal. Lesotho could be vulnerable to accusations of using third-party fabric once the LDC provisions expire. Bangladesh and Jamaica are rated as neutral. In the case of Bangladesh, past difficulties with quota limits to North America and the very size of the industry indicate a certain degree of exposure. Jamaica is also exposed due to past difficulties with US Customs despite significant efforts to monitor its export shipments more closely.

Finally, based on the foregoing factors, some broad conclusions can be drawn as to the overall positioning of the countries in terms of macro costs. Jamaica and South Africa are rated as advantaged. For Jamaica the key factors are market proximity and trade preferences. For South Africa, trade preferences are complemented by infrastructure and support services, and the fact that other factors are either advantageous or neutral. Mauritius and Sri Lanka are rated as neutral, but Mauritius would be rated higher if it were not for distance and shipping time to the US. Bangladesh is generally considered to be disadvantaged in terms of macro costs, as evidenced by the attention given to up-grading in its development plans. Lesotho likewise trades on its low labour costs, but is dependent on its foreign investors.

Table 5.1: US Imports from Sub-Saharan Africa, 2001

Rank	Country	% of Total	Value (US$ million)
1	Mauritius	25.1	238.2
2	Lesotho	22.6	214.8
3	Madagascar	18.8	178.2
4	South Africa	18.3	173.3
5	Kenya	6.8	64.5
6	Swaziland	5.1	48.0
7	Zimbabwe	1.5	14.3
8	Malawi	1.2	11.2
	Other sub-Saharan Africa	0.7	7.1
	Total sub-Saharan Africa	100.0	949.6
	Top eight	99.3	942.5

Source: Calculations based on US Department of Commerce data for HS

Table 5.2: EU imports from Sub-Saharan Africa, 2001

Rank	Country	% of Total	Value (ECU million)
1	Mauritius	62.2	666.8
2	Madagascar	24.8	266.5
3	South Africa	7.3	77.9
4	Zimbabwe	2.0	21.8
5	Botswana	1.8	19.6
6	Lesotho	0.4	3.8
7	Cape Verde	0.3	3.8
8	Tanzania	0.2	2.0
9	Kenya	0.2	1.9
10	Mozambique	0.1	1.5
	Other	0.7	7.1
	Top ten	99.3	1,065.5
	Total	100.0	1,072.6

Source: Calculations based on EUROSTAT data for HS 61 and HS 62

Table 5.3: AGOA – Before and After

Category	AGOA I	AGOA II
Knit-to-shape	The term 'fabric' interpreted by US Customs as excluding components that are 'knit-to-shape' (i.e. components that take their shape in the knitting process, rather than being cut from a bolt of cloth).	Knit-to-shape apparel qualifies for AGOA benefits.
Less developed countries	Duty-free treatment for apparel articles assembled in less developed countries in sub-Saharan Africa, regardless of origin of fabric.	LDC apparel eligible for duty-free treatment regardless of origin of fabric and regardless of origin of yarn.
Botswana and Namibia	Not treated as LDCs because per capita GNP in 1998 exceeded $1,500.	Specially designated as LDCs.
Hybrid cutting	Under US Customs interpretation, cutting of fabric must occur either in the US or AGOA countries, but not both.	Hybrid cutting (i.e. cutting that occurs both in the US and in AGOA countries) does not render fabric ineligible.
Volume cap on duty-free treatment for apparel made from fabric made in AGOA region or for less developed beneficiary countries from fabric made anywhere.	Applicable percentages increase from 1 October 2007.	Applicable percentages doubled.

Source: http://www.agoa.gov

Table 5.4: Distribution of EPZ Employment, 1999–2001 (December)

Industry	1999	2000	2001
Textile yarn and fabrics	4,041	4,672	4,858
Wearing apparel	76,919	75,329	72,145
Of which:			
Pullovers	18,564	18,606	18,447
Other garments	58,355	56,724	53,698
Total textiles and apparel	80,960	80,001	77,003
Total	91,374	90,682	87,607

Source: EPZDA (2002) Tables 2 and 2a; Export Development Zone Development Authority compilation from Central Statistics Office data

Table 5.5: Exports of Textiles and Apparel, 1998–2001 (value (FOB) Rs billion)

Industry	1998	1999	2000	2001
Textile yarn and fabrics	1.1	1.8	1.9	2.5
Apparel	21.1	23.0	24.6	24.9
Total textiles and apparel	22.2	24.8	26.5	27.4

Source: EPZDA (2002) Tables 4 and 4a; Export Development Zone Development Authority compilation from Central Statistics Office data

Table 5.6: Principal Markets for Textiles and Apparel

Country	Export value (Rs billion)			% of Total
	1998	1999	2000	2000
United States	5.8	6.5	6.4	25
France	5.3	5.7	6.1	24
United Kingdom	4.8	5.3	5.7	22
Other	6.3	7.3	7.3	29
Total textiles and apparel	22.2	24.8	25.5	100

Source: Kaidoo (2001), Tables 3 and 4 (data for 2000 are estimates)

Table 5.7: Numbers of EPZ Enterprises, 1999–2001 (December)

Industry	1999	2000	2001
Textile yarn and fabrics	34	45	47
Wearing apparel	251	240	239
Of which:			
Pullovers	32	37	38
Other garments	219	203	201
Total textiles and apparel	285	285	286
Total	512	518	522

Source: EPZDA, Tables 2, 2a

Table 5.8: Evolution of the Textile and Apparel Industry in South Africa, 1990–2000

Item	Units	1990	1995	2000
Clothing industry				
Domestic output	US$ million	1,300	2,100	2,000
Exports	US$ million	55	122	150
Textile industry				
Woven fabric produced	US$ million	355	289	275
Yarn produced	US$ million	320	405	350

Source: Clothing Trade Council of South Africa and CLOFED (data have been rounded)

Table 5.9: Lesotho Apparel Industry Size

Category	Exports 2000–01	Employment 4/2002
# companies for 50%	3	8
# companies for 80%	10	18
Total (24 companies)	$240 million	34,300

Source: Calculated from LNDC (2000)

Table 5.10: Country of Origin of Investors

Country	Number	Workforce* (%)
Taiwan	26	91
South Africa	3	3
Other	4	6
Total	33	100

*Total workforce of 32,750 from 33 companies on which data is available.
Source: LNDC (2000)

Table 5.11: Principal Products

Nominal product	Number of Companies	Workforce*(%)
Jeans	9	35
T-shirts	20	59
Mixed/other	4	6
Total	33	100

*Total workforce of 32,750 from 33 companies on which data is available.
Source: LNDC (2000)

Table 5.12: US Imports from Asia, 2001

Rank	Country	Value (US$ million)	% Total from Asia
1	China	6,429.7	20.8
2	Hong Kong	4,202.0	13.6
3	Indonesia	2,215.0	7.2
4	Korea, South	2,172.0	7.0
5	Bangladesh	1,930.2	6.3
6	Philippines	1,877.0	6.1
7	Thailand	1,839.6	6.0
8	India	1,781.4	5.8
9	Taiwan	1,699.5	5.5
10	Sri Lanka	1,486.3	4.8
11	Macau	1,085.0	3.5
12	Pakistan	934.8	3.0
13	Cambodia	919.8	3.0
14	Malaysia	785.3	2.5
15	Burma (Myanmar)	408.2	1.3
16	Singapore	298.5	1.0
17	Brunei Darussalam	212.4	0.7
18	Nepal	149.4	0.5
19	Mongolia	139.7	0.5
20	Japan	135.3	0.4
21	Maldives	96.5	0.3
22	Vietnam	47.8	0.2
23	Laos	3.6	0.0
	Total: Asia	30,849.4	100.0

Source: Calculations based on US Department of Commerce data for HS 61 and HS 62 (from www.strategis.ic.gc.ca)

Table 5.13: EU Imports from Asia, 2001

Rank	Country	% of Total	Value (ECU million)
1	China	33.4	7,977.9
2	Bangladesh	11.7	2,794.5
3	Hong Kong	10.7	2,552.6
4	India	9.1	2,162.5
5	Indonesia	7.4	1,759.6
6	Thailand	3.5	839.8
7	Sri Lanka	3.2	763.2
8	South Korea	3.2	755.9
9	Vietnam	3.1	738.3
10	Pakistan	2.7	645.5
	Other	12.0	2,863.1
	Top 10	88.0	20,989.8
	Total	100.0	23,852.9

Source: Calculations based on EUROSTAT data for HS 61 and HS 62

Table 5.14: Top Five Exports to the US Market, 2000

	Description	Value (US$ million)
6204	Women's or girls suits, ensembles, jackets, dresses, skirts, etc.	372.9
6203	Men's or boys' suit ensembles, jackets, blazers, trousers, etc.	259.4
6206	Women's or girls' blouses, shirts and shirt-blouses	162.1
6205	Men's or boys' shirts	131.9
6212	Brassieres, girdles, corsets, etc.	107.7

Source: Calculated from Sri Lanka Export Development Board Data

Table 5.15: Top Five Exports to the UK Market, 2000

	Description	Value (US$ million)
6204	Women's or girls' suits, ensembles, jackets, dresses, skirts, etc.	84.1
6109	T-shirts, singlets and other vests	79.1
6107	Men's or boys' underpants, briefs, nightshirts, pajamas, bathrobes, etc.	57.6
6203	Men's or boys' suit ensembles, jackets, blazers, trousers, etc.	46.3
6108	Women's or girls' slips, petticoats, briefs, panties, nightdresses, etc.	42.7

Source: Calculated from Sri Lanka Export Development Board Data

Table 5.16: Distribution of Exports

Size Level		Exporters		Export Value (Rs million)	
Classification	Exports (Rs million)	Number	%	Value (Rs million)	%
Small	0.25 m–100 m	549	64	10 355	5
Medium	100 m–500 m	204	24	48 936	23
Large	> 500 m	106	12	149 362	72
	Total	859	100	208 633	100

Source: Government Sponsored Committee (2002), p. 2 from Sri Lanka Customs/Export Development Board data

Table 5.17: US Apparel Imports from Latin America and the Caribbean, 2001

Rank	Country	% of Regional Imports	Value (US$ million)
1	Honduras	23.4	2,438
2	Dominican Republic	21.4	2,226
3	El Salvador	15.7	1,633
4	Guatemala	15.5	1,612
5	Costa Rica	7.4	771
6	Nicaragua	3.7	380
7	Peru	3.6	370
8	Colombia	3.3	344
9	Haiti	2.2	232
10	Jamaica	1.8	187
11	Brazil	1.0	107
	Other Latin America plus Caribbean	1.1	111
	Top 11	98.9	10,301
	Total	**100.0**	**10,412**

Source: Calculations based on US Department of Commerce data for HS 61 and HS 62. Available at: www.strategis.ic.gc.ca

Table 5.18: EU Apparel Imports from Latin America and the Caribbean, 2001

Rank	Country	% of Regional Imports	Value (ECU million)
1	Jamaica	50.8	84.3
2	Colombia	18.8	31.2
3	Honduras	10.2	16.9
4	Dominican Republic	5.9	9.9
5	El Salvador	4.8	7.9
6	Costa Rica	3.3	5.5
7	Guatemala	2.3	3.9
8	Panama	0.9	1.4
9	Haiti	0.6	1.0
10	Belize	0.5	0.8
	Other	2.0	3.3
	Top 10	98.0	162.7
	Total Caribbean and Latin America	100.0	166.0

Source: Calculations based on EUROSTAT data for HS 61 and HS 62

6

Production and Costing Issues in Selected Commonwealth Developing Countries

6.1 Introduction

The principal business issues faced by the apparel producers interviewed in the six Commonwealth developing countries during the fieldwork were discussed in the previous chapter. This chapter presents findings concerning the principal technical issues facing the apparel industry in these countries. The findings are drawn from interviews with key industry stakeholders and factory observations.

The assessment focuses on the principal factors contributing to indirect and direct costs to an apparel importer in the US and Europe (Birnbaum, 2002). The importance of these issues was confirmed by sourcing executives surveyed in North America. The major indirect cost factors that are assessed are product development capability, full package capability and minimum order size. The assessment of direct cost factors focuses firstly on manufacturing capability and secondly on productivity and performance.

A comparative assessment of the state of development of the apparel industry in each of the six countries and of the principal issues that must be addressed is provided at the end of the chapter.

6.2 Indirect Cost Factors

The issues

The principal contributors to indirect costs, as perceived by the buyers, are related to pre-production activities such as product development capability and full package capability, as well as to minimum order size. The principal capabilities investigated in terms of product development were design capability, sample development, marker making and unit costing. The assessments presented in this section are inevitably general but are believed to reflect the capabilities of the industry at large in each of the Commonwealth countries visited.

Based on the interviews in the selected countries it is also possible to assess general capability with regard to overall full package capability, that is to source and supply fabric as well as to cut and sew. Minimum order size is also an issue of indirect cost and again, based on interview data, the countries can be positioned with respect to this factor. Chart 6.1 shows the relative positioning of the six countries with respect to indirect costs.

Chart 6.1: Comparison of Selected Indirect Cost Factors

Factors	Jamaica	RSA	Lesotho	Mauritius	Sri Lanka	Bangladesh
	Degree of Country Advantage					
Product development	○	●	○	●	●	⊘
Design capability	○	●	○	●	⊘	○
Pattern making	○	●	○	●	●	⊘
Sample development	○	●	○	●	●	⊘
Marker making	○	⊘	○	⊘	●	⊘
Full package capability	○	●	○	●	●	⊘
Minimum order size	○	●	○	⊘	⊘	○
Overall indirect cost level	○	●	○	●	⊘	○

○ Disadvantaged: Issue needs to be addressed on priority basis
⊘ Neutral: Minor up-grade or initiatives are required
● Advantaged: Continued monitoring and fine-tuning are required

Product development

The overall assessment of product development capability is presented in Chart 6.1. The principal capabilities investigated in terms of product development, as stated above, were design capability, sample development, marker making and unit costing. The key issues related to each are discussed in the following sections prior to presenting an overall assessment of capability for the six countries.

In terms of overall product development capability, South Africa, Mauritius and Sri Lanka were found to be advantaged. The use of computer-aided design and related technology appeared to be less widespread in Bangladesh than in Sri Lanka, for example, and so Bangladesh is rated as neutral. In the case of Jamaica, product development is not an issue for most companies since they rely on 807 business with the US. Several companies, however, which had ambitions to develop non 807-dependent business, saw the lack of product design and development and full package capability as a significant constraint: Jamaica is thus rated as disadvantaged. Since the industry in Lesotho is entirely dependent on foreign partners for product development work, it is considered to be disadvantaged in regard to such capability. Assessments of sub-capabilities follow.

Design capability

Most of the apparel manufacturers whose representatives were interviewed during the fieldwork in Mauritius and South Africa appeared to maintain a good level of knowledge on merchandising intelligence and on the current fashion environment. Manufacturers in both countries have successfully developed a direct marketing link with buyers. In addition, South Africa's focus on the domestic market and experience in dealing directly with the demanding local retailers and providing new collections of products for each season are significant advantages.

In contrast, in Sri Lanka and Bangladesh buyers or their representatives handle style and fashions trend issues; there is little or inadequate knowledge about the fashion apparel industry, especially among the SMEs, and design capability is limited to pattern, grading and sample making. Product development is something new to Lesotho and Jamaican factories and has largely been done by the parent or client companies overseas. Lesotho focuses on basic CMT, and Jamaica on making the garment only under the 807 programme. All activities related to product development, raw materials purchasing, marketing and order processing are handled by their head offices/clients. Generally, these are in the Far East for Lesotho and in the US for Jamaica.

The lack of capability in product design and new product development is seen as a major disadvantage and efforts are reportedly under way in many Commonwealth developing countries to rectify this. The creation of a fashion institute is an example in Bangladesh, and there are indications that this is a priority in other countries. But the crucial requirement, as evident from the sourcing survey, is for companies to have a good understanding of the market that they are serving.

Representatives of at least two of the apparel manufacturers interviewed during the fieldwork in Mauritius reported that they work with design studios in London and/or Paris. They use them to develop stylebooks that reflect the needs of the market and present collections as a starting point for discussions with buyers. At least one group had gone so far as to license its own brand.

The design departments also appeared to be well organised and equipped in Mauritius, South Africa, Sri Lanka and Bangladesh, certainly among the larger companies. Some of the factories visited have recognised the opportunities available through the strategic use of information technology, such as implementing CAD/CAM in style creation. The operation and use of this technology, however, was principally limited to pattern making and grading of any given style in order to improve lead time and increase fit accuracy. This system, which has an interface with the marker-making software, allows the pattern to be transferred electronically. The majority of buyers in North America are equipped with computer aided design (CAD) systems that enable them to transfer any design electronically via the Internet to the vendor site using product data management software such as PDM Gerber. These capabilities contribute to reduced production costs and lead time. Continued use of manual systems makes factories vulnerable to the many challenges of the evolving global market.

Design capability is a strength of the apparel industry in both South Africa and Mauritius. Despite being well equipped, Sri Lanka's industry is generally in need of considerable skills up-grading in order to make full use of the technology; its capability advantage is therefore rated as neutral. The general conclusion with respect to

Bangladesh is that design capability is weak overall and is an issue that needs to be addressed on a priority basis. The same applies to those companies in Jamaica that wish to evolve from the 807 situation.

Sample development

All factories visited in selected Commonwealth developing countries, except Lesotho and Jamaica, were equipped with sample rooms and trained staff enabling them to prepare initial samples. Samples are required by buyers for fitting purposes – to approve size grading and the final appearance of the product prior to production. Less evident was linking this activity to efforts to find the most economical and practical work methods for cutting and sewing. Such optimisation of work methods could help to meet the price in the marketplace and could accelerate reaching better performance. This would also highlight areas where quality is critical and could result in reduction in the cost structure throughout the manufacturing process. In regard to Lesotho and Jamaica, initial samples are made by companies' head offices. In terms of comparative assessment, the ratings and needs for priority interventions are the same as for the overall product development capability.

Marker making

Apparel manufacturers in South Africa and Lesotho are generally making the markers manually; none of the factories visited reported the use of any marker-making software. On the other hand, an estimated 45 per cent of the Sri Lankan garment factories surveyed are currently using marker-making software. In Bangladesh, this technology is limited to the large companies. The majority of Jamaican factories do not have any cutting activities since the essence of the 807 programme is assembly of garment parts cut in the United States. The one company visited that was not doing 807-type work did the marker making manually.

Personnel responsible for marker making, either with software or manually, appear to be adequately trained. It seems, however, that insufficient attention is given to the percentage of fabric wastage that is occurring. The software has an interface with the CAD system sharing the same data in relation to pattern making. When this operation is manual, waste tends to be high. Since fabric represents 55–70 per cent of total unit costs, factories could save a considerable amount of money if fabric utilisation levels were reduced. The potential for such savings was highlighted by some US sourcing executives

In terms of overall assessment for marker making capability, Sri Lankan companies in general make good use of the CAD/CAM capability for marker making, which is an advantage. South Africa, Mauritius and Bangladesh were rated as neither advantaged nor disadvantaged. Jamaican companies need considerable up-skilling to handle cutting activities.

Unit costing

In a significant number of apparel factories surveyed during the field research it appeared that the determination of unit labour cost is tied to the current productivity of the factory and not benchmarked against external standards. Applying an external predetermined motion and time measurement system such as that available from General Sewing Data (GSD) would enable companies to objectively find ways to meet the price in the marketplace through work methods and productivity improvement.

Some 70 per cent of the factories visited in Sri Lanka utilise a predetermined time measurement system, such as GSD and 'Easy Sew', that enables them to determine the standard minute value (SMV) per operation. This enables them to finalise the direct labour cost as well as to determine the most economical work methods to make the product. In South Africa, Bangladesh and Mauritius, many companies reported that time studies had been applied to determine the SMV in order to evaluate direct labour costs. In at least two cases, companies had benchmarked in Mauritius against external predetermined time systems. Likewise companies surveyed in Jamaica and Lesotho relied on the foreign companies (head offices) to provide the operations breakdown with the standard minutes' value for efficiency monitoring and operational planning at the factory sites.

Low labour costs and accurate SMV are not enough to produce a competitive unit labour cost – both are tied up with the global performance of the factories. Improving organisation, productivity and infrastructure are the main issues for labour cost reduction.

Another issue, observed during the survey in Sri Lanka, is that factories do not distinguish in their unit costing between CMT and full package orders, and between large and small production runs. Production cost (direct labour plus overhead costs) remains the same no matter what type of orders they are dealing with, but CMT orders do not require any purchasing activity, product data management, etc. *Buyers expect to find cost differences*.

Full package and minimum order size

The other critical factors that contribute to indirect costs are full package capability and minimum order size. These are discussed below.

Full package capability

Taking account of product development and fabric sourcing capabilities, South Africa, Mauritius and Sri Lanka are rated as advantaged, and Bangladesh as neutral. In essence, these ratings follow those for product development. Jamaica and Lesotho are clearly disadvantaged since most export-oriented companies rely on foreign partners for product development and fabric sourcing.

Minimum order size

Many factories in South Africa, with their dependence on the local market, are geared to production of small order sizes. In fact, many companies stated that the large order sizes, as found in basic products for the US market, were beyond their competitive capabilities. Bangladesh, Jamaica and Lesotho, on the other hand, have become efficient producers due to high volumes and so require higher minimums. This is a disadvantage in seeking new business. Mauritius and Sri Lanka can handle a range of order sizes; they are therefore rated as neither advantaged nor disadvantaged in relation to minimum orders.

Overall indirect cost level

Overall positioning in terms of indirect costs, as viewed by apparel importers, is also presented in Chart 6.1. As was the case for the assessment of macro costs, the positioning is a generalised indication and does not take account of the relative weighting between various factors, nor of the product-specific issues. Rather, it is intended as a general indicator through which to focus on the principal issues.

In general, South Africa and Mauritius are seen as advantaged in terms of indirect costs. Sri Lanka is considered as neutral in terms of advantage and Bangladesh still has considerable capability up-grading to reach the levels of the three preceding countries. Again, Bangladesh acknowledges that its competitive advantage lies in its low labour costs. This situation is also reflected by the high reliance on buying houses and agents by most companies, although there are exceptions, located in Bangladesh. Jamaica has a long way to go if it wants to break out of the 807 segment and its reliance on buyers for pre-production services and otherwise compete in terms of low indirect costs. Lesotho is in the same situation.

6.3 Direct Cost Factors

Principal issues

As stated in Section 6.1 of this chapter, the assessment of direct cost factors focuses firstly on manufacturing capability and secondly on productivity and performance. All these factors contribute to the critical criteria required by buyers in selecting manufacturing partners – competitive pricing, quality consistency and lead time. These are assessed in this section.

The principal manufacturing capabilities investigated and reported on here are labour rates, production line set-ups, machinery and equipment, information management, quality management, methods of control and industrial engineering. Productivity and performance are assessed in terms of labour productivity, quality rejection rates, ratios of direct to indirect labour and lead time. Although addressed in separate sections of the report, productivity and performance are directly linked to manufacturing capabilities and hence to direct manufacturing cost.

The relative positioning of the six countries with respect to direct costs is discussed below and summarised in Chart 6.2; positioning with respect to key productivity and performance parameters is presented in Chart 6.3.

Labour rates

The range in nominal labour rates for the apparel industry in the six countries selected for case studies is shown in Table 6.1. The data are based on information obtained

Chart 6.2: Comparison of Selected Direct Cost Factors

Factors	Degree of Country Advantage					
	Jamaica	RSA	Lesotho	Mauritius	Sri Lanka	Bangladesh
Labour rates	○	○	⊘	○	⊘	●
Production systems	●	⊘	○	⊘	⊘	○
Machinery and equipment	⊘	⊘	⊘	⊘	⊘	⊘
Information management	⊘	●	○	●	⊘	⊘
Quality management	⊘	⊘	○	⊘	●	○
Methods of control	⊘	●	○	●	⊘	⊘
Industrial engineering	⊘	⊘	○	⊘	○	○
Overall direct cost level	⊘	○	⊘	○	○	⊘

○ Disadvantaged: Issue needs to be addressed on priority basis
⊘ Neutral: Minor up-grade or initiatives are required
● Advantaged: Continued monitoring and fine-tuning are required

during the field research and supporting documentation from international sources. To facilitate comparison, the typical rates have been reduced to a per hour basis in US dollars. Two caveats are in order, however. First, available data frequently quotes rates on a daily or weekly basis. This has necessitated certain assumptions, as indicated. Second, rates are based on exchange rates prevailing at the time of the field research. Nonetheless, the orders of magnitude of the rates and the differences between countries provide a good illustration of comparative labour cost levels.

The hourly labour rate varies tremendously between the countries surveyed. Bangladesh has the lowest labour cost per hour of the six countries selected at an equivalent of US$0.14–0.16. Bangladesh is followed by Sri Lanka at an estimated US$0.31–0.35, Lesotho at US$0.43–0.54 and Mauritius, averaging US$0.65. The hourly rate for Jamaica is nearly double this, at a reported US$1.50–1.60. For South Africa, the rate for the urban areas ranges from US$1.10–1.40 but is only US$0.55–0.78. in decentralised production units.

It would appear that in South Africa it is common practice to pay apparel industry employees on a productivity bonus system in order to promote performance and reduce absenteeism. Despite the applied incentive, factories are reported to be performing with an average of 70 per cent on traditional continuous flow and around 55 per cent on seasonal production lines. Employee absenteeism and turnover are reported to

Table 6.1: Estimated Representative Labour Rates in the Apparel Industry, 2002

Country	Rate US$/hour
Bangladesh	0.14–0.16
Jamaica	1.50–1.60
Sri Lanka	0.31–0.35
Mauritius	0.65
South Africa (urban areas)	1.10–1.40
South Africa (other areas)	0.55–0.78
Lesotho	0.43–0.54

Sources: Bangladesh – Rahman (2002), p. 11 and US Department of Labor (2000); Sri Lanka – Rahman (2002), p. 11 and US Department of Labor (2000); Mauritius – Coughlin *et al.* (2001), p. 37 and US Department of Labor (2000) (assuming 10 hours per day); South Africa – Coughlin *et al.* (2001), p. 37, interviews in June 2002 and Moodley and Velia (2002), p. 3; Lesotho – Coughlin *et al.* (2001), p. 37 and interviews in South Africa, June 2002; Jamaica – interviews in February 2002

be high. One respondent cited a turnover of up to 20 per cent and absenteeism of 9 per cent. Production delays averaging 15 per cent due to machinery breakdown, line balancing, re-working defective units and other issues are reported.

Factories in Mauritius, Jamaica and Lesotho have also adopted incentive plans. Those that are tied to line output, as used by some companies, have contributed to achieving higher productivity. This is in contrast to Sri Lanka and Bangladesh, where some of the factories visited have also adopted incentive plans but success has been limited. This is largely due to the lack of support provided to the workers and to the basis on which the incentives are structured.

In general, Bangladesh has a distinct advantage in labour rates and Jamaica, South Africa and Mauritius are disadvantaged.

Production line set-up

Production line set-ups vary in the countries surveyed but exhibit some common characteristics and deficiencies. The overall situation in each country is discussed below. The issue is how to move from production of large orders of basic styles to smaller orders and changing styles following the industry trend, particularly for countries where labour cost is relatively high.

In the factories surveyed in Jamaica, production lines have been set as progressive bundle lines where a bundle of pieces moves from one workstation to another. This kind of system requires a new machinery set-up for every new style, but is suited to large orders. In Jamaica, the lines operate with 16 workstations and 16 operators. In Lesotho, a typical line has 27 workstations and 27 operators. In both countries production lines are manageable, resulting in continuous flow, less production delays, better line balancing and maximisation of workstation output. Due to the mass production nature of the business, this type of set-up is ideal for both countries

In the absence of mass production, the factories visited in Sri Lanka, Bangladesh, Mauritius and South Africa appeared to be vulnerable to problems resulting from use of the progressive bundle system, employees performing sewing operations by speciality rather than working in multi-skilled teams. This increases work-in-process inventories, lead time and risk of misbalance in the flow of work through the manufacturing chain – all of which contribute to lower productivity.

In Sri Lanka the industry is working on small production runs focusing on fashionable goods. Production orders typically vary from 300 units to 5,000 units per order. Production set-up involving a day of almost no output can occur as often as every five days. There is a substantial potential gain here in shifting to flexible production systems from the traditional production line approach. Production lines are too large, employing large numbers of employees averaging 36 workstations, 26 operators and ten helpers. This makes it very difficult to handle orders of less than 3,000 units with proper line balancing and production loading at each workstation on a continuous flow basis.

The production lines observed in Mauritius typically run traditionally, by skill under a progressive bundle system and there is little or no flexibility among the employees. As a result, a high factor of absenteeism and/or a small order could make the resulting operations very costly. This type of set-up does not help to handle small orders efficiently; however Mauritius will have to focus on this type of business, leaving the large run basic business to Madagascar and elsewhere.

Sewing operators in South Africa reportedly lack knowledge about how to adjust their sewing machines in order to meet product quality requirements and to avoid production delays. As a result of the progressive bundles system, there is a lack of flexibility, which is particularly a problem due to the high absenteeism. Cutting rooms of the companies visited in Johannesburg and Cape Town are reportedly still running manually with skilled employees.

Overall, production systems are assessed as being adequate for current business but are clearly vulnerable as volumes drop and required response times diminish also. More critically, significant opportunities for up-grading have been identified, as indicated in the above discussion.

Machinery and equipment

Spreading and cutting.

There are no spreading and cutting activities in the major plants in Jamaica due to the reliance on 807 programmes. Factories in Lesotho, Bangladesh and South Africa tend to operate their cutting rooms using manual spreaders and knife cutters. They have generally chosen not to invest in high-tech equipment due to lack of support from the banks and/or to lack of order continuity to assure the return on investment. In Sri Lanka, however, most large and some medium-sized enterprises have abandoned low-tech spreaders and cutting equipment and adopted total-edge cutting solutions in order to improve production planning, lead time and cutting quality, and reduce fabric wastage and labour costs. In Mauritius, the majority of apparel enterprises are knitting factories with high-tech knitting equipment. Woven factories visited during the field-work worked with manual spreaders and cutters. Cutting rooms of the companies visited in South Africa and Lesotho are reportedly still running manually using skilled employees, unlike in Bangladesh and Sri Lanka where it is possible to still find a high ratio of unskilled labour.

Sewing machinery.

According to most respondents interviewed in Sri Lanka, the average age for factory sewing equipment is one to five years (67.2%). A few (2.8%) noted that their equipment was less than a year old, and a small number of factories (30%) noted that their equipment was more than six years old. The factories visited in Jamaica, Lesotho and South Africa are generally operating with sewing equipment over six years old rather than the latest technology.

Regardless of the age of the sewing machines, they are generally still adequate for the job they are performing. However, there are disadvantages if factories are not equipped with the essential functions that the industry looks for to improve operation cycle and reduce handling. For example, if machines do not have thread cutters and automatic bartack this adds to the cost of direct labour. The difference between modern machines and adequate machines older than six years is that modern machines have more pre-programmed sewing cycles to perform some specific straight seams with a constant speed and, in some cases, they also have higher revolution per minute (RPM). Despite the enhancement of the modern machines, none of the factories surveyed have taken full advantage of these new capabilities, and it seems that the old and the new are performing the same job.

Positioning

In terms of machinery, all the countries surveyed are positioned as neither advantaged nor disadvantaged, but this is really an issue that relates to the companies and the nature of their business. As companies take on responsibility for fabric, savings on fabric will become more important.

Quality management

Jamaican factories have high quality products in comparison to industry criteria and quality programmes have become accepted elements in the management of successful factories, regardless of size or market position. The Jamaican garment industry has also made great strides in adopting quality programmes and has achieved measurable success due to the expertise of its expatriate production supervisors and production managers. A similar situation exists in Lesotho, but there is a very high proportion of foreign workers acting as line supervisors and inspectors. This is not the case in the other countries.

Mauritian factories regard 'total quality management' and workforce cross-functional training as critical issues. In addition, improving product quality and logistics programmes appear to be priorities. Three out of seven factories in Mauritius are certified by the International Standards Organisation (ISO) and there are others in the process of obtaining certification. Lack of ISO 9000 certification may not, however, be a major drawback for the American market, since US buyers are more concerned about operational quality standards than the assurance of quality reliability of the supplier. Despite this, a 4 per cent rejection rate was reported in some factories visited at the final quality audit. This may be due to deficiencies in sewing operator training on quality criteria and adaptability, and is readily rectifiable.

According to the factories operators surveyed in South Africa, the only advantage left for them is their production quality. Products quality appears to be very good. There are some reports of rejection rates as high as 6 per cent, however, which would indicate a need to improve the in-line quality process.

Some of the Bangladeshi garment factories were only slightly more successful at implementing product quality programmes than the industry as a whole. However, the need to focus on 'improving product quality' is evident.

Factories in Sri Lanka have high-quality products in comparison to industry criteria. The industry has made great strides in adopting quality programmes and has achieved measurable success – but at a high cost. Regardless of this success, quality is still suffering internally at all levels and as a result rejection rates of over 14 per cent after final sewing operations have been reported. A rejection rate of 4 per cent at the final quality audit before shipping is also typical. However, all factories clearly identified the need to focus on 'improving product quality'. Despite all the stages of checking, quality is still suffering at all levels. This is largely due to lack of knowledge of the quality standards and flexibility on behalf of the sewing operators. Quality knowledge is limited only to the quality staff, and sewing operators have no training on quality criteria and adaptability. Thus these standards should be built into the production line.

Overall, Sri Lanka is rated as being advantaged in quality issues, an attribute that would appear to be recognised by the buying and sourcing representatives met in the course of the survey in the US and Canada. Lesotho and Bangladesh are disadvantaged and this is perhaps most critical for Bangladesh in view of the fact that most companies are independently run, in contrast to the closely managed foreign plants found in Lesotho. The other countries are rated as neither advantaged nor disadvantaged on quality issues.

Information and control systems

Information management

It would appear that factories in Mauritius and South Africa have generally benefited from the implementation of management information systems that range from simple accounting packages to enterprise wide systems (Enterprise Resource Planning (ERP)). Used successfully, they can streamline processes, such as order processing and tracking of production, eliminate waste and ultimately create a competitive advantage. The

Mauritian garment industry has struggled with the issue of linkage problems between suppliers and retailers. It would appear that most of the factories have not benefited from the opportunities that could result from supply chain integration by redefining business processes, and implementing electronic data interchange, scanning and Extranet systems. However, South African garment factory operators interviewed believe that they must pursue e-business strategies in order to maintain competitiveness and improve operating efficiencies. Much of the development in IT in the South African industry has been due to the pressure of local retailers in regard to the integration of EDI, linking the manufacturer to the buyer through the supply chain. Most of the factories use the Internet to optimise their supply chain, while industry leaders continue to invest in e-business and move towards achieving their strategic objectives.

Apparel manufacturers in Lesotho and Jamaica work with personal computers, generally connected via the Internet and some have a software interface with their head office mainframe located in-market to update the production schedule and productivity achievement. In these cases, ERP and EDI are used by head offices overseas but not the factories.

However, the majority of the factories assessed in Sri Lanka and Bangladesh were found to have concentrated their efforts on implementing more traditional forms of information systems and procedures. For example, Sri Lankan factories seem to be adopting management information systems regardless of their appropriateness, instead of selecting systems that best suit their needs. Some 65 per cent of Sri Lankan factories have implemented resource planning systems for production planning and order tracking through the manufacturing chain. From observations in the factories surveyed it was noted that use of manual data capture and manual updating systems result in excessive time-constraining procedures and that information is often corrupted due to error at the employee level. Despite the information management systems, Bangladeshi and Sri Lankan manufacturers employ large number of employees to control and evaluate each activity through the chain. Such practices increase the unit cost tremendously.

The procurement process has traditionally been characterised by a reliance on paper-based, telephone and fax transactions and e-mail for communication that contribute to high overhead, labour and processing costs. Factories are often unaware of the procurement processing costs they incur and often regard these costs as uncontrollable.

The utilisation of scanning technology to manage inventories and bar-coded shipping labels as requested by some buyers is generally sub-contracted locally in the factories visited. An exception was in Jamaica where bar coding is handled at buyer sites in the US.

Methods of control

Inadequate cost controls were identified as an issue during the study. Costs associated with purchasing, development, producing and holding inventory are so significant that cost control measures must be enforced to ensure competitive unit prices and profitable returns. Factories would be in a much better competitive position if they strategically adopted management information systems with the objective of reducing paper work and reports, speeding up data access and allowing information to be accessed online.

Shop floor cost control is of particular concern. Such a system is the basis from which to calculate labour productivity in order to pay performance bonuses, track production orders, control line balancing and compare actual cost to estimated cost. The reports are generated by the capture of production data off the production floor in real time or by batch daily. The absence of a shop floor control system or any activity-based costing method will not help in enhancing the accuracy of product profitability information.

Factories in Jamaica, South Africa and Lesotho apparently manage costs successfully. To do so, they have adopted shop floor control and distinguish between direct and indirect costs. They have adopted some stand-alone programmes such as shop floor control software in order to monitor the individual performance of the direct labour; as well as software to control and track all orders and to monitor the performance of the direct labour through the manufacturing lines. The basis of this system is production coupons which are attached to each bundle after the cutting, collected by the direct labour and submitted to the office for scanning into the information system.

In Mauritius, five of the factories surveyed report that they have implemented shop floor control software in order to monitor productivity online. They do not, however, appear to have used such software as a tool to combat high unit costs. In Bangladesh, and particularly in Sri Lanka, factories generally appear to consider the workforce to be a fixed cost. There is no costing analysis to determine direct and indirect labour inputs, and control is used only to calculate the number of pieces produced. As a result, factories have difficulty in evaluating and improving product profitability. This is causing an increase in unit prices at all levels of production. In fact, a number of factories have yet to implement initiatives geared towards reducing overhead and set-up costs, improving productivity outputs and shortening lead time.

Positioning

In terms of information management, South Africa and Mauritius are positioned as having an advantage, with the other countries being essentially neutral. This does not mean that there is no room for improvement that could impact on costs. Lesotho is again rated as disadvantaged due to almost total dependence on expatriate management. Positioning for methods of control is similar to that for information management.

Industrial Engineering

A lack of industrial engineering capability has also been identified as another competitive disadvantage for the garment industry in Commonwealth developing countries. This was manifested by reports of unbalanced production lines resulting in low productivity and profitability, high work in process inventories among the workstations and between manufacturing sectors, and lack of creativity in finding new ways to reduce the cost of direct labour through engineered work methods.

Production managers and supervisors in the South African factories appeared to be competent in day-to-day management. Industrial engineering capability within the industry, however, seemed to be limited. In some cases it was reported that this was due to a thinning-out of management ranks as the companies downsized due to loss of business.

Production supervisors in Bangladesh and Sri Lanka appeared to lack technical and operational knowledge. Production supervisors tended to act as general workers, chasing orders online instead of promoting work methods, improving line balancing, and improving and achieving quality norms. Factories face tremendous excess overtime and/or missed delivery deadlines because of poor production planning and operations control – a result of lack of skill on behalf of the supervisors. Line staff and middle management are not objective oriented in relation to cost and performance. Objectives assigned by top management to middle management in order to monitor and ensure that targets for cost of labour are met are at best inadequate and often non-existent.

Mauritius appeared to rate very well in relation to senior management. Concerns were expressed about lower level staff, however. Many company representatives interviewed claimed that they experienced difficulty in recruiting skilled technicians and that supervisors had low levels of knowledge with respect to work methods and costing. The limited labour supply was also viewed as a constraint in implementing possibly unpopular measures aimed at tightening productivity.

In Jamaica, the skill of supervisory and management personnel is limited and many smaller factories managers interviewed claimed that they have difficulty in recruiting skilled technicians. Jamaican factories rely on the work methods developed and transferred to their sites by US manufacturers and with the assistance of US engineers employed in Jamaica. In contrast, in Lesotho there is almost total reliance on expatriate production supervisors for management and line supervision functions. These workers tend, at least for the Taiwanese-owned factories, to come from Taiwan or China. Casual observation would indicate one expatriate supervisor per production line, plus higher-level management. The official ratio is five expatriates per 100 employees, according to the Lesotho National Development Corporation, and the extent to which local workers are trained to advance in the management hierarchy is uncertain. One company referred to the hope of starting a local training programme in the near future.

Overall, in terms of industrial engineering and management capability, South Africa and Mauritius rate best, but even here there are strong deficiencies in the ranks below top management. This is a serious constraint to sustained and continuous improvement. Jamaica has implemented good management practices under the guidance of the, largely, US clients, but again this is limited among nationals. Lesotho is entirely dependent on expatriates and so is disadvantaged in the sense that substantial development is necessary in order for it to become autonomous. Sri Lanka and Bangladesh also need substantial up-grading to improve production methods, planning and management to levels where they can substantially contribute to cost reduction.

Overall positioning for direct cost

Overall positioning in relation to direct cost factors is presented in Chart 6.2. In terms of overall manufacturing costs, Jamaica, Lesotho and Bangladesh are rated as being neither advantaged nor disadvantaged with respect to global competition. What Jamaica loses due to high unit labour rates it makes up for with higher productivity; but this system only works for high-volume business and makes the country's industry vulnerable to lower-cost producers. South Africa, Mauritius and Sri Lanka are disadvantaged, largely as a result of relatively high labour rates, and they should make significant efforts to measure and up-grade productivity.

6.4 Productivity and Performance Parameters

The net result of enhanced manufacturing capability, as discussed in the preceding section, is measured in productivity and performance. This section therefore attempts to position the apparel industry of each country with respect to key performance parameters. The primary factors addressed here are grouped into five broad categories. These are operator performance, productivity turnover, quality rejection rate direct to indirect labour ratios and lead time.

Operator performance

General situation

In general, sewing machine operators in the selected Commonwealth countries surveyed are not performing as well as they could, despite their great dexterity and high speed. Due to lack of systems and work methods, this speed has not been put into continuous motion, with resulting high productivity, and is a major contributor to delays and poor performance. The high percentage of employment turnover in some countries also adds to poor productivity as a result of the need to train new staff and the length of time required for such staff to achieve optimal performance levels.

Another major reason, however, for poor productivity, as claimed by respondents, is lack of follow-up by the engineering department on operator performance. This is in addition to the non-standardisation of work methods noted above.

Sewing operators lack flexibility due to utilisation of traditional production line processes developed for large runs. Today's orders consist of small runs of faster-changing fashions and require more skills and expertise in sewing among the sewing operators in order to overcome the effects of absenteeism and turnover. Such flexibility will also facilitate improved line balancing, reduction in production delays and improved quality of the product. Comments on the specific countries follow.

Measures of operator performance used in this comparison are employee turnover, absenteeism and employee performance (in seasonal production, with shorter runs and in mass production). The relative positioning is presented in Chart 6.3.

Chart 6.3: Comparison of Measures of Manufacturing Productivity						
Factors	Degree of Country Advantage					
	Jamaica	RSA	Lesotho	Mauritius	Sri Lanka	Bangladesh
Employees turnover	●	○	●	⊘	⊘	⊘
Absenteeism	●	⊘	●	●	○	⊘
Employees performance (Seasonal production)	n.a.	⊘	n.a.	●	●	○
Employees performance (Mass production)	●	⊘	○	●	⊘	⊘
Productivity turnover in factory	●	⊘	⊘	●	⊘	⊘
Quality rejection	●	⊘	○	⊘	●	○
Direct to indirect labour (C & M)	●	n.a.	●	n.a.	⊘	⊘
Direct to indirect labour (FOB)	n.a.	●	n.a.	●	⊘	⊘
Fabric lead time	n.a.	○	○	n.a.	○	⊘
1st sample for approval incl fabric	n.a.	●	n.a.	●	○	○

○ **Disadvantaged:** Issue needs to be addressed on priority basis

⊘ **Neutral:** Minor up-grade or initiatives are required

● **Advantaged:** Continued monitoring and fine-tuning are required

Country-specific illustrations

Examples taken from Jamaica, Lesotho, Bangladesh and Sri Lanka of the countries assessed during this study illustrate avenues for up-grading operator performance. Similar issues were found in the two other countries included in the survey – Mauritius and South Africa.

In the export sector of the Jamaican apparel industry, direct labour is well trained, structured and organised. This is a result of the integration of US manufacturers in Jamaica, where technology and knowledge have been transferred to the factory level. Incentive plans tied to line output, as used by some companies, have contributed to achieving high productivity. As an example, it is reported that productivity at a major US-owned plant was 120 per cent of the average of similar US-owned operations in the region. The high-volume, single-product environment in which most companies work has resulted in Jamaican labour being very efficient, focusing only on sewing activity. Sewing operators lack operational flexibility to perform as well in new market niches such as 'fashionable goods'. This is due to utilisation of the progressive bundle system on account of mass production. For more fashionable high value-added products, the number of unskilled labourers is very high and the number of technicians and super-visors is low. Absenteeism and employee turnover has been reported as being lower than in the other countries surveyed.

In Lesotho, Taiwanese manufacturers have not transferred operational and technical knowledge to local direct labour. Thus Lesotho is still low on the learning curve on the production floor. Productivity reportedly averages 65 per cent on mass production, which is low compared with international industry standards, for example as found in Jamaica. The industry representatives interviewed believe that in a short period of time productivity will improve. Manufacturers in Lesotho focus on a progressive bundle environment where they could achieve higher productivity but at the expense of flexibility.

Lack of flexibility is not considered a disadvantage, however, since the whole focus is on mass production. The pattern for the development of the Lesotho garment manufacturing industry is identical to that of Jamaica's apparel industry in the late 1980s and early 1990s, when US manufacturers led the entire industry. If the LDC provisions under AGOA are not extended, Lesotho will find itself in the same position as Jamaica now is: that is, lack of flexibility and limited design capabilities, management and technical knowledge will leave the industry very exposed. Indeed, even if the LDC provisions are extended, the country will be dependent on the goodwill of others, as is evidenced by the Jamaican experience.

In Bangladesh, labour costs are low but so is productivity. There are far too many unskilled employees on the production floor acting as helpers and assistants for the sewing operators. Observation indicates that up to 35 per cent of labour is used on unnecessary activities due to the absence of work methods, lack of technical knowledge among the direct labour and poor levels of supervision. In Bangladesh, and to a lesser but still significant extent, in Sri Lanka, high overall labour costs, resulting from poor productivity, has adversely affected the competitiveness of manufacturers.

Factories in Sri Lanka employ large numbers of workers, some of whom do not add any value to the product. Too often, factories are unknowingly investing significant amounts of resources into unprofitable product lines or activities, rather than concentrating efforts on more profitable products and value-added activities. Moreover, when unit prices increase, employee productivity rates are often inappropriately blamed. High absenteeism ratios of up to 11 per cent and high employee turnover of up to 10 per cent have been reported. This leads to an increased number of employees in training and reduced contribution to production. As a result, factories face excess overtime, missed delivery deadlines and the obligation to resort to airfreight. All these factors add to the production cost.

Other factors

The other performance and productivity factors assessed in Chart 6.3 are productivity turnover, quality rejection rate, direct to indirect labour (for C and M and FOB), fabric lead time and time to get first sample.

6.5 Summary

Country positioning

The relative country positioning is summarised in this section as a prelude to the proposal of a number of generic framework initiatives to assist companies and countries to remain competitive in the global ready-made garment industry.

Chart 6.4: Country Positioning: Textiles and Management Capability

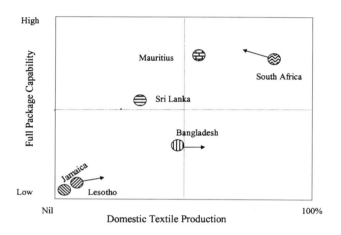

Chart 6.4 indicates an approximate positioning of the countries visited in relation to full package capability and to domestic textile production. Jamaica and Lesotho are at the bottom-left corner, being almost entirely dependent on their buyers for fabric and, in the case of Jamaica, for cutting as well. Lesotho is developing some integrated textile capability, moving it upwards, as represented by the arrow. Bangladesh, Sri Lanka and Mauritius are all more or less in the same position with regard to domestic textile production (although the actual percentages differ); Mauritius has the greatest full package capability, Bangladesh the least and Sri Lanka is positioned midway between the two. South Africa scores high on domestic textiles and full package capability, but there is a looming danger of a lack of AGOA-eligible fabric – thus the arrow shows a trend to slip back as the absolute output increases.

Chart 6.5 positions the countries with respect to productivity and speed to market. Speed to market reflects both the time to acquire fabric, the product development capability and shipment time. Lesotho is positioned low in terms of productivity and speed to market. Bangladesh and Sri Lanka are positioned higher in terms of productivity and slightly higher in terms of speed to market. Mauritius and South Africa rate well, with South Africa slightly ahead as a result of local fabric and shipping times, at least to the US.

Chart 6.5: Country Positioning: Productivity and Speed to Market

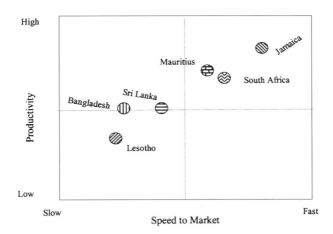

The positioning of Jamaica, in terms of current activity, is perhaps misleading. It is very productive at sewing and close to the US market. Its activity, however, is largely limited to 807-type sewing from US-cut parts.

The principal finding from the field research in selected Commonwealth developing countries is that production costs are too high in the apparel industry despite the relatively low levels of actual labour costs. These costs are largely due to inefficiencies in production systems and the need to better adapt to handle the transfer from large basic orders to smaller, higher-valued orders. The principal cause of this inefficiency is lack of knowledge and adaptation of modern production systems, and related engineering, control and management systems. There are also limitations due to poor management and the limited depth of production engineering personnel. Approaches to overcome these are presented in Chapter 8.

7

Up-grading Initiatives and Lessons Learned

7.1 Introduction

This chapter highlights the measures that have been initiated at national and enterprise levels in selected Commonwealth developing countries to prepare for and adapt to the evolving apparel industry. Emphasis is placed on initiatives in one country that might be applicable elsewhere. At the national level, the discussion focuses on eight key topics that are common to the Commonwealth countries surveyed. The selection of these issues is supported by the findings of the sourcing survey undertaken in North America. These issues are also of concern to sourcing executives. They are:

- strategy studies;

- role of government;

- co-operative measures and clusters;

- training;

- market development;

- third-country production;

- improved textile supply;

- consolidation and alliances.

At the enterprise level, emphasis is placed on highlighting how selected companies in the apparel industry have adapted to the challenges facing the industry.

The chapter ends with a summary of lessons learned that could be instructive for apparel factory operators and for strategists and managers in national trade and industrial agencies and industry associations.

7.2 National-level Initiatives

Strategy studies

Many of the countries surveyed during the field research had formally undertaken strategy studies with close involvement of both government and industry. In the case of Mauritius and Sri Lanka, the work has been carried out by *ad hoc* committees involving a broad-based representation from industry and government and in close consultation with trade associations. Jamaica appears to have taken a similar approach. Aided by a major export development funding assistance programme from the World Bank, Bangladesh commissioned an international consultancy to prepare a strategy study. The degree of documentation and level of detail are perhaps greater using this latter approach, but at least at first glance the results are equally effective. Apparel industry stakeholders interviewed reported that a key result of their initiatives was to generate support from government for those key elements of the strategies that depend on government intervention.

The strategy development initiatives adopted by these countries appear to be reaping benefits in terms of encouraging competing industry interests to collaborate for the greater long-term benefit of the industry as a whole. In Sri Lanka, for example, industry stakeholders saw the involvement of the leading industry representatives as one of the first indications of working together for the betterment of the industry, as opposed to remaining focused on their individual companies. Ensuring follow-up and implementation, however, remains a challenge.

Role of government

As stated above, one of the key results of the strategic planning efforts conducted in a number of countries has been to clearly formulate and generate a belief in what is required of government. Thus, in Sri Lanka one of the outcomes has been to seek improvement to a range of macro issues such as those related to utility rates, port efficacy, labour laws and infrastructure. In the case of Jamaica, where firms are faced with bank loan interest rates of 25 per cent, the government is supporting the industry's emerging full package companies with loans at 12 per cent interest. Similar examples can be cited for the other countries.

Co-operative measures and clustering

A common theme that has emerged in most of the countries is that there is a need for enhanced co-operation within the industry. One of the reasons for this appears to be the realisation, as in Sri Lanka, that there is a danger of losing the critical mass that has driven the development of relatively good shipping links to major markets. The same can be said in respect of buyer visits, a concern expressed in Mauritius and South Africa. If business drops, the whole industry is in danger of embarking on a downward spiral.

One of the key examples of co-operation is the focus on the development of textile and apparel clusters. In Mauritius, the apparel industry and its supporting institutions have reportedly discussed the benefits of some form of enhanced collaboration in order to strengthen their chances of survival. The challenge has been how to achieve this in practice and this has led to the adoption of the concept of development of clusters for the apparel and textile industry. Technical assistance was launched in 2002, under the auspices of the National Productivity and Competitiveness Council and the Clothing Technology Centre, with consulting expertise from France. The focus is on SMEs and the provision of critical facilities that can be accessed by all the companies involved. In Bangladesh, the government is reported to have agreed in principle to develop cluster areas for garment industries, so that centralised common facilities, including waste water treatment facilities, can be created and compliance requirements more easily met. In South Africa also, the government is reported to be assisting in the development of local apparel clusters involving the smaller companies in the industry and aimed particularly at the local market.

Training

There is a generally recognised need for enhanced training, and various initiatives are underway in Commonwealth developing countries. The Ministry of Textiles in Bangladesh, for example, is reported to have taken a decision to up-grade its Textile Diploma College so that it becomes a world-class institution imparting training on fabric processing, fabric use, design development and other related matters. The apparel manufacturers association, BGMEA, also plans to strengthen its Fashion Institute to develop the required human resources. Jamaica has a well-entrenched basic training programme that is now moving into more technical areas such as pre-production. In Sri Lanka, initiatives have been launched to train marketing professionals for the industry and to increase productivity and technology at the enterprise level.

Market development

Enhanced market development is a common theme emerging from the strategic reviews, as evidenced by the range of initiatives in the countries visited. As an example, initiatives have been launched in Sri Lanka to enhance market intelligence and market development, as well as to train marketing professionals for the industry. Mauritius has established in-market representation through the Mauritius Industrial Development Authority, which recently opened a liaison office in New York for marketing purposes. An America, with long experience in marketing to the apparel industry heads the office.

In many of the Commonwealth developing countries surveyed, initiatives for market development fell under the aegis of the national export development agency. A noteworthy exception would appear to be South Africa, where the Clothing Industry Export Council has been at the forefront of export development. The Council has encouraged companies to take the plunge into exports, despite the challenges of breaking away from the comfort of the close-knit domestic market. It has instigated a number of targeted marketing initiatives including to France, the UK and Ireland, as well as to the east coast of the US. The council is funded by the industry.

One initiative used by a number of countries to attract attention is to mount export-oriented fashion shows in collaboration with the local fashion design community. Such an event was held in South Africa as a joint effort of the Fashion Designers' Association and the South African Fashion Council; Jamaica hosts Caribbean Fashion Week, a series of major shows featuring local designers.

Third-country production

Companies in South Africa, Mauritius and Sri Lanka have set up production facilities in other countries in order to benefit from advantageous macro and direct costs. The focus in South Africa has been the neighbouring states that benefit from LDC status under AGOA; companies have also established operations outside the major cities, where wage rates are lower. Several Sri Lankan companies have also set up overseas operations to benefit from various quota and tariff preferences, for example in the Maldives and, more recently, in Kenya and Madagascar as well as elsewhere in Asia.

Establishment of such third-country production bases is most developed by companies from Mauritius, where Madagascar was seen as the logical production base for a Mauritian industry afflicted by high labour costs and unable to benefit from the AGOA LDC provisions. This strategy of delocalisation apparently had government support, even though this led to a partial loss of employment in the apparel sector in Mauritius. More recently, Mauritian companies have continued the process of internationalisation by establishing factories in South Africa and elsewhere in the region.

Improved textile supply

As was evident from the findings of the survey of sourcing executives in North America, the ideal situation from their point of view is to be able to access locally produced fabric. In many countries, however, the realities of the situation dictate other means to address this issue and several examples were noted during the fieldwork in Commonwealth developing countries.

The Bangladeshi apparel industry has made a major effort to develop local spinning and weaving capacity. Despite these measures, however, it is clear that while yarn-spinning capacity is reasonable, there is no realistic way that the weaving capacity (at the time of the study, 30 per cent) can be significantly altered in the immediate future: the investments are too large and the timeframe too short. There are also quality and competition issues. This has given rise to a scheme to create bonded warehouses. These facilities will allow for import of duty free finished and grey fabrics for supply to garment dyeing and printing factories, respectively, as and when needed. A separate central bonded warehouse will also be allowed for duty free import of chemicals for supply to dyeing and finishing mills. This is a nationwide approach to the 'virtually vertical' solution expounded by a number of the executives interviewed in the United States.

Another approach is to strengthen relationships with fabric suppliers in the source countries. Thus, Bangladesh gets much of its fabric from India and Pakistan and is working towards EU acceptance of the notion of regional cumulation for interpretation of the rules of origin of yarn and fabric. An alternative approach was evidenced by one Sri Lankan apparel company that has developed excellent relationships with fabric mills in Korea, resulting in the ability to start cutting fabric within two or three weeks of ordering. The key, it is reported, is that there is sufficient volume between the two countries to warrant direct shipping, thereby avoiding delays due to transhipment.

Consolidation and alliances

The recognition of the need for consolidation, alliances and sub-supplier relationships is particularly advanced in Bangladesh and Sri Lanka. It is generally recognised that small firms will find it increasingly difficult to survive in price-sensitive market segments because they do not have economic scales of operation. It is also felt, however that they are likely to be more viable if they go through a process of merger and integration. This leads to the issue of collaboration, as discussed above. The need for consolidation is also a view that was echoed in the sourcing executive survey in North America. A related issue, as reported in Sri Lanka at least, is that under existing labour legislation it is difficult for firms to downsize or, in the final analysis, to close unprofitable units. At the SAARC seminar on post-2004 issues held in Colombo in 2002, the need for a review of such legislation was flagged by a number of those who intervened.

7.3 Enterprise Level Initiatives

Summaries of the salient features of the strategies and business ideas of companies interviewed during the field research are set out below. These are not intended to be definitive descriptions of the companies and their strategies, but rather to illustrate some of the ways in which companies have tried to find competitive advantage. The findings are presented under the following headings, relating to the major thrust of the company initiative:

- offering full service;

- review of continued viability;

- specialised niches;

- specialisation in support functions;

- efficient production.

Offering full service

Six companies that offer a full range of services to customers are described here. They have developed their capabilities through a variety of means, from vertical integration and in-house development to alliances and contractual relationships. They have all recognised the need for strong pre-production and design capability and for increasingly strong management and industrial engineering support. Their approaches to in-market representation differ but point to an increasing need for market presence. The issue of profitability is less easy to access, but there are indications that expansion to cover more steps in the value chain is not a panacea for all ills; the need to be a least cost and efficient producer is still paramount. The cases demonstrate the following strategies:

- **Case 1:** Project an image of excellence

- **Case 2:** Become a regional player

- **Case 3:** Focused strategy tied to duty-advantageous fabrics

- **Case 4:** Build on partnerships and go global

- **Case 5:** Vertical integration, sub-contracting and management

- **Case 6:** Serve customers from in-market warehouses

The first two cases describe companies from Mauritius. Case 1 describes a company that has focused on design and professional image. Case 2 focuses on a similar, although slightly bigger, company which has made innovative moves including acquisition of a design group in Europe. Both companies tried to establish operations in Madagascar, suffered from the experience and were, in mid-2002, in a period of reflection and in the early stages of balancing a Mauritian base with the lower costs of production elsewhere in the region. Case 3 describes a South African company and illustrates the advantage, and perhaps the necessity, of companies with higher wage rates building on favourable market access preferences. A successful company from Sri Lanka, which has grown through partnerships in raw materials, offshore production and above all access to key clients, is the subject of Case 4. This is followed by two cases from Bangladesh, involving vertically-integrated companies that do not see themselves, however, as being very dependent on partnerships. Case 5 concerns the largest group in Bangladesh, one that has recognised that inexpensive skilled labour still requires excellent management supported by technology, and is now moving to strengthen its in-market presence. The other Bangladeshi profile, Case 6 describes a company which, though fully integrated and offering full service, appears to have found its competitive advantage in an in-market sales office and, above all, an in-market warehouse facility.

Case 1: Project an image of excellence (CMT, Mauritius)

A number of companies in Mauritius successfully project an image that mirrors that of manufacturers in their buyers' markets – in this case the US and Europe. They offer detailed design services, have links to European designers and are strong in IT support systems. One such company is the Compagnie Mauricienne de Textile Ltee (CMT). Founded in 1985, the company has grown so that it now employs 4,000 workers at five sites. Having pulled out of Madagascar and decided instead to expand in Mauritius, in June 2002 the company was seeking, with apparent success, 1,000 new workers. The managing director contends that CMT is one of the top 15 companies in Mauritius and the largest in textiles. Exports are divided 95 per cent to Europe and 5 per cent to the US.

CMT has a very impressive design-oriented head office and is opening a new 20,000 sq. ft. design centre. The company works with design studios in London and Paris to develop style books and collections that are used as a starting point for discussions with buyers.

The company can design and deliver in four to five weeks, if necessary. They have 200 knitting machines and spare capacity, plus 1,400 sewing machines. They use the Eaton unit production system (UPS) of racking to eliminate handling. Some orders are air-freighted, especially repeat orders (25–30%). Twenty people work in the IT department and they have developed their own software for various management tasks.

The company focuses on adapting to the changes in the supply chain criteria. Conscious of both AGOA and the relatively long shipping time from Mauritius, CMT is considering setting up an operation in West Africa.

Case 2: Become a regional player (Floréal, Mauritius)

One of the largest apparel vendors in Mauritius, Floréal is part of the Ciel Group, an established Mauritius-based holding company. Despite the difficulties faced by the industry globally, the company appears determined to continue from its base of operations in Mauritius and to become a regional player. This is in contrast to companies with less strong roots in the country, as discussed in Case 7.

Floréal has a spinning operation and produces knitwear, T-shirts and fine knits. Other members of the group make shirts and bottoms. Founded in 1971 as a Hong Kong-based investment, it was later taken over by Mauritian interests. Since 1987–88, Floréal has also owned a Paris-based brand, Harris Wilson. Production in 2001 was 7.5 million units, distributed among 15 factories. France accounts for 40 per cent of exports, the UK for 25 per cent and the US for 15–20 per cent. At one time France took 80 per cent of Floréal's total exports.

The company has worked hard to adapt to changing supply chain patterns. It has its own design team, as well as calling on specialists from Europe. There is also a small marketing office in New York. Floréal creates two collections a year to stimulate customers, who then suggest minor changes. At the time the field research was being undertaken the company sold 40–50 per cent of its own product range, but this is now changing; the reason for this is that so much of the differentiation in products is a function of fabric and finishing, expertise that Floréal does not offer. It has, however, developed a link to a UK production base and sends raw grey garments to a UK plant, which dyes them to order and then ships them to Marks & Spencer.

The company was a major player in Madagascar and suffered as a result of the pullback in 2002. Its parent company, Ciel Group, has also invested in a significant knitwear company in Cape Town, South Africa and is undertaking a major up-grading.

Despite these moves, the company is reported to be financially shaky. Part of the difficulty is attributable to the fall-out from Madagascar, but it is worth noting the conclusions of Gibbon (2000) that attempts by Mauritian companies to move up the value chain have not been successful. There is a sense that the company has not yet found the right formula, but that that they are strongly committed to the garment industry in Mauritius, albeit in part using expertise developed in Mauritius to manage and provide credibility for operations elsewhere in Africa.

Case 3: Focused strategy tied to duty-advantageous fabrics (Transvaal Clothing, South Africa)

One of the larger, well-established suppliers to the upper tiers of the local South African market, Transvaal Clothing has targeted specific segments of the US market that enable it to benefit from duty preferences under AGOA for use of synthetic fabrics. The focus is woven two-way stretch garments for women. It has two factories, employing 750 and 350 workers, and it also outsources to other factories which account for an additional 700 jobs.

Transvaal Clothing started its export programme to the US in 1998, and its client list includes many key retailers and international buying houses. The principal advantage, it claims, of working through a buying house is risk sharing and risk reduction through its inspection programmes.

They anticipated the advantages offered by AGOA and built a relationship with textile companies. Thus availability of fabric is not a problem. Local textiles account for 95 per cent of its fabric; imported poly-viscose is still AGOA-eligible as it is on the 'in-short-supply' list. Without AGOA benefits, the company claims, it could land product in the US at the same price as Korea. With AGOA, it clearly has better margins.

Case 4: Build on partnerships and go global (MAS Group, Sri Lanka)

MAS Group is possibly the largest apparel manufacturer in Sri Lanka, with a total of 15,000 employees. The development of the group is an excellent example of how to use partnerships to acquire market access, technology and know-how.

The company has a series of joint ventures and partnerships; perhaps the most important of these, in market terms, is with MAST, a leading US buying house. MAST is owned by The Limited, a leading apparel wholesaling and retail group. MAS Group operates a number of factories in Sri Lanka in joint venture with MAST. In the late 1990s the group began a backward linkage in joint venture with a UK company to produce elastic. The elastic plant has now taken on a life of its own. It has developed its own customer base and has established plants in Mexico, India and China. By 2000 MAS established a knit-fabric joint venture for their 'intimates' business. It is now the major supplier to Victoria's Secret.

To remain competitive and to meet customer requirements, the group began to establish factory operations in other countries. It now has plants in Sri Lanka, India, Vietnam, Madagascar and the Maldives. With such dispersed facilities, management is a critical issue. For this reason the company has implemented an order-tracking system that allows for vendor-managed inventory control.

Case 5: Vertical integration, sub-contracting and management (Beximco, Bangladesh)

Beximco Textiles and Garments is the largest and fastest-growing division of the Beximco Group, the largest and most diversified industrial conglomerate in Bangladesh. Major investment in recent years has been in textiles and garments, which in 2002 accounted for at least half of the group's annual business turnover of more than US$200 million.

With the entire supply channel vertically integrated, from research, design and product development through spinning, weaving, knitting, processing, garment production and washing, Beximco offers the most technically advanced and efficient resource in the country for textile and apparel buyers the world over. Beximco's formula for success is to maximise the output of its inexpensive skilled labour with the help of good management supported by technology. Industrial engineering and work-study play an important role, with necessary software support for data-driven production management for maximising efficiency. Beximco also has strong design and product development teams for both textiles and apparel.

The company does not operate through buying houses, but instead sells direct to retailers/buyers abroad; it is setting up its own marketing offices and showrooms in the US, Europe and Japan. Through these it will be able to provide a quick response and better service to business partners based on personal presence and first-hand knowledge of customer needs.

Case 6: Serve customers from in-market warehouses (N.R. Knitting, Bangladesh)

N.R. Knitting is a leading and fully-integrated group of companies in the knit sector. The group's annual business turnover in 2002 was around US$20–25 million. At the time of the research, 95 per cent of its exports were to Europe and 5 per cent to the US and Canada. An estimated 80 per cent of exports are to buyers' design and specification, while 20 per cent are to the company's own design. The company has established a warehouse in the United Kingdom, and as a result of being to offer quick service by shipping from this facility, 40 per cent of its European sales are made from the warehouse. The remaining European sales are serviced on an order basis, usually within 70 days including shipping time.

Review of continued viability

Two companies encountered during the fieldwork are reflecting on their place in the industry and the best strategies to follow. This includes consideration of giving up or drastically reducing their apparel operations in, respectively, Mauritius and Jamaica. Given the generally anticipated consolidation in sourcing, the option of exiting the industry, or at least downsizing, is clearly one that many companies should consider, if only to confirm their decision to re-structure and re-invest. The cases are:

- **Case 7:** Focus investment elsewhere
- **Case 8:** Review participation in the industry

Case 7: Focus investment elsewhere (Novel, Mauritius)

Faced with the tightening labour situation in Mauritius, the growing textile demand in the region under AGOA and some of the clear benefits, at least in the short term, of manufacturing in AGOA-eligible LDCs, one option is to move on. Novel is an interesting example of a company that is not as anchored in Mauritius as some of the, by now, indigenous companies and is refocusing its centre of activities elsewhere. It is part of a Hong Kong-owned group, Novel, listed on NASDAQ . The company appears to be very strong financially.

Novel began in Mauritius with European orders in 1973/74 post-Lomé, then made a major investment in textiles in 1988, in spinning weaving and dyeing denim and chino fabric. In 1990, it further expanded into garment manufacture. In the late 1990s, 80 per cent of production went to Europe and 20 per cent to the US, but by the second quarter of 2002, the balance had shifted so that 70 per cent went to the US and 30 per cent to Europe. The portfolio of customers includes Hilfiger, Gap and Levi. Orders are developed from Hong Kong, where many buying offices are located. The group also has a marketing office in the US. The company views AGOA as a lifeline and states that without AGOA it would have been difficult to continue profitably or to grow.

Despite this success, the company is now focusing its investment elsewhere. Novel had major investments in Madagascar, but pulled out and moved to South Africa, making a serious investment in integrated operations. These included investing in a spinning mill in 1998 and more recently in an integrated denim and garment production facility in Cape Town. The company also owns a big fabric mill in China – Novel Dying and Printing, with a capacity of 4 million metres per month. It is planning to integrate spinning and weaving operations there and will add garment sewing with machines pulled out of Madagascar.

Labour costs are greater in South Africa, but the infrastructure is better. Electricity makes up 25 per cent of the cost in Mauritius and building costs are much lower. South Africa is also approximately two weeks ahead on shipping time to the US (most ships stop in both Durban and Cape Town).

Case 8: Review participation in the industry (Hart Group, Jamaica)

The Hart Group is one of the leading locally-owned garment manufacturers in Jamaica. The strategy of the company is indicative of the difficulty of retaining a substantial industry based solely on low labour costs.

Until 1987, Hart's garment activities were largely oriented to the home market. It started manufacturing for export when it received an order from Sara Lee-Haines. At its peak, the company had five factories and 2,800 employees making T-shirts, boxer shorts and so on. By 2002 business had declined substantially and a number of plants were closed, although the company still produces 100,000 dozen units per week – 50,000 T-shirts and 50,000 panties.

Key factors cited as causes of the decline in business are the advent of NAFTA and the rise of Mexico as a source of supply, as well as the fact that its major client, Sara Lee, consolidated its operations in the Caribbean region. Hart's managing director has doubts about the future of his group in the apparel industry. He foresees that in the coming years the commodity business will move to China, so the company is backing away from the garment business as the centre of its future investment.

Specialised niches

Three companies, one in Jamaica and two in South Africa, provide instructive examples of deciding on core competence and as a result focusing on niche markets. The cases also illustrate the importance of proper in-market representation. The cases are:

- **Case 9:** Specialised niche and end-use customer focus
- **Case 10:** High value-added garments
- **Case 11:** Local design for the tourist market

Case 9: Specialised niche and end-use customer focus (Gross & Co., South Africa)

Founded in the late 1960s, J. Gross & Co is a second-generation family company that would appear to have moved successfully from industrial workwear into an international speciality, chefs clothing. Having developed both businesses locally, about seven years ago Gross began exporting its professional chef lines of clothing and is now exporting to 20 countries. The clothing is marketed under the Chef Works brand, which the company owns. It also prints its own catalogue.

Internationally, Gross targets the hospitality industry, especially major casinos and cruise lines. The key to its success in the US has been having a local distributor who handles much of the marketing. The company has 300 employees and out-sources to four factories which have a combined total of 2,000 workers. One of the plants is in the Durban area and others are in LDC-eligible countries such Malawi and Lesotho. The company prefers to use Chinese fabric, since it is substantially cheaper, even though there is a 27 per cent duty into the US. However, with clothing made in Lesotho and other LDCs they benefit from AGOA and this is a positive advantage.

Case 10: High value-added garments (Dansam, South Africa)

South Africa has an established reputation as a producer of suiting fabric and suits. There are estimated to be three major fabric mills and six major suit manufacturers, and they are reported to be operating at full capacity. The traditional export market was the UK, but under AGOA a number of companies have established a significant export presence in the US. A good example of this is Dansam Clothing.

Dansam Clothing decided to target the US market on account of AGOA and to make the necessary investment in manufacturing and appropriate ways of doing business. Key points are a new factory in one of the decentralised zones, a US agent and an exchange rate hedging programme.

The company used Lectra equipment for pattern making and for grading. It can make a pattern and get a sample back to a wholesaler in ten days. Lead time from acceptance of an order to shipment is 120–150 days. Of this, time to get fabric is 90 days. Dansam hired systems consultants for costing and, based on a time study carried out to overseas standards, calculated that the factory operates at 80 per cent of capacity. The factory works seven days a week for local and US markets. Dansam is uncertain about the long-term future, but aims for five to seven good years in the US market while AGOA remains in force.

Case 11: Local design for the tourist market (Sun Island, Jamaica)

Despite the generally depressed situation in the apparel industry in Jamaica, one company believes that it has found a route to success. This is Sun Island, which grew out of a billboard business and advertising operation in the early 1970s. It is the largest of the local full-package companies offering creativity, plus some local make-up. Several industry representatives interviewed in Jamaica cited the company as a potential industry success story. Sun Island had the capital and wisdom to back the business, according to one observer.

From 1977 to the 1990s, Sun Island was a local manufacturing company, operating under the high tariff barriers of the time; it opened to imports in the 1990s. Its key technologies are embroidery and printing and its principal markets are local tourism and cruise ships. Exports (mainly regional) account for 30 per cent of business and the local market accounts for 70 per cent, of which tourist clientele represents a further 70 per cent or more. The company designs its own basic styles and sources volume finished goods from China, Indonesia and Thailand. It also designs and licenses logos and patterns from others, including some that are internationally recognised. The staffing level is approximately 200.

Faced with the evolving business environment, the company has developed a full-package capability and is targeting the US market. A US company, Sun Island USA, has been set up for clearance and distribution. Two collections a year are developed and presented at trade shows. The company also works closely with local hotel shops.

Fabric sourcing is a key strength. There is a representative for fabric sourcing in the Far East and the company also has links to a mill in China through a Hong Kong connection. The managing director is optimistic that they have found a way to move forward profitably. He believes that 'the great textile revolution is yet to happen', referring to printing technologies that make it economically feasible to print one-off or low-volume designs on white garments. This he sees as a key opportunity for the future.

Specialisation in support functions

While there are several examples of vertically-integrated textile and apparel groups, the case of Tania Textiles illustrates the potential for success from the critical operations of textile printing and finishing.

Case 12: Fabric production and finishing (Tania Textiles, Bangladesh)

Tania Textiles is part of a leading conglomerate with diverse interests. Total investment of the group is around Taka 2500 million (about US$44 million at the rate of exchange at the time of the fieldwork), of which approximately 50 per cent is in the textile sector. Tania Textiles is the manifestation of this investment and a relatively new addition. It started its modest journey in 1989, with dyeing, printing and finishing near Dhaka and quickly grew to its present composite structure by creating spinning and weaving facilities. Today, Tania Textiles is rated as one of the leading quality fabric suppliers to the apparel industry in Bangladesh.

All the machinery installed in the mill is new and state of the art, and was mostly imported from Germany and Japan. Production capacity of dyeing, printing and finishing is between 70,000–75,000 metres per day, while that of the spinning and weaving sections is 8–10 tons per day and 1.1–1.4 million metres per month, respectively. Ten or 12 export-oriented ready-made garment factories take all of the fabric, so this production is considered as *deemed export*. In its overall production of finished fabrics, Tania Textiles usually uses 40 per cent grey fabrics, mostly imported from China and 70 per cent of their own fabrics, locally spun and woven.

Efficient production

Many companies have been faced with a changing market environment and the need to change the ways in which they do business. Five cases are presented as illustrations. They are:

- **Case 13:** The tyranny of 807

- **Case 14:** Select your buyers

- **Case 15:** Invest to become an efficient low-cost producer

- **Case 16:** Make the necessary changes

- **Case 17:** Quota acquisition to vertical integration

The extreme example, presented here in Case 13, is an efficient Jamaican producer perpetually squeezed by clients and the nature of the business. This is a particularly relevant case for companies in other countries that are solely dependent on a very limited number of providers of and limited to the minimal assembly operations. An example of one strategy to avoid this situation is to be selective with clients, as in Case 14. Two examples follow of investing in order to remain in business, Cases 15 and 16. The final illustration, Case 17, concerns a company that has moved from an invest-in-quota strategy to one of vertical integration and full service, but realises that the transformation is not complete. The example of Beximco, in Bangladesh (Case 5) is also relevant to the issue of efficient low-cost production. The company has made significant investment not only in technology, but also in management and industrial engineering.

Case 13: The tyranny of 807 (La Moda, Jamaica)

La Moda is a locally-owned company that has been in business, under various names, for over 30 years. The present company was created in 1985 and has been exporting since 1992. It is located in a reasonably modern facility, in an impressive factory compound with evidence of good management and attention to workers.

The company originally made local women's leisure wear and a locally-branded line for men. Early exports were 807-type for fashion/active sportswear for a US-based manufacturer that then moved its business to Sri Lanka. At the time of the field research, the company was producing T-shirts for Sara Lee, which needed extra production capacity and was reportedly very impressed with Jamaican capability. Another local company in Montego Bay is also working with Sara Lee, but both are in competition with plants in Mexico, Honduras and Haiti. La Moda employed 350 people, although they had at one time employed up to 500. Output was 15,000 dozen units per week.

The principal shareholder believes that the company systems and practices are good and cannot be cut further. Through specialisation, La Moda cut the Standard Minute Value (SMV) from $0.10 to $0.08 per minute, but prices in Haiti are $0.07 and in El Salvador $0.07. The challenge is how to break out of this downward spiral with cost as the sole criteria and allow the many positive factors of the company to be taken into consideration. The company is at the point where it is operating at a loss in order to match competing prices. The principal shareholder recognised that the way forward is probably through full package, but added that nobody in Jamaica is currently doing this. One major constraint is lack of capital. Furthermore, on account of the almost exclusive focus on 807 parts assembly, the company has dismantled the cutting department, even though the people who worked there were excellent workers.

Case 14: Select your buyers (Star Knitting, Mauritius)

Star Knitting, a family-owned medium-sized integrated knitwear company, reported being very selective with regard to dealing with US buyers. Current operations employ 1,800 people, of whom 550–700 are foreigners; a new facility, aimed partly at the US market, was expected to add 1,000 people.

Star Knitting's company director stated that the company had never tried to develop a market in the US, but after half a dozen trips he had selected a buyer (a major chain) with whom he thought he could work. He did not proceed, however, because the buyer wanted to control the total operation down to stationing inspectors in the factory. More generally, his attitude is that he will deal with buyers who show a clear interest by travelling to Mauritius. Industry-wide, he noted, buyers try to get manufacturers to sell cheap; but there are only a few places where there is capacity, and so there is little interest in doing so.

Another company, Tara, made a similar point: 'One large US client could take 80–90 per cent of your volume; but then he dictates your business'. The challenge, therefore, is to identify business in smaller and more specialised market segments.

Case 15: Invest to become an efficient low-cost producer (Lolita Clothing, South Africa)

The partners of Lolita Clothing invested a considerable sum in developing from a 'survival mode' operation into an export competitor. According to the company's president, the company was traditionally a producer of underwear and baby wear tied to the whims of retailers who drove prices low to the point of no return. This led to an export drive in order to try and survive.

Lolita Clothing realised that product line rationalisation was essential since previously the company had been making virtually any product, with up to 50 styles in a month. They decided that the way forward was to consolidate and to become competitive in a limited number of products. This would give the company continuity and long runs. They would like to see exports go to 50–50 per cent and then to 70–30 per cent. The changes made included becoming fully computerised, starting eight years ago with investing in an automatic pocket-making machine and obtaining ISO 9000 certification. They now benchmark against actual world-class standards as determined by an independent outside testing house. They were approached by a mill about an export prospect, making sports uniforms for the US market and decided to gear up for it or other business. The resulting triangular relationship between US buyer, fabric mill and factory is key, but Lolita's direct market contacts are limited and the venture is dependent on this one project.

Case 16: Make the necessary changes (Timex, Sri Lanka)

Timex is a well-established company that has made considerable strides in moving to meet the new criteria of buyers. It has nine factories, of which seven make women's fashion wear such as dress suits and co-ordinates. It also has a children's wear plant. Although for the last 15 years it has been dealing directly with customers, as opposed to going through a buying house, it realises that changes are required to survive beyond 2005.

Over the past two or three years the company has become aggressive in changing how it does business. Its strategy has been to make the necessary production and management changes so that it can profitably handle small quantities, high value and fashion items on short lead times. Examples are lined dresses, embroidery and hand beading.

It has strengthened its relationships with key buyers through frequent visits to the US and Europe, established a design team in Sri Lanka and is moving some production lines to a modular system. It has also developed strong linkages with fabric suppliers and has been able to drastically reduce lead times. With shipping reduced to 10–11 days from Korea it has been able to ensure a two- to three-week turnaround time for a garment orders.

Case 17: Quota acquisition to vertical integration (Ha-Meem Group, Bangladesh)

Ha-Meem Group is presently the fifth-largest group of apparel manufacturers and exporters in Bangladesh, with an annual turnover of around US$70 million in 2002. It holds large amounts of quota, resulting in exports of 80 per cent of its products to the US with the balance going to the EU.

Ha-Meem started operations in 1988 and since then has been utilising its expertise to expand and diversify its garment export business. At the time of the study, Ha-Meem Group had seven garment factories and a number of supportive units such as a washing plant, sand-blasting plant, packaging factory, poly industries plant, printing factory and covered truck company. It has also set up a sweater factory and at the time of the study was setting up a denim fabric mill. This means that the Ha-Meem Group is now capable of producing a wide range of standard items and has become almost self-sufficient in its overall operations. It has fabric sourcing/liaison offices in China, Hong Kong and Singapore.

Ha-Meem Group has an experienced team of quality controllers and inspectors. Its sample section is also very strong, equipped with CAD/CAM and other computerised pattern-making facilities, and with 20 pattern makers capable of producing about 100 samples a day to meet the specific requirements of buyers. Usually individual pattern makers work for each buyer to develop understanding and keep better track of feedback comments.

The Ha-Meem Group is quite optimistic about the future. It feels confident of its capability, consistency and efficiency and is hopeful that it will do equally well, even in the post-MFA competitive situation. It is, however, aware of its weaknesses, including the need for more in-house design development and direct contact with buyers.

7.4 Summary

There is something of value to be learned from each country visited and from each company included in the survey. Some are more successful than others in terms of market positioning and, more critically, in terms of profitability. But they are all instructive as models from which to take inspiration or from which to learn of pitfalls to avoid. Some of the principal lessons, as perceived by the authors of this report, are highlighted in this section.

The impending changes in the environment within which the apparel industry will work post-2004 appear to have served as a catalyst for building greater understanding between government and industry on the key issues. This enhanced understanding of the issues is complemented by a widespread sense that increased co-operation is required between companies, and between the private sector and government. In this sense, the specific outcomes of the high-level strategic planning activities that many countries have undertaken are perhaps less important than the actual planning exercises that have resulted in such a consensus. Time will tell, however, whether the desire to move in these new, collaborative, directions is enough to bring about successful results. It is probable that a considerable amount of detailed expertise and assistance in the planning and implementation will be required as a prerequisite of success.

Many strategies call for enhanced market presence and use terms such as 'niche products for niche markets' – still leaving a wide gap between stated intent and realisation. Many of the enterprise-level examples presented above underscore the importance of market presence and particularly of an in-market sales capability. The example of Mauritius opening an in-market liaison office is an encouraging step, but the success of this endeavour will probably depend on co-operation between competing commercial interests and the government agency that controls the office. In this connection, the South African approach of an industry-driven export council is of interest as an institutional model, but its strengths and weaknesses and applicability to other markets clearly require more study.

The corporate case studies put forward in this chapter illustrate the manner in which a number of companies have taken on more functions in the supply chain, including development of design and other product development and pre-production capabilities. It should also be noted that most of these successful companies assessed the market, determined how to proceed and then set structures in place to achieve their commercial objectives.

These moves must be coupled with an ability to keep production costs low by seeking more favourable macro costs, such as duty advantages, and lower direct costs. The move by Mauritian companies to Madagascar and now to Southern Africa is motivated by this requirement. MAS, in Sri Lanka, has also moved production to remain competitive in terms of macro and direct making costs.

The cases from Bangladesh provide some of the best examples of how to address the issue of fabric supply. Bangladeshi mills now meet close to 80 per cent of their yarn requirements for knitted garments and some 30 per cent of fabric requirements. It has been recognised that a substantial increase in fabric production is unrealistic at this time. The industry in Bangladesh has therefore looked to other approaches, including creation of bonded fabric warehouses, coupled with development of the textile finishing capability. A further element of the fabric strategy is to seek trade preferences that encourage regional trade in fabric. The linkages and relationships developed by Timex in Sri Lanka that have led to sharply reduced delivery times for fabric from Korea are another example that the 'virtually vertical' approach to fabric supply can work. It is worth noting, however, that Sri Lankan companies report that fabric from India and Pakistan takes longer to arrive than fabric from Korea – a clear challenge to regional-level logistics and import-export procedures.

The importance of making the necessary moves to become an efficient and least-cost producer is illustrated in the last set of case studies. The Jamaican factories that are competitive have become so because they produce a very limited product line, thus enabling the sewing machine operators to become extremely efficient at what they do. This need to generate economies inherent in a limited product line was also recognised by Lolita Clothing (Case 15) in South Africa. More critical, it is argued, is that both Lolita and Beximco (Case 5), to name but two, have placed major emphasis on the tools and techniques of industrial engineering. Several companies, including MAS, Beximco and CMT, have also placed emphasis on internal management and management information systems.

The notable weak link in many of the plans and strategies encountered is an inadequate recognition by many companies and by the agencies that support the industry of the importance of the cost-saving potential from correctly applied industrial engineering and middle-management processes. Guidelines for moving forward on these issues will be a key focus of subsequent sections of this report. The other critical issue is that of national and industry-wide efforts to become closer to the market. Lack of market connections was a factor in the difficulties faced by Jamaica where dependence, in many cases, on one buyer left the manufacturers with little market or industry knowledge when that business was withdrawn. There are success stories on an individual basis, as the case studies describe. Yet, as was learned during the survey of executives in the United States, the time for US buyers to seek new partnerships has probably passed. More critical still, not all buyers want to relinquish supply chain functions and the control associated with carrying out these functions themselves or through trusted associates. So not all apparel manufacturers can or should aspire to be full service integrated vendors. This is unrealistic.

It is also evident, however, that those apparel manufacturing companies in Commonwealth developing countries that have found the right mix of customers and that have been able to develop an optimal mix of capabilities in selected supply chain functions, including being a low-cost maker, have succeeded. One of the challenges for industry and supporting agencies, particularly as they seek to promote enhanced collaborative efforts, is to find cost-effective ways to deliver the various supply chain functions as and when clients require them. At the same time, it is critical to facilitate industry consolidation and, where necessary, to facilitate the task of local vendors establishing operations outside their home country so as to benefit from additional cost advantages that may prevail.

In the final analysis, there is convergence between the successful strategies adopted at the enterprise and industry level and the criteria and attributes sought by sourcing executives. The successful enterprises cited above have gone a long way towards not only reducing indirect costs by taking on additional supply chain functions, but also towards working on becoming efficient professional producers with competitive direct costs. Macro costs are in large measure, as pointed out earlier, the domain of government. One of the key successes reported from the strategic planning efforts is that many governments now appear to recognise both the importance of the apparel industry for their economies and the necessity of significant improvements in infrastructure, services and the overall business climate for the successful continuation of the industry. There is hopefully also a realisation that market access alone is not enough, and that while trade agreements with duty benefits in major markets are a start, there is much more that must be done and that can be done to maintain a viable and increasingly professional apparel industry.

8

Strengthening the Apparel Industry in Commonwealth Developing Countries

8.1 Introduction

From the findings of the surveys of sourcing executives in North America and of apparel manufacturers in selected Commonwealth developing countries it is evident that there is a considerable degree of convergence between the attributes sought by sourcing executives and many of the strategies agreed for implementation in developing countries. The field research shows, however, that almost without exception apparel manufacturers are struggling to lower costs and to increase productivity, and that government and industry are faced with decisions on how best to support the apparel industry in their respective countries. For apparel manufacturers from developing countries a key issue is how to acquire the management and technical skills and systems that will enable them to reduce direct costs through increased productivity and lower production costs. The findings from the field research also shows that manufacturers are struggling to decide how and if they should acquire the skills and systems that will enable them to take on more of the supply chain functions that could lead to reduction of a buyer's *indirect costs*. For all too many manufacturers, however, the economically viable solutions are not clear. Government also has to address these issues in order to determine the support to provide for training, finance and other requirements.

This chapter provides guidelines to help countries and companies address these issues. In particular, the guidelines are intended to help them to assess their position in the industry and to establish priority actions either to *sustain* the current level of business or to *expand* the level of business to new products and market. The entity (government, industry association or company) then needs to set goals and a schedule of achievement. The principal national-level issues are first addressed, followed by enterprise-level issues. These address both macro, direct and indirect cost factors.

A central element of the strategic framework is a series of positioning checklists. These are designed to assist a company to assess its position in relation to buyer criteria and to articulate how to move forward. In practice, this may well result in an iterative process considering several possible objectives, and indeed, detailed analysis at the product and market level. A three-level rating system is proposed: weak, moderate and good. Within this framework, a *weak* rating indicates that the capability/perceived capability is inadequate and that a major up-grade or initiative is required. A *moderate* rating signifies that the capability/perceived capability is generally acceptable, although some minor up-grade or initiatives are required to fully meet buyer expectations. A *good* rating signifies that the country-level capability/perceived capability meets or exceeds buyer criteria but that continued monitoring and fine-tuning are required to maintain this situation.

Guidelines are also presented to help companies and government to identify actions to be taken on a priority basis to overcome perceived weaknesses and a framework is proposed to set out priority actions and the milestones for their achievement. Subsequent steps in the process are to integrate the overall findings of the strategic review, to cost the effort (and to revise if necessary) and to obtain endorsement by the appropriate authority. This appropriate authority would normally be senior executives and the board of directors in the case of a company, and senior government officials and ministers in the case of national-level and government-related issues.

In the sections that follow, national level guidelines are first presented. These are followed by guidelines for industrial enterprises. A case study is then presented to illustrate how the assessment guidelines were used to drive the up-grading efforts of a significant apparel manufacturing group in one of the selected Commonwealth developing countries. More specifically the discussion that follows is structured around the following headings:

- **National-level issues**
  - Positioning the country
  - National-level actions

- **Enterprise level**
  - Positioning the enterprise
  - Enterprise-level actions

- **Case study**

- **Summary**

8.2 National-level Issues

Positioning the country

Drawing upon the findings of the survey of sourcing executives, three groups of attributes are seen to be most critical in sourcing decisions at national level. These categories are listed below and discussed in the paragraphs that follow. The attribute categories are:

- basic country attributes;

- industry support services;

- opportunities for regional partners.

Basic country attributes

The checklist for positioning in relation to country-level criteria is presented in Table 8.1. The attributes listed are those rated as important by the respondents to the survey of sourcing executives (see Chapter 4) and concern the following:

- human rights and labour codes;

- local raw material supply;

- business climate;

- security and customs conformity;

- country reputation and capability appropriate for products;

- trade and investment agreements;

- product development and design capability.

Respect for human rights and labour codes of conduct is almost a prerequisite, whereas country reputation and capability addresses the perception that the buyer community has of a country, even though it may differ from reality and from the performance of an individual vendor. Of the other factors, it should be noted that availability of local raw materials, and especially of fabric, varies in importance according to the nature of a buyer's operation. Many respondents to the survey indicated that they were open to negotiation on options to ensure timely fabric supply, at least for certain product lines. Others indicated that domestic fabric production was essential to their business model. Design capability is also an issue that is tied to the business model of the buying company. Capability in design, as well as knowledge and understanding of fashion trends and colours, is preferred by many buyers, even if not deemed to be essential. Respondents from some major buying companies, however, stated that this was their core strength and that they only sought capability to execute an order efficiently and at low cost (buyer attitudes are discussed in Chapter 4, Section 4.4.

The priorities, responsibilities and timeline to improve the positioning with regard to country conditions should be agreed and summarised once the positioning and vision of the future are determined.

Industry support services

National support strategies are the enabling framework in which the individual corporate strategies can function and flourish. The following attributes are considered in the assessment of the capability and adequacy of industry support services:

- management training;

- production management training;

- industrial engineering skills;

- marketing and sales capability;

- trade promotion;

- lobbying effectiveness;

- investment promotion;

- intra-industry collaboration or clustering;

- support for regional collaboration;

- expertise and funding.

These factors have emerged as critical issues during the course of the research. They are reflected in the comments of sourcing executives interviewed and also in discussions with apparel industry executives and supporting agency representatives in selected Commonwealth developing countries. Indeed, many of these factors are also identified in industry strategies as of priority importance. The checklist for positioning in relation to industry support services is presented in Table 8.2.

Regional partners

A critical issue emerging, particularly from findings of the work in Southern Africa and South Asia, is the opportunity that could be afforded by enhanced regional-level collaboration. These benefits relate particularly to increased use of opportunities to source yarn/fabric in one country of the region and to have the garments designed and assembled in other countries. These benefits may be tied to trade preferences, as in the case of Southern Africa's AGOA eligibility, or may just relate to the ability to enhance the definition of 'local' fabric supply, as could apply between countries in South Asia or Southern Africa, for example. Support for regional collaboration is one of the attributes rated in Table 8.2. It is worth exploring specific options further before deciding on specific initiatives, and the checklist in Table 8.3 provides a framework for doing this. Three categories of collaboration are considered: collaboration for fabric supply (fabric); collaboration in manufacturing (make); and collaboration in furnishing technical expertise (tech.).

National-level actions

Assessment of where the country stands is only one part of the process however, since it is also necessary to propose solutions to overcome identified weaknesses or competitive disadvantages. Although many of the required actions will have been identified, at least in outline form, during the positioning exercise, others will require further consideration. This is necessary because there may be several ways to address a particular issue. The findings of this study have provided insights into key issues both from the perspective of the producer and that of sourcing executives, particularly on trade policy issues, national support strategies and the question of expertise and funding to implement any up-grading plans. Possible actions are discussed within the following framework:

- institutional issues;

- trade policy;

- market development support;

- expertise and funding.

Institutional issues

It is necessary to look further at the institutional issues to find differences and to observe what works and does not work. Perhaps more critically, what works in one moment of time may not be replicable, but lessons learned from it may be useful in the future. The South African industry-driven, industry-appointed export councils are an example worth learning from – especially the lobbying skills of these councils and their precursors. The lobbying game is played in-market and must be sensitive to in-market issues. The rising anti-globalisation movement is of direct concern for the apparel industry and requires closer attention. This is particularly the case where countries have a positive social story to tell and where relatively minor investments can yield substantial benefits on social and quality of life issues.

In the case of Southern Africa, and perhaps also other regions, the issue of collaboration across national boundaries is also relevant. The model of the Mauritian industry in Madagascar can be extended throughout the region (see Chapter 5). Obvious poles of expertise are in Mauritius and South Africa, but others can develop, and not only in Southern Africa. In terms of the textile industry, which is the weak link in the AGOA chain at present and is a constraint in Commonwealth South Asia, this is particularly so. On a different front, given the impressive productivity noted in Jamaica but the lack of full package capability, it would be interesting to find a mode of collaboration that would re-establish Jamaica's presence in the US market.

Trade policy

Trade policy initiatives are a continuing issue, driven by the United States in many cases, but which have a profound impact on Commonwealth developing countries. The lobbying efforts mentioned above are crucial here; but perhaps of more immediate impact, and more tractable, are issues at the regional and inter-LDC level. Exchange of raw materials and semi-finished goods within the context of regional production agreements and related rules of origin is one key issue. Enhanced business climate and better performing infrastructure are others. The size of investments required for yarn and fabric production also points to enhanced intra-regional co-operation whose governing framework and facilitation depend on government.

Market development support

Companies need a presence in the marketplace in order to develop business, particularly as they move away from basic items and seek to strengthen relationships with customers. This can be achieved through a mix of market visits and permanent representation or agency arrangements, possibly combined with a showroom facility. The essential issue is to avoid one-off activities. Market presence must be sustained and when not introducing new firms or new collections, company representatives should be focusing on follow-up and feedback.

The level of activity in the marketplace by all exporting countries points to the need for all concerned agencies, associations and institutions to develop a co-ordinated and concerted approach to business development in major markets such as the US and the

EU and in emerging markets. To learn more about market requirements, exporters and national support agencies should visit trade shows as potential exhibitors, rather than as actual exhibitors. If some national firms are already exhibiting, a complementary programme of non-exhibiting visits could be organised.

The national support agencies should also encourage the larger vendor groups to establish permanent offices or representation agreements in the marketplace in order to develop further, particularly value-added, business. The primary role of such vendor groups would be to maintain regular contact with target buyers in order to develop new business for the exporter. A consortium approach by selected firms might be advantageous and would permit a more complete representation office to be established. This could also apply to clusters of apparel industry companies. This representation should be above and beyond anything put in place by national support agencies and national associations. One representational option would be to hire, for the US for example, a senior and experienced national with broad contacts in the industry.

Additional training would be helpful in marketing and marketing management in a North American/European context.

Expertise and funding

Access to resources, both human and financial, is critical if identified deficiencies are to be rectified. This access can be achieved through a number of means appropriate to the specific country or enterprise situation. These include use of external centres of expertise. An alternative is to access the required skill sets through inter-company co-operative mechanisms, or to bring about corporate consolidation that would then make the necessary resources, both financial and human, available in-house. International technical assistance and financial support is also a critical issue. The examples from Bangladesh, with cost-shared funding made available under an export diversification project with the World Bank, are worth closer consideration for replication elsewhere.

The country positioning exercise will have identified priorities for intervention in terms of country conditions and industry support services. These will be key inputs to the process of deciding what solutions to implement. Once the national-level actions to improve country conditions, industry support services and other requirements have been agreed, agreement should be reached as to the timeline and responsibility for implementation.

8.3 Enterprise-level Priorities

Positioning the enterprise

Drawing upon the findings of the survey of sourcing executives, three groups of attributes are seen to be most critical in the sourcing decision at the enterprise level. These categories are listed below and discussed in the paragraphs that follow. The attribute categories are:

- basic vendor attributes;
- skills and financial attributes;

- management attributes;
- market development capabilities.

Basic vendor attributes

The findings of the sourcing executive survey indicate that there are a number of basic attributes sought in a vendor. These attributes are:

- competitive pricing;
- code compliance and security;
- consistent quality;
- speed to market;
- references/reputation;
- on-time delivery;
- service;
- completeness of orders.

Several of these are reflected also at the national level and it should be noted that perception of a particular vendor's situation is as critical as the reality. Conformity to codes, including security codes, is a prerequisite, although buyers did indicate willingness to work with vendors to achieve the required levels, as they will for other factors. A checklist for positioning in relation to required vendor attributes is presented in Table 8.4. Again, initiatives can be prioritised using the guidelines mentioned above.

Skills and financial attributes

Most sourcing executives interviewed during the survey in North America elaborated on their preferences for pre-production and corporate capabilities. The specific attributes, as discussed in more detail in Section 3.4 of Chapter 3, are:

- full package as opposed to CMT;
- dealing on the basis of LDP as opposed to FOB;
- vendor financial capability;
- product development/design capability;
- willingness and ability of vendors to form partnerships;
- willingness and ability to hold fabric in inventory.

The attitude of respondents differed from company to company. Not all companies, for example, required product development capability and while none required LDP capability, there were strong indications that it is increasingly used in some markets. In preparing to assess how a vendor is positioned, it is necessary to address the specific requirements of current buyers as well as those targeted for the future. This requires that those undertaking the strategic review should also undertake a careful review of their customer base and the attitude of customers to these issues, both now and in the near future. If the aim is to move to new customers, or new types of business, these same questions must be posed. A checklist for positioning in relation to required vendor skill and financial attributes is presented in Table 8.5. Concurrently with assessing the positioning from the macro level of Table 8.5, it is appropriate to assess positioning in relation to key underlying capabilities, as detailed in the discussion concerning product development and unit costing.

The priorities for initiatives designed to improve positioning in relation to vendor skills and financial attributes can be agreed once the positioning is determined and the vision of the future determined.

Management attributes

Management is a particularly critical factor as the supply chain becomes more complex and the drive for supply chain optimisation increases. This was reflected in the sourcing executive survey, where issues that are difficult to quantify such as those represented by the general term *quality of vendor management*, were raised by most respondents. The specific attributes to which they referred, and which constitute the basis of the positioning exercise for management issues, are:

- management professionalism;
- continuous improvement;
- communication;
- understanding of market and customers;
- integrity, trust and attitude;
- delivery of proper documentation.

With respect to many of these attributes, and particularly to continuous improvement and communication, there are really two issues: *ability* and *willingness*. Thus, not only do buyers want vendors to display the necessary abilities, they also want to be reassured that the required improvements and timely and appropriate communication that they have requested will actually take place. For a number of issues, proper documentation for example, there are associated technology investments and management information systems that have to be in place. The checklist presented in Table 8.6 provides a framework for determining the positioning of an enterprise in relation to a range of management attributes. Concurrently with assessing the positioning from the macro level of Table 8.6, it is appropriate to assess positioning in relation to key underlying capabilities, as set out in the discussion concerning production management and industrial engineering as methods of control and improvement.

The priorities for initiatives designed to improve positioning in relation to vendor management attributes can be agreed once the positioning and vision of the future are determined.

Market development capabilities

Most respondents to the sourcing survey displayed ambivalence concerning market development activities by vendors. On the one hand, they wanted them to be knowledgeable about fashion and style trends and to 'understand their customers'. On the other hand, they generally claimed that the job of finding new suppliers was the responsibility of the local agents or regional offices. This being said, it was also evident that there is a balance here and that it is necessary to compare one's strengths with the requirements of current and potential customers. The following attributes describe the strength and nature of market development capabilities:

- relations with local agents and buying houses;
- relations with regional sourcing offices of customers;
- relations with corporate sourcing directors;
- relations with buyers and merchandisers;
- relations with key customers, at all levels;
- presence in the marketplace;
- marketing and sales knowledge of key personnel.

A framework for assessment of positioning in relation to key market development issues is set out in Table 8.7. The options discussed for national-level market development are among the solutions that could be applied. These include a permanent office, a representative or agent in the marketplace and participation in various industry-wide events. The crucial issues to be addressed, as indicated in Table 8.7, concern the strength of relationships with customers and their hierarchy of representatives, from agents through buyers and merchandisers to sourcing executives. Particular attention should be given to relationships with key customers, those with whom the company does its most important business. The marketing and sales knowledge of staff is also a critical issue.

The priorities for initiatives designed to improve positioning in relation to market development attributes can be agreed once the positioning and vision of the future are determined.

Enterprise-level actions

The findings from the field research show that, almost without exception, Commonwealth apparel manufacturers are struggling to meet cost and lead time expectations of their customers and would-be customers. This is a unifying theme, and one that calls for critical professional interventions. Enhanced enterprise-level attributes contribute towards this objective but in the final analysis they play out in the planning and management of the pre-production and production processes. This section therefore focuses on the factory-level evaluation that is required in order to plan and implement integrated strategies to reduce lead time and unit costs. Successful strategising requires that manufacturers determine objectives, gaps and areas for improvement on their sites in terms of 'where they want to be'. This must be based on buyers' criteria, business trends and competition and, in particular, on the following key factors:

- product development activities;

- unit costing;

- administrative processes;

- production systems;

- production management and industrial engineering;

- manufacturing management;

- methods of control.

The central tool presented here is a series of evaluation charts designed to assist enterprises to assess where they stand in relation to time and unit cost-based buyer criteria and to articulate how to move forward. The senior managers can use these evaluation sheets to determine gaps and areas for improvement at the factory level. They can also be applied to the garment industry in general for evaluating operations performance in relation to competition and market criteria.

The capabilities required depend on the type of business in which the factory is engaged, both in terms of the type of product and the terms of trade. The evaluation framework thus differentiates between basic and fashion products, as well as between operating on a cut and make basis and what is termed an FOB basis, also known as full package. The critical difference between C & M and FOB is the self-sourcing activity of raw material under FOB, which in turn requires staff in merchandising, purchasing and logistics to execute, manage and monitor the raw materials sourcing process.

With reference to the tables, the critical difference between *basic* and *fashion* is that fashion products imply seasonal production, small-run orders and lower lead times. Basic products suggest more continuous production, with large quantities of the same type of product and longer lead times. Not all capabilities are required for each combination of product type and business term (C & M or full package). Those cells where such capabilities are judged to be important have a *green* background. Those cells where the capability is not required have a *red* background. The answer to each question should be either *yes* or *no*. For a fully capable factory, the answer to each question should be *yes* where the capability is required (*green* cells). Otherwise, the factory must improve or up-grade the capability. If the response is *no*, uncertain or only partially applicable, then the gap between the current and required capability must be documented and interventions planned to address it.

These results of the assessment at this level should be used to complete the strategic positioning exercise and specification of enterprise level intervention priorities as discussed in the section concerning required management capabilities and financial attributes.

Product development

Product development activities have been identified as a critical area where offshore manufacturers can contribute to reduction of a host of indirect costs to the buyer. The critical issues related to product development capability, based on the survey findings and industry best practice, concern the capability of the vendor in relation to:

- computer aided design;
- grading and garment fit;
- internal specification sheets;
- product data management software;
- making of first samples;
- dissemination of quality standards;
- sample making.

The checklist presented in Table 8.8 outlines the required product development capabilities in terms of equipment and skills as a function of product and type of business. Completion of this checklist will enable an enterprise, or higher-level entity, to determine its position in relation to these capabilities.

Computer aided design (1): CAD tools support the designers in the creation and drawing of a sketch of the pieces of the product. These pieces are then available for pattern making, grading and then marker making. This tool enables a big reduction to be made in the time spent on the creation and the corrections of the patterns.

Grading and garment fit (2): If the factory is not equipped with a CAD system, the least they should know is how to grade manually meeting the buyer specifications. If not, they will have to rely on the buying house or overseas buyer to execute these functions.

Internal specification sheets (3): Factories should develop a standard technical sheet for internal use rather than relying on one provided by the buyer. This form will eliminate any conflict and misunderstanding of the given data. The sheet should carry all the final measurements of the garment, as well as the method of measuring and appropriate sketches.

Product data management software (4): Full package companies need to implement product management software to maintain fabric details and garment images and to receive and send these between factory and client. These images are then available for visual line review by product development functions, such as merchandising, specification, costing and sourcing/production. Fabric is then electronically shared with printing, knitting and weaving to increase efficiency in sampling and production.

Making of first samples (5): The sample makers should consult production supervisors about proposed sewing operations, since production supervisors will be able to provide input on sewing tricks and more economical methods.

Dissemination of quality standards (6): The design department should communicate all the quality standards to the production lines. This includes standard stitches per inch and seam width. They should also transmit any changes that arise.

Sample making (7): It is important to have a sample room with flexible sewing operators instead of using direct labour from the production lines. The sewing room should be part of the overhead and not part of the direct labour.

Unit costing

In most instances, the basis for establishing the sales price for an apparel sewing order is the agreed Standard Minutes Value (SMV) or Standard Allocated Minutes (SAM) for the direct labour (sewing machine operators) multiplied by a value per minute. The SAM and SMV are defined in the Glossary. In addition to direct labour cost, this value per minute includes indirect labour, other overhead costs and profit. The unit costing and hence the SAM are determined through a logical analysis of the breakdown of sewing operations for any given product by the work studies department, allocating time for bundle handling, manipulation of pieces and the sewing cycle to each operation. This includes allowances for rest periods, worker fatigue and so on (Abernathy *et al.*, 1999: 28). An error in computation of the SAM, or a misallocation between indirect and direct labour, can either lead to a loss or make the sales price uncompetitive. A critical burden is thus placed on the work-study staff, the techniques used and the management of the process.

Based on on-site observations, it was found that factory SAMs were often higher than the standards of the industry. This is because the establishment of the SAM is all too often based on time studies within the factory, rather than applying a predetermined time system such as GSD as an external benchmark. Use of such benchmarks, coupled with accurate application, is the only way to ensure that factories can meet the competitive challenges post-2004.

Based on the survey findings in Commonwealth developing countries and industry best practice, the critical issues in unit costing include a vendor's capability in relation to:

- analysis by work-study staff;
- use of a predetermined time system;
- improvements to garment construction;
- marker-making software;
- use of fabric utilisation allowance;

- costing formula;
- relation to market prices.

The checklist presented in Table 8.9 outlines the recommended unit costing practices as a function of product and type of business. Using information from this checklist an enterprise will be able to ascertain its relative position in terms of recommended practices and decide how to rectify any deficiencies. The questions listed in the checklist are discussed in more detail below.

Analysis by work-study staff (1): Work-study staff should determine the operations breakdown in a sequential logical order, taking into consideration the bundle handling methods between the operations. This will provide guidelines for setting up the line so as to meet costing objectives.

Predetermined time system (2): Pre-determined time systems should be used so as to provide an external benchmark, as discussed above.

Improvements to garment construction (3): Work studies personnel have a major role in labour costing and in finding the most economical work methods. They should be encouraged to propose changes in construction of a garment, as long as appearance remains the same, so as to arrive at a more competitive price.

Marker making software (4): Fabric costs typically represent 45–55 per cent of the total unit cost. A marker making software programme can determine the efficiency of fabric utilisation and help to reduce cost of fabric wastage.

Fabric utilisation allowance (5): The costing department should communicate the assumed wastage tolerance in fabric to the marker making operator based on what has been estimated in the unit costing. This basic step is essential if factories are to avoid over-use of fabric or inability to complete an order.

Costing formula (6): As discussed in the introduction to this section, correct allocation between direct and indirect labour and other overheads is essential when the direct labour SAM is the basis for calculation of payment. It should also be noted that the overhead assigned to C & M work should be less than that for FOB work.

Relation to market prices (7): Buyers are not willing to pay for lack of performance, absenteeism, employment turnover and other production delays in factories as a result of lack of management and improvement capabilities. Factories in Commonwealth developing countries should focus on the price offered by the industry in the marketplace rather than the costs derived from factory operations that include current inefficiencies. It is up to the management to find ways and tools to improve their current situation rather than absorbing the loss. This market knowledge becomes even more critical when engaging in various bidding processes.

Administrative processes

The management structure and the way in which issues are analysed and decisions made are important contributors to the efficiency of a factory and to reduction in costs. Based on the survey findings and industry best practice, the critical issues in assessing the degree of bureaucracy, or lack of it, in a vendor's management and staff functions include:

- how development activities are carried out;
- levels of management;
- order processing;
- office staff flexibility;
- use of computerised management information systems.

The checklist presented in Table 8.10 addresses recommended administrative practices as a function of product and type of business. On completion of this checklist, an enterprise or higher-level entity will be able to determine its position in relation to the recommended practices and decide how to rectify any deficiencies. The questions listed in the checklist are discussed in more detail below.

Development activities (1): Typically, 70–80 per cent of the time to market is absorbed in the design and development process. Significant profits flow from a reduction of this time. Thus the simultaneous execution of activities can reduce the design and manufacturing time. Dealing directly with key people instead of following the formal organisation can further speed up the process.

Levels of management (2): If the factories have more than two levels in management, this indicates the unwillingness of managers to trust lower-level staff to make decisions regarding issues about which they should be knowledgeable. This hinders timely intervention to rectify issues and taking the most appropriate decisions. More generally, a management philosophy of fostering positive relations with production line staff could contribute more to the product, and to lower costs, than enforcing rules and discipline.

Order processing (3): If the managing director handles the orders and assigns objectives, this could indicate that no one has any decision-making authority and that management is ineffective. More generally, if personnel are called upon to contribute toward the product and given an opportunity to show initiative and freethinking, they are more likely to contribute to the overall improvement of the business.

Office staff flexibility (4): Although it is useful to have specific job descriptions, office employees should be multi-functional and able to handle several tasks in case of need. If they are limited only to their primary job function, as described in a job description, delays could result in a process when people are absent or otherwise unavailable.

Management information systems (5): The most progressive factories that were observed in selected Commonwealth developing countries are implementing zero-paper solutions to manage the entire process of orders using integrated computerised management information systems. These systems are resulting in tremendous time savings, improved communication in relation to orders, better tracking of production, better control of inventories and avoidance of conflict in data manipulation.

Production systems

Even in environments with low labour rates, the procedures and systems in use on the factory floor are important contributors to the efficiency of a factory, to enhanced quality and to overall reduction in product costs. Based on the survey findings and industry best practice, the critical guidelines for efficient production systems should address the following issues:

- empowerment;
- size of production line;
- cutting room planning;
- operator machine skills;
- operations skills of operators;
- dissemination of productivity targets;
- collaboration among operators.

The checklist presented in Table 8.11 addresses these issues concerning production practices and capabilities as a function of product and type of business. The questions listed in the checklist are discussed in more detail below.

Empowerment (*1*): Empowerment of a line team implies the shift of some of the decision-making responsibility from middle management to line people. This can lead to a team developing capability in handling any order in terms of productivity, quality and balancing without supervision. This is to be contrasted with the situation observed in some factories in Commonwealth developing countries, where sewing operators are grouped on a line working on one product at a time.

Production lines (*2*): Running fashion orders of less than 3,000 units through production lines regrouping more than 15 employees will generate lack of balance between the workstations, as well as a high value in bundle handling. This results in considerable costs that could be eliminated by shortening the production lines. Lead time and production turnover can also be improved.

Cutting room planning (*3*): In fashion manufacturing, production lines should be flexible, handling several types of product, and the cutting room should cut according to a plan designed to meet the delivery date target. If production lines are not flexible, the cutting schedule will depend on the availability of the specialised line which can lead to delays. One order could be split over several teams in order to meet the target and reduce the overtime cost on production lines.

Operator machine skills (*4*): Balancing production lines is a major problem faced by factories in Commonwealth developing countries, particularly for the smaller order lots associated with fashion products. This leads to delays between workstation and lost time. For better balancing, sewing operators should be moved from a push system used for basic products, to a pull system. Under this approach they could pull production in, operating on other machinery in order to reduce waiting delays.

Operations skills (5): Enhanced skills in the various operations will contribute further to the flexibility sought on production lines, as discussed above for multi-machine competency.

Dissemination of productivity targets (6): Productivity targets and achievement should be communicated to the line people and could be done individually. Factories should, as part of this approach, provide further training to under-performing employees to improve their efficiency. This is a tool that is applicable to both basic and fashion products.

Collaboration among operators (7): In a flexible manufacturing system, sewing operators are empowered to support each other in order to pull the production through the line as well as to reduce the work in process inventories. More generally, flexibility is a major solution for absenteeism.

Production management and industrial engineering

Interviews with senior representatives of apparel manufacturing companies in Commonwealth developing countries and findings of the sourcing survey in North America led to the conclusion that almost everywhere production management and industrial engineering capabilities need to be up-graded. This conclusion applies as much to the manufacture of basic products as to the manufacturer of fashion products. Guidelines for production management and industrial engineering capabilities, as set out in Table 8.12, include the following:

- implementation of SAMs;
- monitoring of work methods;
- performance reviews;
- analysis of production delays;
- sewing operator performance;
- clarifying who intervenes to plan work methods;
- dissemination of work methods and quality standards;
- capabilities of production managers;
- causes of quality problems.

The checklist addresses these issues, which are drawn from the survey findings and from industry best practice concerning production practices and capabilities, as a function of product and type of business. Assessment against the checklist will enable an enterprise, or higher-level entity, to determine its position with respect to the recommended practices and decide how to rectify any deficiencies. The questions listed in the checklist are discussed in more detail below.

Implementation of SAMs (*1*): As discussed in the section on unit costing, the costing of direct labour is based on the total SAM established for each activity. The work studies team should therefore work with the line employees executing the operations in order to ensure that the intended work methods associated with a SAM are followed.

Monitoring of work methods (*2*): Once the work methods are implemented, work studies staff should monitor the progress of the methods and correct any deviation caused by improper employee habits. Otherwise, employees could implement their own methods with a resulting increase in cost.

Performance reviews (*3*): Production managers should meet with individuals performing below the target efficiency to find the reason(s) for the lack of performance and to take remedial action. The employee's supervisor should also participate in this meeting. Such performance review can be critical to success in improving performance.

Production delays (*4*): When production delays occur, production managers should, on the same day, evaluate the causes and take mid-course corrective actions. When an employee is not productive, every minute of delay is a loss in revenue. To determine the losses, managers could evaluate the total minutes of the delays multiplied by the production cost per minute, adjusted for the target efficiency of the plant. This will yield the total revenue lost.

Operator performance (*5*): Improving efficiency is not limited to production managers and employees. Work studies staff should carry out a performance follow-up on underperforming employees identified as discussed above (Performance review 3). This review will determine causes of the poor efficiency and provide assistance to the production supervisor to improve efficiency. This process must be followed if the desired continuous improvement in productivity is to be achieved.

Work methods planning (*6*): Work studies staff should ensure that the method of piling the pieces and bundle manipulation between workstations corresponds to that established for the SAM. Cutting room staff should also be aware of the bundling system specified by the work-study staff.

Dissemination of information (*7*): Work-studies staff should transfer the conclusions of the work-method studies to the production supervisors. This will allow for better monitoring on the production floor. Quality standards should be communicated to the supervisors. If they understand the requirements of the buyers regarding the quality standards and how to train and follow-up the sewing operators effectively, the cost objectives are more likely to be met.

Capabilities of production managers (*8*): Production managers should be knowledgeable about operational planning, how to balance their production lines and control of the operations. All too often, in the factories studied, the engineering department does the planning with little or no involvement of the production manager.

Quality problems (9): Management should monitor defects per type of operation and the causes of instances where defects are excessively high. They should then implement action plans to resolve the problem. Implementation should then be monitored until the problem is resolved.

Manufacturing management

The questions set out in Table 8.13 serve as a guide for the assessment of the adequacy of the production management and industrial engineering solutions that have been implemented. These questions apply as much to the manufacture of basic products as to fashion products. The checklist presented in Table 8.13 is developed from industry best practice concerning production practices and capabilities. Assessment against the checklist will enable an enterprise, or higher-level entity, to determine its position with respect to the recommended practices and decide how to rectify any deficiencies. The items in the checklist are discussed in more detail below.

Required productive minutes (1): With revenue based on the number of minutes earned, it is essential to determine the number of minutes required per day for the plant to be viable, and to achieve this target.

Measurement of minutes earned (2): Many of the factories surveyed in selected Commonwealth developing countries calculate performance based on the output of the plant compared to the target. With such a measure it is very difficult to determine where and how to improve productivity. Since revenue is based on minutes earned by the direct labour, this must be captured daily. Otherwise the factory management will not be able to monitor performance, improve efficiency and reduce delays.

Synchronisation to SAMs (3): Factories should determine the ratio of employees to machines that yields the best equipment utilisation and balancing. This requires undertaking studies to separate the operations sequences proportionally according to the total given SAM per product. On basic production lines, each employee executes from one to several operations on one machine. The number of operators should be determined based on the output from each operation. On fashion production lines, total given SAM should be split according to the number of employees per team.

Maximum quantity in process (4): In order to get the first bundle out in two hours (see point 6, below) management should establish a target of quantity per bundle per workstation and monitor this work in process in order to guarantee the productivity output.

Quantity balancing (5): When there is no quantity balancing between the manufacturing activities, employment ratio per activity is wrong. This situation affects the lead time and adds more cost to the product.

Bundle turnover time (6): Factories lose a considerable amount of time, often a day, in laying out their equipment for each new order. This situation disturbs the other activities linked to the sewing and can result in more employees being involved than normally required to complete production orders on time. From factory observations it is clear that running flexible teams of less than 15 employees can achieve a bundle turnover of less than two hours. The time could fluctuate according to the number of units per bundle, so this number must be known (see point 4 above). It can be expected, if properly implemented, that there will be a great improvement in lead time and better distribution of employees between the production areas.

Machine adjustment by operators (*7*): Based on factory observations it was noted that sewing operators rely heavily on sewing machine mechanics to adjust their equipment. Operators should be trained to do this; in so doing they will become more aware of the importance of the linkage between good adjustment and quality sewing.

Use of incentive programmes (*8*): It also emerged from the survey that employees tend to prefer factories that provide incentive pay for performance and productivity merits. Implementation of such measures could greatly reduce employee turnover and increase productivity.

Basis of incentive programmes (*9*): Based on the findings of the survey it is recommended that incentive programmes are not paid only on performance outputs as this could affect quality. The incentive system should tie quality, attendance and productivity together as one target.

Ratio of quality inspectors to operators (*10*): From observations, some factories have a fixed number of final checkers attached to the production line. In an efficient system, the number of checkers should vary according to the type of product and to the productivity of the production line. As a rule of thumb, factories should not exceed a ratio of more than 17 per cent of final checkers as compared to sewing operators.

Quality monitoring (*11*): To improve quality, the factory should generate records of quality rejects by type of defects in order to target areas for improvement and reduce the cost of the non-quality items.

Methods of control and improvement

The questions set out in Table 8.14 serve as a guide for the assessment of the adequacy of the methods of control and improvement that have been implemented. These questions apply as much to the manufacture of basic products as to fashion products. The checklist was developed from industry best practice concerning production practices and capabilities.

The questions given in the checklist are essentially self-explanatory. Assessment against the checklist will enable an enterprise, or higher-level entity, to determine its position in relation to the recommended practices and decide how to rectify any deficiencies. Whether they are computerised or manual, use of such control and improvement indicators will provide management with the information required to up-grade lead time, quality and productivity. More critically, they will help management to attain target unit cost levels and maintain these levels.

Determination of priority actions

Using the information from the assessment checklists (Tables 8.8–8.14), the gaps in capabilities and procedures at the level of a specific factory or for groups of factories or industry segments, as the case may be, can be identified. Many of the necessary up-grades can be implemented with the resources at hand and others will require relatively modest degrees of training and external assistance. Where the required up-grading in capability could have significant investment implications or uncertain impacts throughout the manufacturing chain, external advice should certainly be sought.

8.4 Case Study: An Up-grading Intervention

An intervention using the tools and approaches set out in this chapter is described in this section. The case describes the up-grading efforts of a significant apparel manufacturing operation in one of the selected Commonwealth developing countries. The example illustrates many of the points raised in the preceding paragraphs and shows that substantial benefits can be attained at relatively little investment.

There are two key issues to be addressed particularly at the enterprise level in embarking on an up-grading programme. The first is the question of acquiring the resources, both human and financial, to implement the priority actions. The second is to determine the benefits or feasibility of addressing these priorities. The determination of benefits will depend on the specific situation of the company, its factories, its customer base and its business plan. An indication, however, of the scope for improvement can be gleaned from the following case. The principles outlined in this chapter were applied throughout the intervention.

Background

The case concerns a conglomerate with seven factories and 12 sub-contractors employing a combined total of around 6,400 people. The group was mostly limited to CMT capability. The objective of the intervention was to help the group re-structure and re-engineer so as to move into full package operations on basic and fashion items. The company would have to be able to produce both small and large runs, have a low rejection rate for poor quality and meet agreed delivery dates. Most critically, however, senior management decided that cutting and making value per minute should not exceed $0.04.

The principles outlined in this chapter, and particularly the enterprise level framework, formed the basis of the approach to this challenge. The issues raised by this case study are typical of many such operations in Commonwealth developing countries. The project was carried out by an external expert assisted by a team drawn from the work studies staff of the company. They were trained for the purpose. At the time of the study the first phase was completed but further work will be required to fully achieve the target cost level.

Prior to the intervention, the cost per minute for C & M was $0.10 +/- $0.05. The factories had four levels of management between the managing director and line management personnel. Factories operated with production lines regrouping 27 sewing operators and four manual workers (helpers) per line, working on one style at a time. Every production line had a structure of indirect labour as follows: one production supervisor, one quality control supervisor, two in-line quality checkers, three end-lines quality checkers, one production leader and one garment technician in addition to the direct labour. Plant efficiency averaged 41 per cent, and production delays exceeded 35 per cent as a result of the large number of employees. There was no line balancing and as a result downtime was too high. Quality rejection rate in-line ranged from 11–19 per cent, and at auditing prior to shipping was 6 per cent. Production supervisors and sewing operators had limited knowledge of quality standards, relying on the quality personnel. Absenteeism averaged 11 per cent, and employment turnover was 7 per cent. Cutting room efficiency averaged 56 per cent due to poor planning, wrong fabric and delays in markers.

Communication of product and orders data was carried out manually, with paper records. This task required a large number of employees. Management focused only on delivering on time and at any cost. They had no idea about the costing value and the cost of the labour. The major role of production supervisors was to distribute the work on the floor and handle discipline on the production lines. The company knew that they had to address all these issues in order to reach, or even approach, a competitive price level, which they had determined to be $0.04 per minute, for direct labour. There was, however, no improvement plan with regard to productivity or employee efficiency and no cost control method. The indirect labour in the manufacturing process was high, estimated at 44 per cent of all plant labour, due to the burden of paper work, data capture, manual control methods, unnecessary activities and so on.

Principal interventions

The structure of the business has been redesigned. Factories are now specialised by family of product so that, for example, one factory works only on intimate apparel, another on fashion women's wear. Production lines at each factory have been rebuilt as a function of the products, order sizes and style complexity. As a result, some lines consist of seven employees, some ten and others up to a maximum of 15 employees. A new organisation chart was designed for each factory and all internal procedures were restructured to match the new production process and to eliminate all duplicate tasks and paper work. As part of this process, an order information system was installed allowing online access through the network by each manager or section head. The production planning system and production management activities were up-graded in collaboration with management and line personnel.

Production supervisors were trained on work methods, operations balancing and quality standards. In factories with modular units, production supervisors handle the operational planning and there is no indirect labour at all throughout the modular team cells.

Marketing, merchandising, pattern making, costing and sample making for the entire group have been centralised at head office, where they are split by type of product. A master planner position was created at head office to manage and assign the orders to the factories. These improvements reduce the overheads of the entire group. Factory-level management has been reduced to a single factory manager, eliminating a general manager position at each plant. The factory activities consist of managing the stores and raw materials inventories, marker making, cutting, sewing, packing and shipping.

Product data (pattern sketches, bill of materials and orders information) are transferred electronically to the factory from the head-office. The marker is made at the factory and is then plotted for the cutting room. A CAD system has been implemented at the head-office, and GSD predetermined time system software has been installed to establish the SAM at the head-office for labour costing purposes. Each factory is equipped with shop floor control software to mange the cost performance of each individual line, employee and plant in addition to order tracking online. Data from all the factories are linked to the head office main frame.

Principal results

Improving the product process and re-engineering manufacturing activities resulted in major improvements in resource utilisation and in the production process, including a reduction in production overheads and an increase in productivity. Improving the production process also improved the product flow and line balancing among all departments. As a result, unnecessary labour has been eliminated and, more critically, many employees previously considered as indirect labour have been transferred to operations where they become chargeable under the SAM and their time is effectively calculated and costed.

Some of the results achieved in terms of various performance measures are as follows. Productivity has increased by 22 per cent, quality defect cost has been reduced by 9 per cent, production delays due to unbalanced lines have been cut by 25 per cent and time lost due to line set-ups has been cut by 15 per cent. In addition to reduction of the size of production lines and transfer of personnel from indirect to direct labour, quality control personnel have been reduced by 33 per cent. The bundling system at the cutting room has been improved to reflect the new production process and overall bundle handling throughout the manufacturing process has been reduced by 36 per cent. Non-added-value activities related to raw material have been eliminated.

These results were obtained in the six months following the start of the restructuring. As a direct result of all these achievements the cost per minute has been cut substantially from the original level of $0.10. The group is on track to attain the target unit cost per minute of $0.04 as the implementation proceeds and personnel become more familiar with the new ways of doing business.

Lessons learned

The success of this case study validates the framework for up-grading measure at the enterprise level and is based on the findings of the survey and the observations and recommendations made throughout this study. It also shows that when implemented these measures can help to produce positive results. This case study clearly demonstrates that substantial improvements in costs can be attained through application of improved management procedures that reduces inefficiencies at both the production and enterprise levels.

What is borne out in this case study is the fact that much improvement can be undertaken at the enterprise level in Commonwealth developing countries if manufacturers are willing to commit time and resources and are serious about addressing issues related to the survival of their operations post-2004.

8.5 Summary

The focus of this chapter has been to provide a number of tools to assist enterprise-level management, or higher-level entities such as industry associations and government agencies, to assess capability and to position the enterprise, industry and country in relation to critical issues and attributes. A framework for setting out priorities at each step was also provided.

As the findings of the survey of sourcing executives made clear, the first level of decision making is focused at the country level, and more specifically on the perceived attributes of the country. In most cases, as discussed in this chapter, country-level issues affect macro-cost levels and are the responsibility of government. There will almost certainly be opportunities, however, for industry and the wider business community to play a role in helping to make government aware of the issues and of the benefits that will be generated if they are resolved. During the course of the research, numerous examples were encountered where industry had been the apparent prime mover in generating support from government and the wider business community. More generally, there is much that can be done by industry and indeed by companies or groups of companies.

The challenge for industry associations and national support agencies is to see the up-grading activities expanded from individual corporate groups to a wider spectrum of the industry. This requires articulation of enterprise-level needs at the national level, including training programmes, pilot projects and creation of industrial engineering and production management teams. The precise methods adopted will depend upon the state of the apparel industry in the particular country, the existing support institutions, available expertise, and available funding and commitment.

Table 8.1: Rating of Basic Country Attributes						
Attributes	To sustain current level of business			To expand level of business		
	Weak	Moderate	Good	Weak	Moderate	Good
Human rights and labour codes						
Local raw material supply						
Good business climate						
Security and customs conformity						
Country reputation and capability appropriate for product						
Trade and investment agreements						
Product development and design capability						

Weak: Capability is inadequate. Major up-grade or initiative is required

Moderate: Generally acceptable. Minor up-grade or initiatives are required.

Good: Meets criteria. Continued monitoring and fine-tuning are required

Attributes	To sustain current level of business			To expand level of business		
	Weak	Moderate	Good	Weak	Moderate	Good
Management training						
Production management training						
Industrial engineering skills						
Marketing and sales capability						
Trade promotion						
Lobbying effectiveness						
Investment promotion						
Intra-industry collaboration (clustering)						
Support for regional collaboration						
Expertise and funding						

Table 8.2: Rating of Industry Support Services

Weak: Capability is inadequate. Major up-grade or initiative is required
Moderate: Generally acceptable. Minor up-grade or initiatives are required.
Good: Meets criteria. Continued monitoring and fine-tuning are required

Country	To sustain current level of business			To expand level of business		
	Fabric	Make	Tech.	Fabric	Make	Tech.
1						
2						
3						
4						
5						

Table 8.3: Collaboration Possibilities with Regional Partners

Fabric: Possibly advantageous to obtain fabric
Make: Possibly advantageous to have some production done in that country
Tech.:   Possibly advantageous to obtain technical and management support. Could also extend to formal or informal vendor alliances

Table 8.4: Rating of Required Vendor Attributes	To sustain current level of business			To expand level of business		
Attributes	Weak	Moderate	Good	Weak	Moderate	Good
Competitive pricing						
Code compliance and security						
Consistent quality						
Speed to market						
References/reputation						
On time delivery						
Service						
Completeness of orders						

Weak: Capability is inadequate. Major up-grade or initiative is required
Moderate: Generally acceptable. Minor up-grade or initiatives are required.
Good: Meets criteria. Continued monitoring and fine-tuning are required

Table 8.5: Rating of Required Vendor Skill and Financial Attributes						
Attributes	To sustain current level of business			To expand level of business		
	Weak	Moderate	Good	Weak	Moderate	Good
Full package as opposed to CMT						
LDP as opposed to FOB						
Vendor financial capability						
Product development/ design capability						
Partnerships: willingness and ability						
Hold fabric in inventory: ability and willingness						

Weak: Capability is inadequate. Major up-grade or initiative is required
Moderate: Generally acceptable. Minor up-grade or initiatives are required.
Good: Meets criteria. Continued monitoring and fine-tuning are required

Table 8.6: Rating of Required Vendor Management Attributes						
Attributes	To sustain current level of business			To expand level of business		
	Weak	Moderate	Good	Weak	Moderate	Good
Management professionalism						
Continuous improvement ability and willingness						
Communication: ability and willingness						
Understanding of market and customers						
Integrity, trust and attitude						
Delivery of proper documentation						

Weak: Capability is inadequate. Major up-grade or initiative is required

Moderate: Generally acceptable. Minor up-grade or initiatives are required.

Good: Meets criteria. Continued monitoring and fine-tuning are required

Table 8.7: Rating of Market Development Attributes						
Attributes	To sustain current level of business			To expand level of business		
	Weak	Moderate	Good	Weak	Moderate	Good
Relations with local agents and buying houses						
Relations with regional sourcing offices of customers						
Relations with corporate sourcing directors						
Relations with buyers and merchandisers						
Relations with key customers, at all levels						
Presence in the marketplace						
Marketing and sales knowledge of key personnel						

Weak: Capability is inadequate. Major up-grade or initiative is required
Moderate: Generally acceptable. Minor up-grade or initiatives are required.
Good: Meets criteria. Continued monitoring and fine-tuning are required

Table 8.8: Assessment of Product Development Capabilities

Description of Capability		Response		Application Guide			
				C & M		Full Package	
		YES	NO	B	F	B	F
1	Do you use any computer-aided design system to digitalise a product, develop first pattern and grading?			■	■		
2	Are your design staff knowledgeable about grading and garment fit?			■			
3	Are you capable of preparing an internal specification sheet for any given product beside the one provided by the buyer?			■			
4	Do you use any 'product data management software' (e.g. PDM from GGT)?			■	■		
5	Are your production supervisors involved at the stage of making the first sample?			■		■	
6	Are the garment quality standards communicated to the employees on the production lines?						
7	Do you have a sample room for sample making?			■			

Please respond to questions using a check in 'No' or 'Yes' box.
Red cells: Capability not required.
Green cells: Capability required.
B: BASIC
F: FASHION

Interpretation of response where capability is required (green cells/boxes):
No: Weak, inadequate. Major up-grade or initiative is required
Yes: Meets criteria. Continued monitoring and fine-tuning are required

Table 8.9: Assessment of Unit Costing Capabilities							

Description of Capability		Response		Application Guide			
				C & M		Full Package	
		YES	NO	B	F	B	F
1	Do your work studies staff analyse the operations sequences of the new product?						
2	Do you use a predetermined time system to establish the SAM per operation?						
3	Do your work-studies staff propose changes in the construction of the garment designed to reduce time and cost?						
4	Do you use marker-making software in order to analyse the material requirement per unit?			■			
5	Do you assign any percentage for fabric utilisation on the making of the marker that meets the buyer estimate?			■	■		
6	Is your costing formula split into direct labour and plant overhead per type of order?						
7	Is your unit costing analysis based on the target price in the marketplace?						

Please respond to questions using a check in 'No' or 'Yes' box.
Red cells: Capability not required.
Green cells: Capability required.
B: BASIC
F: FASHION

Interpretation of response where capability is required (green cells/boxes):
No: Weak, inadequate. Major up-grade or initiative is required.
Yes: Meets criteria. Continued monitoring and fine-tuning are required.

Table 8.10: Assessment of Administrative Processes

Description of Capability		Response		Application Guide			
				C & M		Full Package	
		YES	NO	B	F	B	F
1	Are your development activities such as fabric costing, labour costing, sample making, etc. done simultaneously?			░	░		
2	Do you have more than two levels in management to reach the line people?			░	░		
3	Does the management director handle the order information through their staff and assign objectives regarding the order?			░	░		
4	Are your office employees multi-functional and able to do several tasks?						
5	Do you use integrated computerised management information systems to process and manage the orders?						

Please respond to questions using a check in 'No' or 'Yes' box.
Red cells: Capability not required.
Green cells: Capability required.
B: BASIC
F: FASHION

Interpretation of response where capability is required (green cells/boxes):
No: Weak, inadequate. Major up-grade or initiative is required.
Yes: Meets criteria. Continued monitoring and fine-tuning are required.

Table 8.11: Assessment of Production Systems

Description of Capability		Response		Application Guide			
				C & M		Full Package	
		YES	NO	B	F	B	F
1	Do you emphasise teamwork?			■		■	
2	Are your production lines regrouping not more than 15 employees?			■		■	
3	Does your cutting room plan against delivery dates and production line availability?			■		■	
4	Do sewing operators have the technical knowledge to operate efficiently at least two types of sewing machine?			■		■	
5	Do sewing operators have the operational knowledge of sewing more than four operations?			■		■	
6	Are direct employees aware of productivity targets and what they have achieved?						
7	Do sewing operators help each other in order to balance their production line and reach the productivity targets?			■		■	

Please respond to questions using a check in 'No' or 'Yes' box.
Red cells: Capability not required.
Green cells: Capability required.
B: BASIC
F: FASHION

Interpretation of response where capability is required (green cells/boxes):
No: Weak, inadequate. Major up-grade or initiative is required.
Yes: Meets criteria. Continued monitoring and fine-tuning are required.

Table 8.12: Assessment of Production Management and Industrial Engineering Capability

	Description of Capability	Response		Application Guide			
				C & M		Full Package	
		YES	NO	B	F	B	F
1	Does your work-studies staff work with your sewing operators to implement the work methods associated with a particular SAM?						
2	Does your work-studies staff monitor and correct deviations in the implemented work methods?						
3	Does the production manager meet with the line people in regard to their performance?						
4	Do you analyse and monitor daily the causes of production delays?						
5	Do you do any follow-up with sewing operators in order to improve their performance?						
6	Does your work-studies staff determine the bundling methods for delivering the pieces from one workstation to another?						
7	Are the production supervisors knowledgeable about quality standards and work methods set by the work-studies staff?						
8	Are production managers capable of planning and controlling their production lines?						
9	Does your management work to eliminate the causes of problems in quality?						

Please respond to questions using a check in 'No' or 'Yes' box.
Red cells: Capability not required.
Green cells: Capability required.
B: BASIC
F: FASHION

Interpretation of response where capability is required (green cells/boxes):
No: Weak, inadequate. Major up-grade or initiative is required.
Yes: Meets criteria. Continued monitoring and fine-tuning are required.

Table 8.13: Assessment of Manufacturing Management Capabilities

	Description of Capability	Response		Application Guide			
				C & M		Full Package	
		YES	NO	B	F	B	F
1	Have you determined the number of productive minutes required daily for the plant to be feasible?						
2	Do you capture daily the minutes earned by the direct labour as a measure of performance?						
3	Is the time of sewing operations synchronised between the sewing operators according to the SMV?						
4	Have you determined the maximum quantity in process between workstations to respond to the productivity time output?						
5	Do you monitor the balancing of operations on a daily basis through the manufacturing chain?						
6	Does first bundle output off the production line take no longer than two hours?			■		■	
7	Are your employees capable of adjusting the stitches per inch and the tension on their sewing machines?						
8	Have you implemented any individual or group incentive bonus programme?						
9	Is your incentive bonus programme based on these three criteria: productivity, attendance and quality?						
10	Is the number of employees in the quality department less than 17% of the sewing operators?						
11	Do you monitor quality by type of defects?						

Please respond to questions using a check in 'No' or 'Yes' box.
Red cells: Capability not required.
Green cells: Capability required.
B: BASIC
F: FASHION

Interpretation of response where capability is required (green cells/boxes):
No: Weak, inadequate. Major up-grade or initiative is required.
Yes: Meets criteria. Continued monitoring and fine-tuning are required.

Table 8.14: Assessment of Methods of Control and Improvement Capabilities

	Description of Capability	Response		Application Guide			
				C & M		Full Package	
		YES	NO	B	F	B	F
1	Competitive product development and target cost achievement of every cost?						
2	Price structure (direct labour, overheads, etc.) seasonally?						
3	Effectiveness of key business systems based on costing objectives, daily?						
4	Daily results of production lines and employee performance?						
5	Do you monitor the balancing of operations on a daily basis through the manufacturing chain?						
6	Responsiveness to customers' needs at the end of each activity?						
7	Daily manufacturing activities and operations?						
8	Daily quality improvement programmes?						
9	Daily analysis of direct labour versus actual cost?						
10	Daily analysis of production delays and reduction?						
11	Daily plant efficiency?						
12	Order tracking frequently?						
13	Shipping schedules?						
14	Delivery performance?						
15	Inventories of raw materials and work in process?						

Please respond to questions using a check in 'No' or 'Yes' box.
Red cells: Capability not required.
Green cells: Capability required.
B: BASIC
F: FASHION

Interpretation of response where capability is required (green cells/boxes):
No: Weak, inadequate. Major up-grade or initiative is required.
Yes: Meets criteria. Continued monitoring and fine-tuning are required.

9

Conclusions

9.1 The Importance of the Commonwealth Apparel Industry

A critical industry in many countries

The manufacture of ready-made apparel for export to the United States and Europe is of critical importance to many Commonwealth developing countries, contributing substantially to export earnings and employing large numbers of workers, up to 90 per cent of them women. Apparel exports account for 10 per cent or more of export earnings in ten Commonwealth developing countries and for three countries, Sri Lanka, Mauritius and Bangladesh, apparel exports account for between 50 and 77 per cent of export earnings. Any reduction in the level of activity in the apparel industry in these countries could have a significant socio-economic impact.

.... but not a dominant role globally

The countries of the Commonwealth, as a group, play a significant role as suppliers of ready-made apparel to Europe and the US. Commonwealth member states supplied, in 2001, close to 16 per cent of all EU and more than 18 per cent of US apparel imports. To put this in perspective, however, the total imports from the Commonwealth are of the same order of magnitude as imports from the leading supplier countries. Mexico, for example, accounted for just under 14 per cent of US apparel imports in 2001 and China (including Hong Kong) accounted for in excess of 18 per cent.

In 2001, six Commonwealth countries had a market share in the EU or US of more than 1 per cent. India and Bangladesh reached or surpassed the 3 per cent threshold postulated by Birnbaum (2001) for both Europe and the US, and Sri Lanka was close for the US, with a share of 2.5 per cent. Three other Commonwealth countries had market shares slightly in excess of 1 per cent, namely Pakistan in both markets, Malaysia in the US and Mauritius in Europe. Despite low individual market shares, Commonwealth countries are significant players in ready-made garment exports in two key regions: South Asia and sub-Saharan Africa. The relative market shares of these regions differ dramatically, however. South Asia supplied 11 per cent of US ready-made garment imports in 2001, whereas sub-Saharan Africa, including Mauritius, accounted for only 1.6 per cent.

Some countries are particularly vulnerable

In terms of implications, the greater the market share the stronger the links between supplier and buyers in that market. Conversely, the larger the share of apparel in a country's export earnings, the greater the sensitivity of the economy of that country to a downturn in such exports. The research findings indicate that countries that are particularly at risk in the changing apparel industry environment are those where *apparel accounts for more than 50 per cent of exports and where market shares are less than 3 per cent* (Birnbaum (2001). In 2001 apparel accounted for more than 50 per cent of the exports of Bangladesh, Mauritius and Sri Lanka. In terms of market share, only Bangladesh and India reached the 3 per cent threshold, although Sri Lanka, Mauritius, Pakistan and Malaysia also have sufficient market share. It is in this context that the impacts of the changing forces in the apparel industry must be viewed.

9.2 Sourcing Executives' Expectations

The survey of apparel industry executives carried out in North America as a key part of this study represents a valuable assembly of information and insights into their sourcing criteria.

An increasingly competitive marketplace

The MFA quota system has served to protect the apparel industry in Commonwealth developing countries from many of the pressures of the marketplace. With its demise, this protection will be removed but not eliminated, because tariff preferences offered under the proliferation of bilateral and regional trade preferences will still play a critical role. Manufacturers in the countries with such favourable market access agreements can use these temporary advantages to implement other competitiveness-creating measures while the trade benefits last. For countries and regions that do not have favoured market access there is still a window of opportunity. This window is afforded by the apparent intention of sourcing executives to continue to maintain a widespread sourcing base in the early post-2004 years as a hedge against anticipated trade disruptions.

Sooner or later, however, apparel manufacturers in Commonwealth developing countries' ready-made garment industries will be fully exposed to global market forces. They must understand these forces and adapt to them. Key among them is that the competitive retail environment, particularly in the US, has fuelled a continued drive for lower costs and greater speed to market.

The shift to a total cost viewpoint

The review of the changing forces in the apparel industry presented in Chapter 2 and the results of the survey of sourcing executives indicate that low wages alone are no longer enough to ensure the survival, let alone growth, of an apparel industry. Increasingly, buyers are moving to optimise costs throughout the supply chain as opposed to simply seeking the lowest cost for cut, make and trim. That is, they strive to optimise the sum of what Birnbaum (2001) has termed:

- *macro costs* (tariffs, costs related to doing business in a country);

- *indirect costs* (those costs associated with the various stages of pre-production as well as costs due to delays, late deliveries and returns);

- *direct costs* (costs of actually making the garments, including fabric, sewing costs, factory overheads and agents' commissions).

Birnbaum argues that the potential gains from reduced labour costs are minimal and almost irrelevant when compared to the gains to be made from reduction of macro and indirect costs.

Apparel importers compete with different business models

The new sourcing environment could place increased burdens on vendors and require them to undertake additional tasks within the value chain, requiring considerable investment. It must be noted, however, that a key finding of this survey is that *there is no single formula for success in this new sourcing environment.*

One major conclusion based on the survey of sourcing executives in North America is that moving up the value chain will not necessarily produce enhanced results for apparel manufacturers in Commonwealth developing countries. The reason for this is that the sourcing criteria differ from company to company. Different buyers seek differing products, have differing clients, differing approaches to business and differing core competencies, as well as differing levels of willingness to give up control by allowing suppliers to take responsibility for more functions in the value chain.

A reduced but loyal supplier base

The greatest impact of the elimination of the quota system, according to sourcing executives interviewed, is that *the supplier base will be reduced*. Thus, on a company-by-company basis, it is expected that there will be significant shrinkage of the vendor base following removal of quotas. Much of this reduction, but by no means all, will favour China. However, sourcing executives in the US foresee a period of instability tied to the various possibilities for trade retaliation against China and other countries deemed to be disrupting the equilibrium. For this reason, coupled with prudent strategies for risk-sharing in view of geo-political factors, buyers will hedge their bets and continue to maintain a diverse supplier base around the world. This will not be as diverse as that dictated by the quota system. A critical factor, however, is that as part of the supply chain optimisation drive, good vendor relationships will continue to be valued by those responsible for sourcing. On account of this, where good business relationships have been developed with suppliers, these links could be retained, provided that the suppliers remain competitive.

Strategic sourcing: a total cost perspective

A key finding of the survey of sourcing executives is the confirmation of the move from a first cost basis (lowest CMT, for example) to optimisation of the supply chain and lowest total cost. Since the late 1990s and early 2000s many leading apparel importers have established new departments responsible for *strategic sourcing*, run by supply chain and logistics professionals. These professionals expect the same degree of professionalism on the part of the apparel manufacturers with whom they do business. This means that apparel manufacturers in Commonwealth developing countries must develop and maintain a comprehensive knowledge of the fashion industry and trends, and of modern production management and industrial engineering approaches. These must be integrated with the technological tools to enable them to fully participate in the successful functioning of the supply chain. To achieve this requires professional management and considerable financial resources.

Chapter 4 presents the findings of the survey and Chapter 8 sets out guidelines for vendors to establish the required professionalism.

9.3 National-level Perspectives

The ready-made apparel industry is important to government because it is a source of significant employment, but requires relatively little direct investment. It is clear from this study that governments in many Commonwealth developing countries have tended to neglect the supporting investment that is required if macro and indirect costs are to remain competitive. In the case of countries that have developed a substantial industry, such as Bangladesh and Sri Lanka, the challenge is to retain these employment levels; whereas for sub-Saharan Africa, the challenge is to leverage the short-term benefits offered by AGOA to create more jobs.

The Jamaican paradox: a sword of Damocles

As countries in Africa take advantage of trade preferences such as AGOA the rapid rise and equally rapid demise of the apparel industry in Jamaica should provide food for thought. The restrictive and constraining nature of the 807 programme pushed Jamaican industry to become highly productive at sewing, remaining competitive despite comparatively high wage rates. But this was to the detriment of capabilities in product development and fabric sourcing, as well as in diversification of market contacts – capabilities that are required for a more resilient industry. This raises the whole issue of how to strengthen a country's position in the highly competitive and global apparel industry.

Countries whose apparel industry is solely dependent on particular trade preferences, such as Lesotho's dependence on AGOA, are clearly vulnerable.

Government support for industry is critical

The findings of this study confirm that duties and other macro costs are major contributors to total costs for an apparel importer. These costs fall largely within the purview of government (Birnbaum, 2001). Government also plays a key role in infrastructure, in education and training, in regulation and more generally in creating a good business environment. Many such initiatives aimed at reduction of indirect and direct costs to the importer can also benefit from industry-wide measures facilitated and supported by government. There is thus a need for industry to work closely with government to achieve the desired solutions.

Effective lobbying by industry and by government

Governments in Commonwealth developing countries clearly have responsibility for market access negotiations, but notable examples were found during the research where the apparel industry associations played an important role in organising and orchestrating the lobbying effort, both within the country and in the marketplace, as well as at international fora. The importance of lobbying, particularly in the context of the US political system and the processes within the European Commission, must constantly be borne in mind. It is incumbent on countries acting alone or in alliances at a regional level, for example, to develop a winning story line and to tell that story. And, as one industry leader said during the survey in North America: *there is a good story to tell*. The apparel industry can and should take an important lead in conveying the right messages to the key constituencies in the major importing countries.

Intra-regional co-operation

Exchange of raw materials and semi-finished goods within the context of regional production agreements and related rules of origin are a key intra-regional issue. This is currently very important in Southern Africa, but could apply elsewhere – particularly in terms of the textile industry, which is the weak link in the AGOA chain at present and is also a constraint in Commonwealth South Asia. Countries should strive for enhanced intra-regional co-operation, particularly in attracting investments in major textile facilities to serve the apparel industry collectively in the countries of that region.

Delocalisation and diversification

A related area for government that is perhaps more difficult but none the less important to support is the movement of factories to lower-cost production areas – to benefit from bilateral trade agreements, for example. This jeopardises some national jobs in the short term but enables the head office and corporate functions to be retained in-country and keeps companies and their profits from migrating completely. Notable examples of this movement were found in Sri Lanka and in Mauritius, and this is an important issue throughout Southern Africa. A related issue, illustrated by the findings in Jamaica, is the possibility of exiting the industry. Although alternative employment strategies are not the focus of this research, it is worth noting that Jamaica was able, when the apparel industry collapsed, to move rapidly to develop call centres and related businesses using existing infrastructure.

Up-grading work practices

Workplace environment and quality of life issues are critical in the apparel industry, particularly to the degree in which they influence market perceptions and hence sourcing decisions. In addition, the reluctance to work in the industry when other less arduous opportunities are available appeared to be a major factor, for example in Mauritius, leading to very significant use of labourers imported under contract from other countries. The recommendations and guidelines set out in this research, particularly in Chapter 8, for up-grading production management and industrial engineering capability can lead not only to reduced costs but also to an improved work place environment and work practices. When production is properly planned and managed, squeezing labour costs through extended overtime and related work place practices should no longer be necessary to meet delivery and cost targets. Indeed, the whole approach is to involve line operators in the work flow and quality control process, thereby reducing costs due to lost time and quality rejection. The enthusiasm with which many of the approaches addressed during the research were greeted by manufacturers in Commonwealth developing countries underscores the openness and indeed strong desire to adopt such measures.

9.4 Industry and Government Co-operation

Joint strategic planning initiatives

Faced with the changing environment in the global apparel industry, all the Common-wealth countries surveyed had undertaken strategic planning initiatives. This generally involves close collaboration between government and industry. These initiatives would appear to have helped develop enhanced support within government despite the conflict-ing priorities that governments are called upon to address. Specific regulatory, indus-trial and infrastructure initiatives have been identified to enhance the business environ-ment and up-grade capability to help consolidate the apparel industry. At the time of the study, in most cases these had not moved to the funding and implementation stages.

Clustering and other collaborative measures

One common result of the strategic planning initiatives is a widespread recognition that enhanced co-operation is required among companies and between the apparel industry and government in Commonwealth developing countries. Examples of this enhanced awareness of the need for co-operation at all levels are schemes to develop cluster and cooperatives as well as central fabric warehouse facilities. Such co-operative measures are critical for developing specialisation and hence economies of scale among the smaller manufacturers, but require a high degree of trust in order to succeed. Proper financial and technical support will also be required for such clustering and collabora-tive measures to succeed.

Enhanced market development activities

Many of the enterprise-level examples encountered during the research underscore the importance of market presence and particularly of an in-market sales capability. This has been and should continue to be an area where national trade support networks play an important role. There does appear to be widespread recognition that a stronger presence is required in the major markets and that it is necessary to up-grade skills of market development personnel. This is particularly true as companies move away from basic apparel items and seek to strengthen relations with customers. However, specific means to develop this presence and establish appropriate niche market strategies were frequently wanting.

One avenue to achieve these objectives is through a mix of visits to the target markets and permanent representation or agency arrangements in these locations. These could possibly be combined with showroom facilities. The essential issue is to avoid one-off activities and market presence must be sustained. Enhanced training in apparel marketing is a necessary prerequisite for personnel in Commonwealth developing countries to support the market development initiatives in the target markets.

Permanent presence in the marketplace

The national trade support network should encourage the larger apparel manufacturing groups to establish permanent offices or representation agreements in target markets in order to facilitate market expansion, especially higher valued business. A consortium approach could also be advantageous through cost-sharing in overseas representation. One representational option would be to hire a senior and experienced national who has broad contacts in the apparel industry in the target market.

9.5 Up-grading Manufacturing Capability

Cost-saving potential from up-grading management systems

The case study in Chapter 8 clearly demonstrates that up-grading management systems can lead to significant cost reductions. The observations made during the study in selected Commonwealth developing countries noted an absence in most strategic plans of industrial engineering processes that could lead to cost reductions.

Up-grading for an individual company

In order for individual apparel manufacturers to decide how to up-grade they first need to assess their position with respect to industry trends and buyer criteria. The guidelines presented in Chapter 8 are a tool to facilitate this assessment: to develop an understanding of where the industry is headed, of the buyer criteria and of positioning of the company with respect to these trends and criteria. Before deciding on a course of action, however, the enterprise must determine its core competencies, its current capabilities and what role they can profitably play in the future. They can then establish the priority actions that need to be undertaken. The resources, both human and financial, that are required to undertake the priority up-grading actions must also be determined. The benefits that are expected to result and the feasibility of undertaking the investment should then be determined.

Extension to the industry as a whole

A process similar to that described above for the individual firm should be carried out at an industry-wide level for various segments of the apparel industry. The challenge for industry associations and national trade and industrial support networks is to see the up-grading activities expanded from individual corporate groups to a wider spectrum of the industry. This requires articulation of enterprise-level needs at the national level, including training programmes, pilot projects and creation of industrial engineering and production management teams. The specific up-grading requirements will depend upon the state of the industry in a country, the existing support institutions, available expertise and available funding.

Limitations of supply chain integration

The evolving sourcing environment will place increased pressure on apparel manufacturers in Commonwealth developing countries to undertake additional tasks within the supply chain. This may often require considerable investment.

It is clear from the sourcing survey, however, that apparel manufacturers cannot rely solely on offering increased supply-chain services because many potential clients will still continue to execute functions directly or outsource them to intermediaries. The apparel supply chain has been termed a 'buyer driven' chain, whereby it is the buyer who is the linchpin between the retail customer and the manufacturers. Therefore a manufacturer should not take on additional functions, in effect offering more complete service, without reference to its target customers. Manufacturers must take the necessary dispositions to offer such services and to deliver them when required, but first and foremost they must become efficient, low-cost manufacturers.

The case studies in up-grading initiatives in Chapter 7 illustrate the manner in which a number of companies have taken on more functions in the supply chain, including design and other product development and pre-production capabilities. The limitations of this strategy are, however, underscored by the Mauritius experience in trying to move up the value chain. Indeed, almost without exception, apparel manufacturers in Commonwealth developing countries were found to be struggling with the management and technical skills and systems required to take on more supply chain functions, to increase productivity and to thereby lower both indirect costs and direct production costs. The extant literature on the apparel industry offers very little concrete advice on how to offer more services to buyers; in essence, to move up the value chain. Likewise, there is little in the literature on how to become a low-cost supplier.

The guidelines in Chapter 8 show how the buyer criteria can be translated into concrete actions to reduce lead times and unit costs and thus enable a manufacturer to become a low-cost supplier. The case study presented in the same chapter illustrates the benefits that can result from up-grading the manufacturing process to reduce costs, while at the same time training members of the industrial and production management team.

Companies must collaborate in order to compete

The key ingredient for successful and rapid implementation of the new processes will be the willingness of competing apparel firms in Commonwealth developing countries to collaborate in order to compete in the international market. Individual firms must assess their market possibilities and determine their current capabilities and the gap to be bridged in order to be viable. This may result in a decision to merge with an existing group, to become involved in various production networks and other collaborative schemes, or to focus on sub-contract specialisation.

A conclusion of the surveys of sourcing apparel executives and apparel manufacturers is that there are no 'one-size-fits-all' formulae for enterprise, industry-wide and institutional-level interventions. The examples and recommendations in Chapters 7 and 8 provide a basis from which to start the up-grading process. The experiences of others should be reviewed to find differences and similarities, and what works and what does not work. Perhaps more critically, what works at one moment of time may not be replicable, but there are still lessons to be learned. One of the challenges for industry and supporting agencies, particularly as they seek to promote enhanced collaborative efforts, is to find cost-effective ways to deliver the various supply chain functions as and when clients require them. At the same time, it is critical to facilitate industry consolidation and where necessary also to facilitate the task of local vendors establishing operations outside their home country so as to benefit from additional cost advantages that might prevail.

Pilot projects and institutional support

Much development at the enterprise level can be carried out with commercial financing, but it would be appropriate and most probably necessary that pilot projects, whether for up-grading production capability or for such collaborative efforts as clustering initiatives, will require full public/private sector participation. A limited window exists for the apparel industry in Commonwealth developing countries to enhance their capabilities – but *time is of the essence*. Commonwealth governments must act to reduce the macro costs that are within their control. They must also implement measures to help companies reduce their indirect and direct costs. Companies in countries favoured by tariff preferences will have a greater respite, but sooner or later all will have to compete squarely on the basis of being professional supply chain partners.

9.6 And Now What?

Industry and government both have responsibilities to ensure a professionally managed low-cost environment to serve the global apparel industry. The nature of costs has changed substantially since government and entrepreneurs first acted together to seize the opportunities presented by the quota system. Low labour costs are no longer the critical determinant because major apparel importers have adopted a strategic sourcing perspective aiming to minimise total costs. Likewise, moving up the value chain does not necessarily create higher margins and importers differ widely in their business models with respect to who does what value chain functions, and where.

The role of government

Government has responsibility for most of what are termed macro costs and must therefore act to enhance the business environment. Tariffs, rules of origin and other trade restrictions are major contributors to macro costs and government must lobby and negotiate effectively on this front. Efficient transportation and communications systems, efficient financial systems and excellent human resource development will all contribute both to lower macro costs and to less delays and penalties that trigger indirect costs. Government must also facilitate and provide sustained support to the apparel industry to assist it in making the transition to becoming a low-cost producer and where necessary become capable of taking on an increasing range of supply chain tasks.

The role of entrepreneurs

The burden in this exercise falls, however, on the entrepreneurs who have chosen to remain in the export-oriented apparel industry. The findings of this study have shown that there is much that they can do in their own factories to lower costs and increase productivity, and that this can be done at costs well within the reach of the entrepreneur. The study has also provided examples of companies that have consolidated, integrated backwards to textiles production and established effective pre-production market development capability. Enterprises must emulate them, either acting alone or in collaboration with other companies. Entrepreneurs must also be the driving force for ensuring that action is taken on the macro-cost front and must, acting at the industry-wide level, take the message direct to the importing countries where and when necessary.

Failure will have significant implications in terms of employment and resultant socio-economic impact throughout the economies of apparel-producing Commonwealth developing countries.

This study provides insights and tools to establish priorities at both government and enterprise levels. Use them!

Bibliography

General

Abernathy, F., Dunlop, J., Hammond, J. and Weil, D. (1999). *A stitch in time: lean retailing and the transformation of manufacturing, lessons from the apparel and textile industries*. Oxford: Oxford University Press.

African Growth and Opportunity Act (AGOA). Available at: *http://www.agoa.gov/*

African Growth and Opportunity Act (2000). Proclamation by the President of the United States of America, 2 October.

AGOA Summary Sheet (updated for AGOA II). Available at: *http://otexa.ita.doc.gov/Trade_Act_2000.htm*

American Apparel and Footwear Association (2001). A Quarterly Compilation of Statistical Information on the US. Apparel and Footwear Industries. As obtained from: *www.apparelandfootwear.org*

American Textile Manufacturers Institute (1998). China trade policy testimony of Carlos Moore, executive vice president, before the Committee on Commerce, Subcommittee on Telecommunications, Trade and Consumer Protection, 14 May.

American Textile Manufacturers Institute (1999). *US and European textile and apparel industries urge government action to gain market access to address trade imbalances.* ATMI news release, Washington, DC, 14 July. Available at: *http://www.atmi.org/newsroom/releases/1999archives.asp*

Birnbaum, D. (2000). *Birnbaum's global guide to winning the great garment war*. Hong Kong: Third Horizon Press.

Birnbaum, D. (2001). 'The coming garment massacre', *Canadian Apparel Magazine*, December. Available at: *http://www.apparel.ca/magazine/2001Dec/Garment%20Massacre.pdf*

Bovet, D. and Martha, J. (2000). *Value Nets*. Chichester: John Wiley.

Bureau of International Labour Affairs, US Department of Labour (1997). *The apparel industry and codes of conduct: a solution to the international child labour problem?* Available at: *http://www.dol.gov/dol/ilab/public/media/reports/iclp/apparel/main.htm*

Christopher, M. (undated). The agile supply chain: competing in volatile markets. Cranfield School of Management, UK. Available at: *www.martin-christopher.org/downloads/downloads/agile_supply_chain.pdf*

Christopher, M. (1998). 'Responding to the global supply chain challenge', *Supply Chain Management Review* 2(4).

Christopher, M. and Towill, D. (2002). 'Developing market specific supply chain strategies', *International Journal of Logistics Management*, 13(1).

Christopher, M. and Towill, D.R. (undated). Developing market specific supply chain

Coughlin, P., Rubin, M. and Amedée Darga, M. (2001). *The SADC textile and garment industries: constraints and opportunities, myopia or global vision?*, Southern African Development Community, August.

Diao, X. and Somwaru, A. (2001). 'Impact and the MFA phase-out on the world economy and intertemporal globalgeneral equilibrium analysis', International Food Policy Research Institute. Discussion Paper No. 79, October.

Dicken, P. (1999). *Global Shift: Transforming the World Economy*. Paul Chapman Publishing.

Dickerson, Kitty G. (1995). *Textiles and apparel in the global economy*. Prentice Hall

Economic Commission for Latin America, United Nations (1999). La Industria des Vestido: Inversiones y Estrategias Empresariales en América Latina y el Caribe (in Spanish).

Forza, C. and Vinelli, A. (2000). Time compression in production and distribution within the textile-apparel chain. *Integrated Manufacturing Systems* 11(2):138–146.

Gereffi, G. (1999). 'International trade and industrial up-grading in the apparel commodity chain', *Journal of International Economics* 48:37–70.

Gereffi, G. and Korzeniewicz, M. (eds) (1994). *Commodity Chains and Global Capitalism*. Praeger.

Gereffi, G. (1994). 'The organisation of buyer-driven global commodity chains: How US Retailers shape overseas production networks'. In Gereffi, G., and Korzeniewicz, M. (1994). *Commodity Chains and Global Capitalism*. Praeger.

Gereffi, G. (1997). 'Global Shift, Regional Response: Can North America meet the full package challenge?' *Apparel, the Bobbin Magazine* 39 (3), November.

Gereffi, G. (1999). 'International trade and industrial up-grading in the apparel commodity chain', *Journal of International Economics* 48(1).

Gereffi, G. (2001). 'Global sourcing in the US apparel industry', *Journal of Textile and Apparel Technology and Management* 2(1), Fall.

Gereffi, G. (2001). 'The Transformation of the North American Apparel Industry: Is NAFTA a curse or blessing?', *Integration and Trade* 4(11). August.

Gereffi, G. (2002). 'Outsourcing and changing patterns of international competition in the apparel commodity chain', Paper presented at the Conference on 'Responding to Globalisation: Societies, Groups and Individuals', Boulder, Colorado, 4–7 April.

Gereffi, G., Humphrey, J., and Sturgeon, T. (2003). *The Governance of Global Value Chains: An Analytical Framework*. Institute of Development Studies, January.

Giuliani, E. (2002). Cluster absorptive capability: an evolutionary approach for industrial clusters in developing countries. DRUID Summer Conference on Industrial Dynamics of the New and Old Economy – who is embracing whom? Copenhagen/Elsinore 6–8 June. Available at: *www.druid.dk/conferences/summer2002/Papers/GIULIANI.pdf*

Humphrey, J. and Schmitz, H. (2002). How does insertion in global value chain affect up-grading in industrial clusters? IDS. Available at: *http://www.ids.ac.uk/ids/global/vwpap.html*

Kaplinsky, R. and Readman, J. (2001). *How can SME producers serve global markets and sustain income growth?* Institute of Development Studies, University of Sussex, April.

Kaplinsky, R., and Morris, M. (2001). *A handbook for value chain research*. Institute of Development Studies (IDS). *www.ids.ac.uk/ids/global/valchn.html#manuals*

Kathuria, S. and Bhardwaj, A. (1998). *Export quotas and policy constraints in the Indian textile and garment industries*. SASPR, World Bank New Delhi Office, October.

Kathuria, S., Martin, W. and Bhardwaj, A. (2000). 'Implications of MFA abolition for South Asian Countries', Paper presented at the NCAER-World Bank WTO 2000 South Asia Workshop, 20–21 December, New Delhi.

Lamy, P. (2000). 'EU moves to liberalise textile and apparel sectors', Press release by EU Commissioner of Trade, October–November.

Lee, E.-J. (2001). *Export positions in the apparel commodity chain and product import values*. University of Tennessee at Knoxville. Available at: *http://www.sbaer.uca.edu/Research/2001/SMA/01sma074.html*

Lee, J.-R. and Chen, J.-S. (1998). *Synergy creation with multiple business activities: toward a competence-based growth model for contract manufacturers*. Research in Competence-based Research, Advances in Applied Business Strategy Series, Volume C. Greenwich, CT: JAI Press. Available at: *http://www.ids.ac.uk/ids/global/pdfs/lee.pdf*

Lin, S.-H., Kincade, D.H. and Avery, C. (2002). 'Dimensions of apparel manufacturing strategy and production management', *International Journal of Clothing Science and Technology* 14(1): 46–60.

McCormick, D. and Schmitz, H. (2001). *Manual for value chain research on homeworkers in the garment industry*. November. Available at: *http://www.ids.ac.uk/ids/global/pdfs/homeworkerslinkedforwebmarch.pdf*

Navaraetti, G.B., Faini, R. and Silberston, A., (eds) (1995). *Beyond the Multifibre Arrangement: Third World Competition and Restructuring Europe's Textile Industry*. Paris: Organisation for Economic Cooperation and Development.

Office of Technology Assessment (1987). *The US textile and apparel industry: a revolution in progress*. OTA-TET 332, April. Available at: *http://govinfo.library.unt.edu/ota/Ota_3/DATA/1987/8733.PDF*

Rahman, M. (2002). *South Asia's T & C sector in the context of MFA–phase out: ready or not?*, Paper presentation at Seminar on Implications of the Expiry of the MFA for SAARC/Commonwealth Member States, Post-2005, Colombo, Sri Lanka, December.

Raikes, P., Friis, Jensen, M. and Ponte, S. (2000). 'Global commodity chain analysis and the French Filière approach: comparison and critique', CDR Working Paper 00.3, Copenhagen, February.

Ryan, T. (2003a). 'Sourcing: the need for speed', *Apparel, the Bobbin Magazine*, 1 February. Available at: *http://www.bobbin.com/bobbin/search/search_display.jsp?vnu_content_id=1808801*

Ryan, T. (2003b). Shipment security at the forefront. *Apparel, the Bobbin Magazine*, 1 January. Available at: *http://www.bobbin.com/bobbin/search/search_display.jsp?vnu_content_id=1786045*

Spinanger, D. (1998). *Textiles beyond the MFA phase-out*. Kiel Institute of World Economics; CSGR Working Paper No. 13/98.

Spinanger, D. (1999). *Faking liberalization and finagling protectionism: the ATC at its best*. Kiel Institute of World Economics, June.

Trade and Development Act of 2000 and the Trade Act of 2002. Available at: *http://otexa.ita.doc.gov/Trade_Act_2000.htm*

The Apparel Industry and Codes of Conduct (2002). A report produced by the United States Department of Labour. Available at: *http://www.itcilo.it/actrav/actrav-english/telearn/global/ilo/code/apparel.htm*

Tyagi, R. (2003). 'Apparel globalization: the big picture', *Apparel, the Bobbin Magazine*, 1 January. Available at: *http://www.bobbin.com/bobbin/search/search_display.jsp?vnu_content_id=1786051*

Tain, N. (2002). 'Sourcing extra: back to business in Madagascar', *Apparel, the Bobbin Magazine*, 8 November. Available at: *http://www.bobbin.com/bobbin/reports_analysis/article_display.jsp?vnu_content_id=1758066*

US Customs Service (2002). 'US Customs Service Launches Customs-Trade Partnership Against Terrorism', Press release, Detroit, 26 April 2002.

Available at: *http://www.itsa.org/ITSNEWS.NSF/4e0650bef6193b3e852562350056a3a7/75a670bbf07a2f3e85256ba000623ac9?OpenDocument*

US Department of Commerce (2002). Report to the Congressional Textile Caucus on the Administration's efforts on textile issues, September.

US Department of Labour (2000). *Wages, benefits, poverty line, and meeting workers' needs in the apparel and footwear industries of selected countries*, Tables 1–2 pp. 1–44 to 1–46.

World Trade Organisation–Agreement on Textiles and Clothing. Available at: *http://otexa.ita.doc.gov/wto.htm*

World Trade Organisation (2000). (Minutes of meeting) Trade policy review of Bangladesh. Trade Policy Review Body, 2 and 4 May; WT/TPR/M/68 14 June; (00-2351).

Bangladesh

Hassan, T. (2002). 'Readymade garments vis à vis the textile sector in Bangladesh beyond 2004', Export Promotion Bureau of Bangladesh, presented at SAARC Seminar, December.

Hassan, F. (2002). Country paper, Bangladesh Garment Manufacturers Association, presented at SAARC Seminar, December.

Ministry of Commerce (2001). *Ready made garment sector in Bangladesh: background information for a strategy study*. Government of Bangladesh, July.

Jamaica

Black, S. (2000). 'In praise of parity', *Apparel, the Bobbin Magazine*, 1 September. Available at: *http://www.bobbin.com/bobbin/search/search_display.jsp?vnu_content_id=1432058*

Department of Commerce (2000). US–Caribbean Basin Trade Partnership Act of 2000. Available at: *http://www.mac.doc.gov/CBI/webmain/intro.htm*

Trade Board Ltd (2002). Special compilation: Textile/apparel exports 1990–2000.
Trade Board Ltd (2002). Special compilation: Textile/apparel exports 2001.

Lesotho

Lesotho National Development Corporation (1999). *Annual report 1998/99.*
Lesotho National Development Corporation (2000). *Lesotho: an investor's guide.*
Lesotho National Development Corporation (2002). *Investment, employment and output statistics.*
Lesotho National Development Corporation Special Compilation (2002). Statistical tables series A on Lesotho economy (but not expressly on garment sector).
Lesotho National Development Corporation: Special Compilation (2002). Report on 'Session 1': Role of large businesses in light manufacturing sectors in Lesotho´s PRSP.
Rubin, M. (2001). *SADC study of the textile and garment industries: Lesotho.* Southern African Development Community, March.

Mauritius

Coughlin, P., Rubin, M. and Darga, L.A. (2001). *The SADC textile and garment industries, constraints and opportunities: myopia or global vision.* Southern African Development Community, August.
Export Development Zone Development Authority (EPZDA) (2001). 'Foreign labour', *Industry Focus* 57 (July–August). Port Louis.
EPZDA (2001). 'Le textile', *Industry Focus* 56 (May–June). Port Louis.
EPZDA (2001). Employment by product group and gender. Mauritius Industry Statistics (Table 2). Available at: *http://www.mauritius-industry.com/*
EPZDA (2002). Clustering. Industry Focus, 60(March–April). Port Louis.
EPZDA Enterprises and Workforce Distribution and Percentage Change by EPZ Product Group, 1988–2000 (Table 2a). Mauritius Industry Statistics. Available at: *http://www.mauritius-industry.com/*
EPZDA EPZ exports by section/commodity, 2000-2001 (Table 4). Mauritius Industry Statistics. Available at: http://www.mauritius-industry.com/
EPZDA EPZ exports and percentage change by section/selected groups of commodities, 1997–2000 (Table 4a). Mauritius Industry Statistics. Available at: *http://www.mauritius-industry.com/*
Gibbon, P. (2000). 'Back to the basics through delocalisation: the Mauritian garment industry at the end of the twentieth century', Working Paper Sub-series on Globalisation and Economic Restructuring in Africa; CDR Working Paper 00.7, Copenhagen, October.
Joint Economic Council (2001). 'The economic transition of Mauritius', Report of the JEC Task Force, February.
Kaidoo, M. (2001). The Export Processing Zone–2000. EPZDA. Available at: *http://epzdanet.intnet.mu/epzda/industry/EPZ2000.htm*
Ministry of Industry and International Trade (2002). 'Adapting to the changing environment: strategic plan for the textile and clothing sector 2002–2005', High Powered Committee, Mauritius, January.

Organisation for Economic Cooperation and Development/ADB (2002). *Mauritius: Africa economic outlook*. London: OECD.

Rubin, M. (2002). 'Three new strategies for the Mauritian apparel industry', *Industry Focus* 60 (March–April), 33–38. Port Louis: EPZDA.

South Africa

CLOFED (2000). *The South African Clothing Industry 2000/01 Handbook*. Clothing Federation of South Africa.

Coughlin, P., Rubin, M. and Amedée Darga, M. (2001). *The SADC textile and garment industries: constraints and opportunities, myopia or global vision?* Southern African Development Community, August.

Gibbon, P. (2002). 'South Africa and the global commodity chain for clothing: export performance and constraints', Centre for Development Research, Working Paper 02.7, Copenhagen, April.

Moodley, S. and Velia, M. (2002). 'The South African clothing export value chain: prospects for upgrading?', Industrial Restructuring Project, School of Development Studies, University of Natal, 28 May.

Roberts, S. and Thoburn, J. (2001). *Adjusting to trade liberalisation: the case of firms in the South African textile sector*. United Nations Industrial Development Organisation and Oxford University Centre for the Study of African Economics International Forum.

Sri Lanka

Export Development Board (2002). 'The apparel industry in Sri Lanka', Paper presented at SAARC Seminar, December.

Government Sponsored Committee (2002). *Five-year strategy for the Sri Lankan apparel industry*. Colombo, June.

United Nations Industrial Development Organisation (2000). *Master plan study for the apparel industry*. JICA/UNIDO, July.

Glossary

Activity-based costing: cost allocation methods that assign costs to each process undertaken. Costs 'below the line' are considered in product contribution analysis, thereby enhancing the accuracy and value of product profitability information. Often, companies unknowingly invest significant amounts of resources into unprofitable product lines, rather than concentrating efforts on more profitable products.

CAD (computer aided design): CAD is a product development technology. CAD systems assist in new product designs costing and quality, while minimising the time and resources required, improving the accuracy of grading, and providing better flexibility and lead time compared to manual operations. CAD tools support the design, development and maintenance of fabric and garment images. These images are then available for visual line review by product development functions, such as merchandising, specification, costing and sourcing/production. Images are then electronically shared with printing, knitting and weaving to increase efficiency in sampling and production.

Cellular manufacturing: refers to a type of manufacturing layout that groups machines into 'cells'. Cell groupings are determined by the operations required for items that require similar processing. This avoids costly material handling, faster processing (lowering work in progress inventory levels) and reduced set-up times.

Cost production minute: is a value per minute earned (see Minutes earned) in production. The minute production value includes production overhead, indirect and direct labour cost, in addition to some profits.

Cutting and making value: is the cost per unit charged to the buyer covering production overhead, cutting and making of the product excluding raw materials. The C and M value of a product is calculated as follows: total Standard Minutes' Values of a product multiplied by the minute production value. When raw materials are added to the cost, then the value is called full package (FOB price) (see SMV).

Electronic Data Interchange (EDI): an electronic exchange of instructions and documents between companies with the aim of increasing efficiency and reducing paperwork by streamlining information flow. While this process has existed for 20 years, the Internet is now simplifying EDI and eliminates the need for costly interchange networks.

Enterprise Resource Planning (ERP): regarded as the master plan for efficiently organising, integrating and managing enterprise applications, such as finance, accounting, manufacturing, distribution and human resources. ERP involves centralising and integrating applications and streamlining business processes across an organisation.

Extranets: a private network that uses the Internet to share business information securely and to complete transactions with pre-established suppliers, vendors, partners, customers or other businesses. An extranet can be viewed as part of a company's intranet that is extended to secure users outside the company.

Manufacturing Resource Planning (MRP I): a similar concept to ERP, with a focus narrowed to manufacturing only.

Materials Requirement Planning (MRP II): a similar concept to ERP, with a focus on the planning of fabric and trimmings for orders as well as manufacturing processes.

Marker making: integrated software systems that work with the CAD system for drawing a sketch of the pieces to be cut, ensuring efficiency of fabric utilisation and reduction of fabric wastage. The marker is transferred electronically to the laser cutter and is very cost-effective for small order sizes. This operation is costly if performed manually.

Minutes earned: are the total of units produced per an employee multiplied by the given SMV (see Standard minute value).

Minutes worked: are the total minutes worked by an employee on a daily basis.

Performance: is the achievement result of an employee or production line/plant vis-à-vis the objectives. Employee's performance is calculated as follows: minutes earned (see Minutes earned) divided by minutes worked (see Minutes worked).

Predetermined Time Measurement System: the Predetermined Time Measurement System was developed from motion pictures of industrial operation, and the time standards were first published in 1948. This system is defined as a procedure which analyses any manual operation or method into the basic motions required to perform the operation, and assigns to each motion a predetermined time standard which is determined by the nature of the motion and the conditions under which it is made. This is known as SMV in Asia (standard minute value) and as SAM in North America (standard allowed minute).

Standard minute value (SMV): for unit costing purpose, a breakdown of operations must be created for any given product from the cutting to the finishing. It is desirable to allow a time to each operation in order to calculate the direct labour cost, employee performance and order planning, and to control labour costs and productivity levels. Each SMV is a combination of several elements covering the hand motions of parts handling and sewing cycles. These elements are based on a predetermined time system and are considered as the international standards (see Predetermined time system).

Specification sheet: for production and quality purposes, bills of materials and charts of final measurements must be given to the production people and quality staff to assure the quality of the product corresponds to the requirements of the buyer. The specification sheet contains a sketch of the product, illustrating the methods of measurement per measurement element.